Contents

KV-374-389

The views expressed in this book are those of the authors, and not necessarily of the National Council of Social Service

)C   ilies
... B

edited by Robert Holman

The Bedford Square Press

of the National Council of Social Service
26 Bedford Square, London, WC1

NCSS London 1970
SBN 7199 0795 0

Reprinted 1971
Reprinted with supplement 1973

EDITOR'S NOTE

Socially Deprived Families in Britain was first published in 1970. Three years later, two factors have led the authors (with the exception of Professor Lafitte who was unable to help) to issue this Supplement. First, demand for the book has been maintained. Second, a number of important developments have occurred in social policy and the social services. All that can be presented now is a brief outline of the major developments but consideration will be given in the future to providing a completely revised edition of the book.

September 1973   R.H.

Dr Robert Holman is now Senior Lecturer in Social Administration and Social Work in the University of Glasgow.

Supplement supplied separately for 30p.

Distributed by Research Publications Services,
Victoria Hall, East Greenwich, London SE10 0RF

Design and typography by NCSS Publications Department
Printed in England by Lewis Reprints Limited, Tonbridge.

Introduction

During the 1960s the United Nations expressed concern over the continuance of social deprivation in Western Europe. In 1967 its Division of Social Affairs established, within the framework of the European Social Development Programme, a standing Working Group on Socially Deprived Families. Member nations who agreed to contribute included Belgium, France, Italy, the Netherlands, Denmark, Western Germany. Israel and the United Kingdom. It was envisaged that the group would function for three years, culminating in an international seminar at which findings would be presented.

The objectives of the working group were to make a thorough study of the problem of socially deprived families, and to formulate suggestions to 'stimulate and support effective policies and programmes in this field in different countries'. It decided early that its major contribution would be for each member nation to collect material on the extent and nature of social deprivation in their own country, with particular emphasis on the last ten to fifteen years, plus a description and assessment of the services and methods employed to combat the problems. Thus the intention was not to initiate original research, but to collate existing material.

The British representatives to the working group have been Mr Fred Philp, formerly secretary to the Family Service Units, Dr Harriett Wilson, Research Fellow at Birmingham University, and the present writer who has acted as respondent and editor. It was early perceived that the collection of material was too broad a task for one person, and it was fortunate that Birmingham University contained three experts on the very subjects on which the working group had decided to concentrate, namely social deprivation as it concerns income, housing, and child socialisation. Thus, respectively, Professor François Lafitte, Mr. Kenneth Spencer and Dr. Harriett Wilson undertook responsibility. The quality of their work, the use of some material not easily available to the public, and the opportunity to collect evidence of different kinds of deprivation in one volume, has caused a number of people to encourage publication of the British material.

DEFINITION AND MEASUREMENT

Discussions between the various national representatives in 1967-68 soon revealed differences over the definition of the term 'socially deprived families'. To some it was confined to the small group commonly known in this country as 'problem families', of the type amongst whom Family Service Units have worked. To others the term was broad enough to include all females on the basis that they suffered discrimination and deprivation in the sense of lower wages and fewer employment opportunities. It became clear that the subject matter would have to be narrowed, and hence it was decided to limit the study to deprivation in the fields of income, housing and child socialisation. These were not chosen because they represented needs and conditions more basic and primary than others, but because they offered some hope of measurement allowing international comparison. It was also recognised that the factors may well be interrelated and could not be distinguished as either the cause or effect of social deprivation. For instance, housing deprivation may result from income deprivation, or vice versa; or be caused by some outside factor; possibly by yet some other form of deprivation like ill-health.

Having decided the content of the study, the question arises what is social deprivation, and how can it be measured? With regard to income, housing and child socialisation it is taken as a level generally regarded as causing hardship by comparison with the rest of society, so that society is moved to alleviate these conditions. This is a deliberately loose definition, which allows each contributor to develop his own terms. It also underlines the fact that social deprivation is a relative concept. The standards of housing which a hundred years ago were not regarded as low, will today be regarded as depriving simply because society's standards and expectations have risen. As Aneurin Bevan once aptly put it, 'The causes of housing problems are higher social standards'.[1] Similarly other nations may have different standards, and one of the eventual outcomes of the United Nations study will allow not only comparison concerning different proportions of certain measures, for instance the lack of housing amenities, but whether this lack is regarded as depriving. Finally, it is recognised that any assessment of deprivation involves a subjective judgment. Thus in the field of income deprivation, Professor Lafitte follows the government study *Circumstances of Families* in accepting the lower limit of public assistance (supplementary benefit) payment as the poverty line.[2] Other writers, like Townsend and Abel-Smith, or Coates and Silburn, take an income of so many per cent above this level as the poverty line.[3, 4]

The question of measurement and definition obviously poses severe problems for the contributors. The study is one of families, and hence single persons, childless couples and other couples who live alone, like the elderly, are excluded. Unfortunately some figures available, for instance in regard to housing deprivation, do not distinguish between such types. The method adopted is to make such distinctions where possible, but otherwise to present the full findings. Again, available sources vary in their geographical coverage. Some deal with England, others with England and Wales; others Scotland, and only occasionally Northern Ireland. All the contributors can do is to make clear the various coverages to the reader, so that a misleading impression is not created. Next there is the problem of measurement within each section. For instance, in the field of income, can benefits in the form of kind, like coal to miners or vegetables to farm labourers, be included? Is the income of the main wage earner counted alone, or is any income of the spouse or children also added? The problem is partly solved because the contributors are drawing on available material and are not designing new research projects. Nevertheless, these difficulties are pointed out in order to stress the limitations of this study, for repeatedly the contributors have been restricted by the lack of comprehensive national data.

RESEARCH AND SOCIAL DEPRIVATION

The nature of the study makes it wholly dependent on the quantity and quality of previous research in the fields of income, housing and child socialisation. Thus a brief outline of the development of relevant research in post-war Britain is in place.

Education contributes towards the socialisation of children and as early as the 1950s research was drawing attention to the educational handicaps associated with children from poor environments, especially those in homes characterised ,by overcrowding or lack of household amenities.[5] Larger studies confirmed the picture, as for example those carried out by J. W. B. Douglas.[6,7] The government expressed concern, and a series of government initiated reports, especially the Crowther, Newsom and Plowden Reports, further stressed that social deprivation was by no means vanquished.[8,9,10] The Plowden Report used research to make the important point that factors associated with educational deprivation tended to be found in certain geographical locations which could be defined, and hence given priority help.

The early years of the welfare state witnessed other important research projects, among them research into delinquency, deprived children and the problems of the elderly. Interest in the elderly was so strong that Rodgers says it ' . . . demanded the thoughts of those concerned with the social services . . . An enormous number of surveys were undertaken in the twenty or so years after the war . . . '[11] However, the 1940s and '50s showed a notable absence of research concerning housing deprivation and family poverty. Academics tended to blame the lack of research on the government. Donnison claimed that its lack of housing research led it into serious errors of policy.[12] Professor Titmuss, at the end of the 1950s, complained that the government had made 'no effort' to discover the real incidence of poverty.[13] McGregor went as far as to say, 'British society today exhibits a greater unwillingness to discover, to collect and to face up to the social facts of life than at any time during the last hundred years'.[14]

Such sweeping criticisms could not be made today. The late 1950s and the 1960s saw a plethora of housing surveys and statistics. The whole range is listed by Spencer in the section headed 'Sources' in Chapter 3 so examples need not be given at this point. It is enough to say that knowledge about the nature of housing deprivation was greatly increased by research carried out by the government and by the universities. Similarly, more light was thrown upon family poverty. In 1964, Margaret Wynn accumulated and presented statistics demonstrating the economic difficulties of fatherless families.[15] A year later appeared *The Poor and the Poorest* by Brian Abel-Smith and Peter Townsend which, drawing on government material, argued that poverty existed amongst substantial numbers of the population including many children.[3] Although criticised on methodological grounds, the publication had an impact on the popular press as well as on students of poverty. By this time the government had commenced its own investigations, the Ministry of Pensions and National Insurance instigating one of the first official large-scale poverty surveys published as *Financial and Other Circumstances of Retirement Pensioners*.[16] It was followed by their influential *Circumstances of Families*, a study based on a sample of families receiving family allowance.[2] Its findings are discussed extensively in the following chapters. It suffices here to say that it established the existence of poverty not only among those dependent on state benefits but also amongst those in full-time work. A number of other pieces of research were initiated during this period and the contrast with preceding years is such that their effect has been referred to as 'the rediscovery of poverty'.[17]

It is difficult to explain either why research into the housing and family income aspects of social deprivation was comparatively neglected in the earlier period or why it subsequently increased. The neglect may have stemmed from the assumption of some politicians and some elements of the press that the welfare state had not only made deprivation a thing of the past but was promoting substantial redistribution of income and wealth. Certainly there was not the unemployment of the pre-war years and the words of the prime minister, Harold Macmillan, in 1957, 'They've never had it so good', so caught the mood of the times as to become a catch phrase.* If these assumptions did influence society it may not have been considered necessary to initiate research.

There was by no means a blanket acceptance of the above assumptions.

---

* Macmillan used these or similar words in a number of speeches during his premiership. See A. Sampson, *Macmillan*, Allen Lane, The Penguin Press, 1967.

Professor Titmuss challenged them, especially questioning whether re-distribution of income and wealth was occurring.[18,19] In *The Irresponsible Society*, published in 1960, he said the concept of the welfare state largely benefiting the working class was a myth while there was little evidence to suggest that much progress had been made 'to concentrate help through the public services on those whose need is greatest . . . Those who have benefited most are those who have needed it least.'[13]

The call of Titmuss and others for more research came at a time when Social Administration and Sociology departments were growing in univer-sities and hence a response could be expected. The 1960s also witnessed the election of a socialist government committed to social change and, in many ways, 'research minded'. However, before giving it all the praise for the government research of the succeeding years, it is fair to add that many of the education reports, such as Crowther, were initiated under the previous government which also set up the Committee on Social Studies culminating in the establishment of the Social Science Research Council to support research in the field of social studies.

One other factor stimulating research, and its propagation, in the 1960s was the activities of voluntary pressure groups. Possibly their efforts increased in this period because they expected a socialist government to be more amenable to pressure for social reform. Paradoxically, disappointment with subsequent legislation also appears to have spurred them on. Most notable has been the Child Poverty Action Group, founded in 1965 under the secretaryship of Tony Lynes. Through its magazine *Poverty* and other means it has consistently and skilfully depicted the plight of the poor and the inadequacy of their provision. The Disablement Income Group, formed in 1965, and the Birmingham Claimants Union, formed in 1968, have also drawn attention to the conditions of their members. A number of societies concerned with children, in particular the Council for Children's Welfare and the National Society of Children's Nurseries, were concerned about children separated from their parents for short or long periods. Like other voluntary organisations, they not only urged the government and universi-ties to undertake research but were prepared to initiate their own. They commissioned the Yudkin Report whose findings revealed the adverse social and psychological environments affecting the socialisation of many children.[20]

Whatever the causes, by the end of the 1960s the frontiers of knowledge about social deprivation had been pushed outward. As frequently happens, the research served also to reveal the extent of ignorance about the subject. Further studies have been undertaken, for example exploring the extent and nature of poverty amongst certain deprived groups such as the unem-ployed, large families and the disabled. Even so, gaps in knowledge still exist including the amount of poverty amongst one-child families, the distribution of play space and facilities for children, the geographical location of the socially deprived, the extent of correlation between the different types of social deprivation, and the most effective means of countering it.

The background to the report has been outlined. The succeeding chapters will draw on the research mentioned above, as well as many other studies, to depict deprivation in the three areas of income, housing and child socialisation. In some respects they overlap by drawing on certain basic works, such as *Circumstances of Families*, which include material relevant to all three.[2] The editor has decided not to strike out the overlap where such action would imperil continuity of style or thought. The final chapter will attempt to identify any groupings amongst the deprived and to make some points about the services and means available to help them. It is hoped the material will prove of value to British and European readers as surely as the present contributors will learn from the work of their European colleagues. Needless to say, any views given are those of the contributors and not those of the United Nations or the publishers.

Finally, the contributors wish to extend their thanks to all the persons who have so readily co-operated in making the material available; to the Publications Department of the National Council of Social Service for its help and advice; to Mr J. W. A. Thorburn for editorial services; and to Mrs Marian Batten who typed all the script.

ROBERT HOLMAN

1. Income Deprivation

François Lafitte

INTRODUCTORY

In a community with a wide spread of incomes most families experience some degree of 'income deprivation' relative to families who are better off.

This paper is concerned with income deprivation in a much narrower sense — a level of income sufficiently low to be generally regarded as creating hardship, in terms of the community's prevailing living standards, and so requiring remedial action on the part of public social policy — in other words 'poverty' which is sufficiently severe to be seen as a 'social problem'.

An expert group convened by the British Social Science Research Council has well stated:[1]

'People are "poor" because they are deprived of the opportunities, comforts, and self-respect regarded as normal in the community to which they belong. It is therefore the continually moving *average* standards of that community that are the starting points for an assessment of its poverty, and the poor are those who fall sufficiently far below these average standards. Their deprivation can be measured and their numbers counted by comparisons with average personal income . . . or with a standard of living currently sanctioned by government . . . or with average life chances . . . But "felt" deprivations do not match the "objective" distribution of poverty at all closely.'

This paper reviews what is known about the 'objective' contemporary distribution in the United Kingdom of families with dependent children whose incomes 'fall sufficiently far' below the community's 'continually moving *average* standards' to be regarded as poor.

CHANGING INCOME STANDARDS

What average income standards have actually prevailed in Britain over 1966-68 among manual workers' families? How do these relate to the standards applied in public social policy for income-support of families where the father is unable to work (distribution of social security payments), and for spreading taxes on income with regard to family size and level of income (distribution of tax sacrifices)?

For answers to these questions 1966 is an appropriate starting point. In the summer of that year the government conducted a detailed survey of the levels of income prevailing among families with more than one dependent child.[2] These were compared with the income standards applied by Britain's nationalised assistance service for the relief of poverty among people unable to work. The extent of income deprivation revealed by this survey was one of the factors influencing the Wilson Government's subsequent reforms in social security. Those reforms came at a difficult time. 1966-68 was a period when, for economic reasons, the government was actively restraining the growth of money incomes. Money incomes continued to grow, though perhaps more slowly, but much of the increase was offset by rising prices. In terms of purchasing power the real incomes of many earners in 1968 were probably no greater than in 1966, and some may have been slightly reduced by the increased weight of direct taxes on income.

In 1966, until the autumn, Britain's social security services still retained essentially the structure imparted to them in the great refashioning of 1946-48: *

(1) State *family allowances* payable to every family with more than one dependent child. These were at flat rates regardless of a child's age, had not been improved since 1956, and were very small. For an average manual worker with five children they represented an addition to earnings (before tax) of only 9½ per cent.

(2) State *social insurance* payments during sickness or unemployment, with additions for a man's dependent wife, his first child (not eligible for family allowance), and for his other children (since their family allowances were much below minimum child-support costs). These insurance payments too were at the same flat rates for everyone; and the income they provided together with family allowances was appreciably below the poverty minimum of the assistance service.

(3) State *assistance* payments based on the principle that a man unable to work owing to illness, handicap or unemployment, has a right to have his income raised to a guaranteed level if his resources fall short of that level.[3] The price of food, fuel, clothing and other elementary necessaries does not in Britain vary widely from place to place or season to season. Housing costs (rent, owner-occupiers' costs, local taxation of dwellings) do vary widely and arbitrarily. Accordingly the

---

* The main exception was a trifling earnings-related addition to pensions (1961), with a corresponding earnings-related supplement added to the flat-rate social insurance contribution.

minimum income guaranteed by assistance has a variable and a fixed component: (i) reimbursement of the actual housing costs of an assisted family,* and (ii) uniform national minimum payments (varying by age for non-adults) for non-housing needs.†

From 1966 to the end of 1968 the government's reforms were:

(1) Appreciable enlargement of family allowances in real terms. With five children allowances now add 17½ per cent to the average manual worker's gross earnings.

(2) Improvements in additional payments for children through social insurance, with a more modest improvement of flat insurance payments for adults.

(3) Addition, since autumn 1966, to short-term flat insurance payments for the sick and unemployed of an appreciable extra payment— 'earnings-related benefit' — proportional to yearly earnings between £450 and £1500.

(4) Raising of the real level of income guaranteed through assistance (rates raised in autumn of 1966, 1967 and 1968).

(5) Enlargement of the social security charge on earnings to finance improvements under (2) and (3).

(6) Reduction of income-tax remissions with respect to children to offset for the better-off families the 1968 increases in family allowances.

THE AVERAGE MANUAL WORKER: WORK INCOME AND
SOCIAL SECURITY PAYMENTS

Set in this context of change, the purpose of Tables 1 and 2 is to analyse trends from early 1966 to the end of 1968 in Britain's accustomed income standards and expectations at the level of the average manual worker—the AMW for short. For comparative purposes the following conventions are used:

(1) The normal standard for earnings is the average earnings of adult male manual workers in the main range of UK industries, as officially ascertained for one week in April and October of each year.

(2) In Britain wages and social payments are expressed in *weekly* rates, but levels of income taxation and of earnings-related insurance payments are determined by *yearly* income. For convenience of comparison the tables express all rates in annual terms—the yearly income and tax standards implied by various rates of weekly earnings, social pay-

---

* Reimbursement may be partial if housing costs are 'unreasonably high', but partial reimbursement is rare.

† A family with some exceptional need may get more than the national minimum payment. The right to assistance at full rates remains even if a family has a small amount of income from certain prescribed sources or capital not exceeding prescribed limits; and the capital value of an owner-occupied dwelling is ignored.

ments or charges on income. All weekly rates are multiplied by fifty-two.

(3) The AMW's yearly earnings are taken to be the average weekly wage in (1) above multiplied by fifty-two. This represents the income standard aspired to—and achieved by increasing numbers of workers—of wages derived from full employment throughout the year and with no loss of earnings (or equivalent replacement income) at least during short spells of sickness.

(4) The AMW is assumed to be the sole family earner, supporting his wife and one to five children of primary school age.

(5) Regardless of size, all families at the AMW level are assumed to have the same housing costs—those of the average household whose chief economic supporter is a manual worker with about the average wage.

Technical details are given in the Notes on Tables on page 49.

The salient changes in incomes and income standards between 1966 (Table 1) and 1968 (Table 2) are summarised in Table 3, both in terms of money and, allowing for increased prices, in real values.

(1) For the AMW in full employment the net effect of changes in social payments, income taxation and social security charges has depended on family size.* The disposable income left to the married AMW with no child or one or two children was little or no greater, in terms of purchasing power, in 1968 than in 1966. It may even have been cut a little for this preponderant group of smaller families. But for the minority of larger families it has been appreciably improved.

(2) For the AMW who is sick or unemployed and has to depend on insurance payments and family allowances ('benefits' in the tables), the improvement from early 1966 to late 1968 is much more pronounced, even allowing for a price increase of 11 per cent.

(3) During the first nine months of 1966 a sick or unemployed man was entitled only to the flat 'basic minimum' benefits (insurance payments plus family allowances) shown at line 10 of Table 1. How markedly these were improved, especially for the larger families, by the end of 1968 is seen in Table 3. In 1968 moreover, after two weeks' sickness or unemployment, the basic minimum benefit is enlarged by a substantial earnings-related additional benefit. For the AMW this is at the rates shown at line 11 of Table 2. At the AMW level the combined basic and earnings-related benefits have improved the real income of families with two children by one-half, and that of those with five children by more than one-third (Table 3, line 12). This enhanced total benefit

---

* Income tax falls upon the great majority of earners and is applied to family allowances as well as other income. All earners pay a flat-rate social security contribution and nearly all pay an additional earnings-related contribution. So far as possible income-tax and social security charges are deducted by employers from the wages paid out to men.

standard operates from the third to the twenty-eighth week (inclusive) of sickness or unemployment, leaving only those with very short or quite abnormally long interruptions of earnings to depend only on the basic minimum.*

(4) Men not working who have to depend on insurance and family allowance payments may find, if they have no other resources, that their income is below the official minimum of the assistance service. If so, and if they apply, they are entitled to assistance sufficient to raise them to that level. The assistance standard is Britain's official 'poverty line'. Anyone not in work who is below this level is considered poor enough to need help. Anyone raised up to or beyond this level is considered to have been rescued from poverty. The assistance standard is the upper limit or ceiling (save where needs are exceptional) set on public action for the relief of poverty *not* attributable to abnormally low wages.

The assistance standard is shown at lines 13-15 of Tables 1 and 2, including housing costs at the AMW level. Since early 1966 (when it was admittedly obsolescent) this official poverty standard has been improved in real terms by about 7 per cent (Table 3, line 15), moving ahead of the real improvement in earnings and disposable income.

(5) Both in 1968 and in 1966, Tables 1 and 2 show, the basic benefit standard, even for a family paying no rent at all, was appreciably below the assistance standard. What transformed the situation for the AMW in 1968 was the addition of earnings-related benefit. By the end of 1968 the AMW supported on the total benefit standard (line 12) would be well above the assistance level and so not officially poor— save possibly if his housing costs were abnormally high, his family very large, his children all much older than the tables assume,† or his needs quite exceptional in some other way.

---

* During short sickness large numbers of workers continue to receive either full wages or the balance of wages not covered by social insurance benefits (see ref. 4). Many who fall sick or unemployed, or even go on strike, fairly late in the fiscal year (autumn or winter) receive appreciable reimbursements of income tax. Many have savings to draw on during short interruptions of earning capacity. For the small minority at the AMW level who after twenty-eight weeks have to revert to basic minimum benefits, and who lack other resources, additional income can usually be obtained from assistance.

† The assistance service's annual valuation (late 1968) of a dependent child aged sixteen is £138, against the £81 assumed in the tables for a child aged five to ten, and as against a family allowance, not varying with age, of £47 (first eligible child) or £52 (each other eligible child).

TABLE 1.   AVERAGE YEARLY INCOME STANDARDS FOR MANUAL WORKERS
1966

	Man supporting Wife and Children:				
	1	2	3	4	5
A. NORMAL INCOME IN WORK					
Gross Income	£	£	£	£	£
1. Earnings	1,054	1,054	1,054	1,054	1,054
2. Family allowances	—	21	47	73	99
3. Total:	1,054	1,075	1,101	1,127	1,153
Less Direct Taxes					
4. Income tax	107	70	41	15	—
5. Social security	58	58	58	58	58
6. Total:	165	128	99	73	58
7. *Disposable Income* (3-6)	889	947	1,002	1,054	1,095
8. *Less Work Expenses*	33	33	33	33	33
9. *Net Income* (7-8)	856	914	969	1,021	1,062
B. BENEFIT STANDARDS					
10. Basic minimum	397	456	519	583	647
11. Earnings-related at AMW level	200	200	200	200	200
12. Total at AMW level	597	656	719	783	847
C. ASSISTANCE STANDARDS					
13. General costs (fixed)					
(a) Early 1966	397	467	537	608	678
(b) Late 1966	419	492	565	637	710
14. Housing costs (variable) at AMW level	94	94	94	94	94
15. Total at AMW level					
(a) Early 1966	491	561	631	702	772
(b) Late 1966	513	586	659	731	804
D. TAX STANDARDS					
16. Income free of tax	585	733	881	1,029	1,177
5. Less social security charge (AMW level)	58	58	58	58	58
17. Effective tax floor at AMW level (16-5)	527	675	823	971	1,119

TAX FLOORS AND POVERTY CEILINGS

Table 4 illustrates these changes in a different way. At the AMW level it shows: (i) a slight reduction by 1968, except for large families, in the proportion which disposable income bears to gross earnings; (ii) a very marked improvement in the proportion of disposable income which is replaced by benefits during interruption of earnings; (iii) a more modest improvement in the proportion of disposable income guaranteed by assistance; and (iv) a shifting of the balance between (ii) and (iii) in favour of provision through benefit rather than assistance.

No full-time earner can escape the social security contribution deducted from earnings. But income tax, the main direct charge, is so arranged that income below a certain level, which varies with family size and children's ages, escapes tax altogether. This 'tax floor', below which the state refrains from imposing any sacrifice (save the social security charge), is shown at line 16 in Tables 1 and 2. Line 17 shows the effective tax floor at AMW level including social security charges.

If people's incomes are larger, when distributing tax sacrifices the state will not reduce them below the effective tax floor. If people who are not working have incomes below the assistance standard, that standard represents a ceiling above which the state will not normally raise their incomes. It is arguable that the tax floor should normally stand at a higher level than the assistance ceiling.* For if men whose incomes fall below the official poverty line were nevertheless to be officially regarded as prosperous

TABLE 2. AVERAGE YEARLY INCOME STANDARDS FOR MANUAL WORKERS
1968
Man supporting Wife and Children:

	1	2	3	4	5
A. NORMAL INCOME IN WORK					
Gross Income	£	£	£	£	£
1. Earnings	1,170	1,170	1,170	1,170	1,170
2. Family allowances	—	47	99	151	203
3. Total	1,170	1,217	1,269	1,321	1,373
Less Direct Taxes					
4. Income tax	144	127	111	94	79
5. Social security	67	67	67	67	67
6. Total	211	194	178	161	146
7. *Disposable Income*	959	1,023	1,091	1,160	1,227
8. *Less Work Expenses*	36	36	36	36	36
9. *Net Income*	923	987	1,055	1,124	1,191
B. BENEFIT STANDARDS					
10. Basic minimum	452	525	598	671	744
11. Earnings-related at AMW level	237	237	237	237	237
12. Total at AMW level	689	762	835	908	981
C. ASSISTANCE STANDARDS					
13. General costs (fixed)	471	554	637	721	804
14. Housing costs (variable) at AMW level	115	115	115	115	115
15. Total at AMW level	586	669	752	836	919
D. TAX STANDARDS					
16. Income free of tax	585	687	788	890	991
5. Less social security charge (AMW level)	67	67	67	67	67
17. Effective tax floor at AMW level	518	620	721	823	924

* Though Titmuss, a leading socialist thinker, appears to take the contrary view (ref. 5).

TABLE 3. INCREASE IN MONEY AND REAL INCOME STANDARDS

Averages for Manual Workers   1966 to 1968

	Children in Family	Percentage Increase	
		Money Rates	Real Values
(A) 1968 OVER 1966			
Consumer prices		7½	
1. Earnings		11	3½
2. Family allowances:	3	110½	96
	5	105	94
7. Disposable income:	1	8	½
	2	8	½
	3	9	1½
	5	12	4½
(B) 1968 LAST QUARTER OVER 1966 FIRST QUARTER			
Consumer prices		11	
10. Basic minimum benefits .	2	15	4
	3	31	18
	5	63	47
12. Total benefit:	2	67	50
	3	61	45
	5	52	36
15. Total assistance:	2 ⎫		
	3 ⎬	19	7
	5 ⎭		

Note:

Items numbered as in Table 2. Data from Tables 1 and 2.

enough to sacrifice some of their income in direct taxation, then the state could not avoid appearing to use income taxation to make poor men poorer. Though the tax floor must be founded on some concept of reasonable need or of the reasonable limits to sacrifice, that concept has always seemed to have been one of relative income deprivation, when the deprivation is directly attributable to state action, couched justifiably in more liberal terms than the official standard for that deprivation which constitutes poverty.*

The tax floor could therefore be reasonably expected to be fixed at a distinctly higher point than the assistance ceiling; and this was so until recently. During the period under review, however, the gap between the

TABLE 4. SOCIAL INCOME STANDARDS RELATED TO NORMAL INCOME
Averages for Manual Workers

	Children in Family	1966 Early	1968 Late
1. Earnings =		100	100
7. Disposable income:	1	84½	82
	2	90	87½
	3	95½	93
	5	104	104½
7. *Disposable Income* =		100	100
12. Total benefit:	1	44½	72
	2	48	74½
	3	51½	76½
	5	58	80
15. Total assistance:	1	55	61
	2	59	65½
	3	63	69
	5	70½	75

Note:
As for Table 3.

two standards has been narrowed. At the AMW level, by the end of 1968, Table 2 shows not only that for most families (save very large ones) the tax floor was below the assistance ceiling, but also that the tax floor was for nearly all families below the benefit standard. Thus in 1968 a great many men could be deemed poor enough when not working to be given financial help by the state up to a level at which, if they were working, they would be regarded as rich enough to pay some tax.†

* The criteria by which British finance ministers in their annual budgets determine the floor for income tax are an unexplained mystery. Nearly as mysterious are the unpublished determinants which underlie standards of assistance. Though tax rates and assistance rates are both in the last resort approved by Parliament and not subsequently changed without fresh reference to Parliament, this aspect of their structure is never publicly explained.

† In practice the absurdity seldom arises. Assistance payments are not taxable, nor are insurance benefits for sickness and unemployment. Family allowances and insurance pensions (e.g. of widowed mothers) are, however, taxable. It is fair to add (i) that people with incomes at or close to the assistance standard normally have lower housing costs than the AMW (cf. the low earners in Tables 5 and 6), so that for them the assistance ceiling in fact usually remains below the tax floor if they have three or more children; and (ii) that, although he could not escape a minimum charge for social security, a man with income exceeding the tax floor by not more than £100 annually would sacrifice only 20 per cent of that excess in income tax (fiscal year 1968-69). And see page 45, footnote, on the raising of the tax floor by the Budget of 1969.

THE LOW-EARNING FAMILY MAN

So much for the average income standards which prevail in contemporary Britain. At the level of the average manual worker and using the assistance poverty yardstick, very few men with children today are in official poverty whether in work or living on benefit or assistance.

What of low earners? In 1966 and 1967 (and most likely in 1968) men whose earnings in full-time work amounted to two-thirds or less of the AMW wages surveyed in Tables 1-4 constituted about one-tenth of all manual workers.[6] About one-half of these low earners had earnings not exceeding 60 per cent of the AMW wage. This minority of men were also more prone to sickness and unemployment, so that it is less plausible to assume for them annual work incomes of fifty-two times their normal weekly full-time earnings. Their housing costs average only about four-fifths of those of the AMW, but earnings-related supplements to their insurance benefits are also smaller. Moreover, when out of work, both their benefits and their assistance may be reduced by 'wage-stop' restrictions limiting the total of social payments (other than family allowances) to a man's normal disposable income when in work, reduced to allow for travel and other expenses only incurred when men are working.* On the other hand direct taxes on low incomes are lower.

On the same lines as for the AMW in Tables 1-4, Tables 5-8 set out the situation of this low-earning minority in 1966 and at the end of 1968. The man with two-thirds of the AMW wage has earnings broadly corresponding to those of the lowest decile of manual workers, while the 60 per cent earner is broadly at the level of the lowest half-decile.† For comparison of income standards the same conventions are adopted as in Tables 1 and 2, save that for low earners housing costs are assumed to be 80 per cent of the AMW's.

The salient features of these four tables are:

(1) The discrepancy between the net incomes of low earners in full-time work and the official poverty standard during the main part of 1966. Thus in Table 5, taking the unrevised assistance standard (line 15a) as the measure of poverty, men might be worse off when working (in terms of the net incomes of line 9) than—at least in theory—they could be if supported by assistance. On the table's assumptions this applied to the very low 60 per cent earners with more than two

---

* Earnings-related benefit plus other insurance payments must not exceed 85 per cent of the earnings to which earnings-related benefit is related. Assistance must not exceed normal net income after tax, social security charges and work expenses. Criteria of normal earnings and work expenses, when these cannot be precisely ascertained, have been somewhat liberalised since 1966.

† Decile: the uppermost earner among the lowest tenth.
Half-decile: the uppermost earner among the lowest twentieth.

children and to two-thirds earners with more than four. The more generous official redefinition of poverty in autumn 1966 (line 15b) naturally enlarged the numbers who were judged officially poor even though working. This change widened the discrepancy for the groups earlier mentioned, and extended it to include two-thirds earners with four children. Low earners with lower rents or younger children than the table assumes would be somewhat better placed, those with higher rents or older children somewhat worse placed.

TABLE 5. YEARLY INCOME STANDARDS FOR LOW EARNERS 1966

Man supporting Wife and Children :

	1	2	3	4	5
TWO-THIRDS EARNER					
A. *Normal Income*	£	£	£	£	£
3. Gross income	703	724	750	776	802
6. Less direct taxes	65	47	47	47	47
7. Disposable income	638	677	703	729	755
8. Less work expenses	33	33	33	33	33
9. Net income	605	644	670	696	722
B. *Benefit Standards*					
10. Basic minimum	397	456	519	583	647
11. Earnings-related	86	86	86	86	76*
12. Total	483	542	605	669	723*
60 PER CENT EARNER					
A. *Normal Income*					
3. Gross income	633	654	680	706	732
6. Less direct taxes	51	44	44	44	44
7. Disposable income	582	610	636	662	688
8. Less work expenses	33	33	33	33	33
9. Net income	549	577	603	629	655
B. *Benefit Standards*					
10 Basic minimum	397	456	519	583	647
11. Earnings-related	60	60	60	47*	9*
12. Total	457	516	579	630*	656*
ASSISTANCE STANDARDS FOR BOTH					
15. *Unrestricted Total :*					
(a) Early 1966	472	542	612	683	753
(b) Late 1966	494	567	640	712	785
18. *Restricted Total* (Ceiling = 9):					
(i) Two-thirds earner				697*	723*
(ii) 60 per cent earner			603*	629*	655*

Notes: Items numbered as in Table 2. For details see Notes on p. 49.
* Figure affected by 'wage-stop' provisions.

(2) The continuing discrepancy between benefit and assistance standards. For the low earner the introduction of additional earnings-related benefits has *not*, as with the AMW, sufficed to raise him above the poverty line when living on benefit, though it has diminished the gap (Table 6.)

(3) Where low earners' customary income when in work is at poverty levels, the use of 'wage-stop' rules preventing payment of full benefit or assistance when these men are not working, since these payments may not exceed normal disposable or net earnings (as variously defined). Although the real standards of insurance and assistance provision for low earners improved from 1966 to 1968, the figures with asterisks in Tables 5 and 6 indicate circumstances in which benefit

TABLE 6. YEARLY INCOME STANDARDS FOR LOW EARNERS   1968

Man supporting Wife and Children:

		1	2	3	4	5
TWO-THIRDS EARNER						
	A. *Normal Income*	£	£	£	£	£
3.	Gross income	780	827	879	931	983
6.	Less direct taxes	95	82	73	65	59
7.	Disposable income	685	745	806	866	924
8.	Less work expenses	36	36	36	36	36
9.	Net income	649	709	770	830	888
	B. *Benefit Standards*					
10.	Basic minimum	452	525	598	671	744
11.	Earnings-related	107	107	107	107	107
12.	Total	559	632	705	778	851
60 PER CENT EARNER						
	A. *Normal Income*					
3.	Gross income	702	749	801	853	905
6.	Less direct taxes	89	74	66	57	55
7.	Disposable income	613	675	735	796	850
8.	Less work expenses	36	36	36	36	36
9.	Net income	577	639	699	760	814
	B. *Benefit Standards*					
10.	Basic minimum	452	525	598	671	744
11.	Earnings-related	81	81	81	81	69*
12.	Total	533	606	679	752	813*
ASSISTANCE STANDARDS FOR BOTH						
15.	Unrestricted Total	563	646	729	813	896
18.	Restricted Total (Ceiling):					
	(ii) 60 per cent Earner			717*	778*	832*

Notes:
As for Table 5.

TABLE 7. INCREASES IN MONEY AND REAL INCOME STANDARDS

1966 to 1968

Low Earners

Percentage Increase

	Children in Family	Two-Thirds Earner		60 per cent Earner	
		Money Rates	Real Values	Money Rates	Real Values
(A) 1968 OVER 1966					
Prices					
Earnings			As in Table 3		
Family allowances					
7. Disposable income:	1	$7\frac{1}{2}$	0	$5\frac{1}{2}$	−2
	2	10	$2\frac{1}{2}$	$10\frac{1}{2}$	3
	3	$14\frac{1}{2}$	$6\frac{1}{2}$	$15\frac{1}{2}$	$7\frac{1}{2}$
	5	$22\frac{1}{2}$	14	$23\frac{1}{2}$	15
(B) 1968 LAST QUARTER OVER 1966 FIRST QUARTER					
Prices			As in Table 3		
Basic minimum benefit					
12. Total benefit:	2	39	25	33	20
	3	36	$22\frac{1}{2}$	31	18
	5	32	19	26*	$13\frac{1}{2}$*
15. Total assistance:	2	19	7	19	7
	3	19	7	19*	7*
	5	$25\frac{1}{2}$*	13*	27*	$14\frac{1}{2}$*

Notes:
As for Table 5.

or assistance are restricted to sub-standard levels by 'wage-stop' requirements. The impact of these restrictions was generally less severe in 1968 than in 1966.*

(4) Despite the foregoing, both in real and relative terms Tables 7 and 8 record for low earners since 1966 a notable strengthening of disposable incomes when they are in work and if they have four or more children to support. But for some of the smaller families at these low income levels there was little or no improvement. The tables record

---

* In 1966 the assistance ceiling, shown at line 18 of Table 5, was determined by the net income shown at line 9. In 1968 the ceiling is officially intended to be a little higher than net income as shown in line 9 of Table 6. In determining the ceiling only half the work expenses assumed in line 8 (those for travel to work) would necessarily be deducted (see ref. 7).

also, for all family sizes, substantial improvements in benefit and assistance standards, though this is more pronounced for smaller than for larger families.

Compared with changes at the AMW level, the improvement in disposable incomes, reflecting changes in family allowances and direct taxation, is much more pronounced for low than for average earners. On the other hand, relative improvements in benefit standards, chiefly earnings-related insurance payments, have been more marked for the average than for the low earner. Changes in levels of assistance have been fairly uniform at nearly all the income levels and family sizes considered.

TABLE 8. SOCIAL INCOME STANDARDS RELATED TO NORMAL INCOME
Low Earners

		Two-Thirds Earner		60 per cent Earner	
	Children in Family	*1966 Early*	*1968 Late*	*1966 Early*	*1968 Late*
1. Earnings =		100	100	100	100
7. Disposable income:	1	91	88	92	87½
	2	96½	95½	96½	96
	3	100	103½	100½	105
	5	107½	118½	109	121
7. Disposable Income =		100	100	100	100
12. Total benefit:	1	62	81½	68	87
	2	67½	85	74½	90
	3	74	87½	81½	92½
	5	85½	92	94	95½*
15. Total assistance:	1	74	82	81	92
	2	80	87	88½	95½
	3	87	90½	95*	97½*
	5	95½*	97	95*	98*

Notes:
As for Table 5.

WIDOWED AND OTHER SINGLE-HANDED MOTHERS

The remaining important group of families with dependent children is the fatherless—single-handed mothers who are widows, separated or deserted, or who are unmarried. Such mothers have the same right as other citizens to family allowances if they have more than one child; and, if employed, they may qualify for insurance benefits during sickness and unemployment.

TABLE 9. SOCIAL INCOME STANDARDS FOR WIDOWED MOTHERS   1966

Widow supporting Children:

ASSISTANCE STANDARDS	1 £	2 £	3 £	4 £	5 £
14. Housing costs	75	75	75	75	75
Early 1966:					
13a. General costs	268	338	409	479	549
15a. Total	343	413	484	554	624
Late 1966:					
13b. General costs:					
(i) Two years	284	357	429	502	575
(ii) Long-term	307	380	452	525	598
15b. Total:					
(i) Two years	359	432	504	577	650
(ii) Long-term	382	455	527	600	673
19. Plus 'disregarded' insurance benefit	20	39	54	68	81
BENEFIT STANDARDS					
10. Basic minimum	312	416	520	624	728
Short-term additions:					
20. Extra flat benefit	85	85	85	85	85
11. Earnings-related supplement, if husband:					
(i) AMW earner	200	200	200	200	200
(ii) Two-thirds earner	86	86	86	86	86
21. Short-term total (10+20+11), if husband:					
(i) AMW earner	597	701	805	909	1,013
(ii) Two-thirds earner	483	587	691	795	899

Otherwise, social insurance provides only for the single-handed mother who is also a widow:

(1) Basic minimum benefit (insurance plus family allowances) at the rates shown at line 10 of Tables 9 and 10—the only benefit paid beyond six months of widowhood.

(2) During an initial period of widowhood (three months until autumn 1966, six months thereafter) a temporary additional flat-rate benefit (line 20).

(3) Since autumn 1966, during the same initial six months an earnings-related supplement based on the deceased husband's earnings (line 11).

A widowed mother receiving insurance benefit may, if she lacks other income, find herself below the assistance ceiling. If so, assistance will raise her income up to the levels indicated in the tables without requiring her to seek paid work. During most of 1966 the widow, like any other single-handed mother, was guaranteed through assistance only the total income shown at line 15(a) of Table 9 (assuming the housing costs of line 14). At

the end of that year three improvements were made:
(1) The basic assistance standard was raised.
(2) Widows with insurance benefits who are also receiving assistance now
    have their assistance payments raised after two years on assistance
    (the long-term rates of 13(ii) in Tables 9 and 10).
(3) In settling the amount of assistance payable, a portion of the widow's
    insurance benefits* is ignored. In effect, for the insured widow the
    assistance standard, short-term or long-term, is raised by the 'dis-
    regarded' insurance benefit at line 19 of the tables.

The first two improvements apply to all single-handed mothers, the third
only to widows with insurance pensions.

Extremely little is known about the incomes and circumstances of life of
widowed mothers, still less about those of other single-handed mothers.†

TABLE 10.   SOCIAL INCOME STANDARDS FOR WIDOWED MOTHERS   1968

	Widow supporting Children:				
ASSISTANCE STANDARDS	1 £	2 £	3 £	4 £	5 £
14. Housing costs	92	92	92	92	92
13. General costs:					
(i) Two years	320	403	487	570	653
(ii) Long-term	346	429	513	596	679
15. Total:					
(i) Two years	412	495	579	662	745
(ii) Long-term	438	521	605	688	771
19. *Plus* 'disregarded' insurance benefit	20	39	54	68	82
BENEFIT STANDARDS					
10. Basic minimum	353	471	589	708	826
Short-term additions:					
20. Extra flat benefit	96	96	96	96	96
11. Earnings-related supplement, if husband:					
(i) AMW earner	237	237	237	237	237
(ii) Two-thirds earner	107	107	107	107	107
21. Short-term total (10+20+11), if husband:					
(i) AMW earner	686	804	922	1,041	1,159
(ii) Two-thirds earner	556	674	792	911	1,029

* The increase in children's insurance benefits enacted in 1965.
† The official survey of childhood poverty in 1966 lumped all fatherless families
  together and published no information about their housing costs, work expenses
  and other relevant factors.

To establish what income standards prevail in Britain even for widowed mothers—the purpose of Tables 9-12—involves, save in the case of the benefit standard, a series of hypotheses. These tables, based on the same conventions as Tables 1-8, show the situation of the widowed mother (who almost always has an insurance pension) *if*:

(1) When taking assistance to supplement her benefit her net housing costs are 80 per cent of those of the AMW.

(2) When she takes employment to supplement her benefit with earnings,
   (i) She earns at best half the wage of the AMW or, more likely, one-quarter of that wage because she can take only part-time work;* and
   (ii) Her work expenses, including the costs of child-minding, are at the levels of line 8 in Table 11.

The Notes on Tables on p. 49 explain these and other assumptions.

Given these partly hypothetical circumstances, the salient features of Tables 9-12 are:

(1) The contrast between the widowed mother's benefits during the initial three/six months and her long-term benefits thereafter.
   (a) Even the three-month 'cushion' which was provided during most of 1966 (10 plus 20 in Table 9) sufficed to raise most widowed mothers temporarily above the official poverty line (15a). The ampler six-month cushion later provided (21 in Tables 9 and 10) does so in all cases. If indeed these short-term extra benefits were to run for twelve months instead of six, pensioned widowed mothers at the AMW level would generally be prosperous enough to pay some income tax. For the rates are above the tax floors shown in Table 11.
   (b) Since the assistance improvements of late 1966 widowed mothers' long-term benefits have been below the two-year assistance standard (15(i) plus 19 in Table 10), save perhaps for widows with at least five children, and still more below the long-term assistance standard (15(ii) plus 19).

(2) This reflects:
   (a) The very modest real improvement since early 1966 in widowed mothers' benefits (2-2½ per cent in real terms) indicated in Table 12. For the family supported by a father, even a very low earner, during sickness or unemployment the improvement has been much greater (total benefit, line 12, Tables 3 and 7). Sickness and unemployment are for most men short-term dependencies; widowhood is very often a long-term dependency. The six-month cushion of

---

* Women's full-time earnings among manual workers average half those of men.

earnings-related benefits suffices for most men, but affords only an
initial spell of comfort for a great many widows.

(b) An impressive enhancement of the real levels of assistance for
widowed mothers ('full assistance' standard in Table 12), with a
somewhat lesser improvement for other single-handed mothers,
who do not profit from the widow's 'disregarded' benefit. This
enhancement goes well beyond that effected for father-supported
families, even of very low earners, and is not restricted by wage-
stop rules.

TABLE 11.   EARNING AND TAX STANDARDS FOR WIDOWED MOTHERS

1966 and 1968

Widow supporting Children:

	1	2	3	4	5
INCOME IN WORK					
1966	£	£	£	£	£
(i) With Half of AMW *Earnings*					
3. Gross Income	839	943	1,047		
6. Less direct taxes	77	68	57		
7. Disposable income	762	875	990		
8. Less work expenses	62	98	124		
9. Net income	700	777	866		
(ii) With Quarter of AMW *Earnings*					
3. Gross income	576	680	784	888	992
6. Less direct taxes	16	9	3	2	2
7. Disposable income	560	671	781	886	990
8. Less work expenses	62	98	124	150	176
9. Net income	498	573	657	736	814
1968					
(i) With Half of AMW *Earnings*					
3. Gross income	938	1,056	1,174		
6. Less direct taxes	106	83	80		
7. Disposable income	832	973	1,094		
8. Less work expenses	77	125	151		
9. Net income	755	848	943		
(ii) With Quarter of AMW *Earnings*					
3. Gross income	646	764	882	1,001	1,119
6. Less direct taxes	20	16	11	7	2
7. Disposable income	626	748	871	994	1,117
8. Less work expenses	77	125	151	177	203
9. Net income	549	623	720	817	914
TAX STANDARDS					
16. Income free of tax: 1966	482	630	778	926	1,074
1968	527	675	823	971	1,119

(3)   The contrast between long-term benefit and assistance standards for
widowed mothers is clear in Table 12. The proportion of her late husband's disposable income which the widowed mother recovers from
social security benefits is generally low and has changed very little
since 1966. The proportion guaranteed by assistance is larger and has
been appreciably raised since 1966. For widows of low earners with
large families it can now even exceed former disposable income.

TABLE 12.   CHANGES AFFECTING WIDOWED MOTHERS   1966 to 1968

(A) MONEY AND REAL INCOME STANDARDS
    (1968 fourth quarter over 1966 first quarter)

	Children	Percentage Increase			
		Money Rates		Real Values	
10. Benefit (basic minimum)		13 to 13½		2 to 2½	
15. Full assistance		(i)	(ii)	(i)	(ii)
+	1	26	33½	13½	20½
19.	2	29½	35½	16½	22½
	3	31	36½	18	23
	5	32½	37	19½	23

(B) SOCIAL INCOME RELATED TO NORMAL INCOME

		Percentage of Husband's Disposable Income			
		AMW Earner		⅔ Earner	
		1966	1968	1966	1968
		Early	Late	Early	Late
10. Benefit (basic minimum)	1	35	37	49	52
	2	44	46	61	63
	3	52	54	74	73
	5	67	67	96	89
15. Full assistance:					
+ (i) Two years	1	39	45	54	68
19.	2	44	52	61	79
	3	48	58	69	90
	5	57	67	83	110
(ii) Long-term	1	39	48	54	72
	2	44	55	61	83
	3	48	60	69	94
	5	57	70	83	113

Notes:
Full assistance: Total assistance (15) plus disregarded insurance benefit (19).
Assistance (i) = first two years; (ii) = long-term.
Data from Tables 9 and 10.
Husband's disposable income: AMW earner as in Tables 1 and 2.
                               Two-thirds earner as in Tables 5 and 6.

(4) The genuine financial gain to the widowed mother who is able to combine caring for her children with paid employment (net income, line 9, Table 11)—*if* she can limit her work expenses to the levels indicated. Although social security benefits are intended to enable the widow to care for children without taking paid work unless she wishes, the low proportion of disposable income they provide, in particular for mothers with one or two children, is hardly compatible with that intention.

Most widowed mothers can be better off if they are earning even a low part-time wage. The incentive to earn will be particularly strong where they can enlist relatives or friends to help with care of the children, rather than rely on costly and scarce facilities such as nurseries. The incentive is strengthened by the fact that a single-handed mother receiving assistance may, by part-time work, have net earnings of £104 a year without reducing her income from assistance.

Among single-handed mothers the widows are the best-treated group.* Even when on assistance, income standards are somewhat lower for the abandoned wife, the prisoner's wife and the unmarried mother, and these groups are outside the scope of family support through social insurance unless they take paid work.

POVERTY IN 1966

This lengthy review of income norms is a necessary prelude to examining what is known about income deprivation among British families. By far the most important source of information is the government's own survey of childhood poverty in the summer of 1966.² Some of its main findings are summarised in Tables 13 to 17.

Taking a representative sample of families with dependent children, the survey tried to ascertain their income from every source (including wives' earnings), which it then compared with the official assistance yardstick of poverty. The sample, taken from families entitled to family allowances, was confined to families with two or more *dependent* children, but omitted families where no dependent child was aged under sixteen.† Allowing for non-response and incomplete response, the data obtained related to about 80 per cent of all families with two or more dependent children in Britain. The survey's findings were converted into national estimates (i) by adjustment to allow for the uninvestigated 20 per cent (predominantly better-off

---

* Widows of men who die in consequence of war or industrial injury have better social income and tax standards than the great majority of widows depending on ordinary social insurance.

† Children over fifteen but under eighteen remain eligible for family allowances if they are in full-time education or apprenticeship.

families), and (ii) by adding an incomplete estimate of poverty among one-child families. These national estimates might for various reasons some-what overstate the amount of measured poverty* Against this, however, the omission of Northern Ireland—the survey refers only to Great Britain —tends to some understating of poverty in the UK as a whole.

The poverty yardstick applied was the unrevised assistance standard which prevailed during most of 1966 (*old poverty standard* in Tables 13-16). Since that standard was improved late in the year, however, the survey added summary estimates of the extent to which measured poverty would be increased by applying the new yardstick (*new poverty standard* in the tables). The family income related to these yardsticks was the net income of earners after deducting direct taxes and work expenses (broadly the *net income* of line 9, Tables 1, 2, 5, 6) and all other income *except* assist-ance. From a family's 'initial net resources' so defined, its actual housing costs were then deducted (cf. line 14 in Tables 1-8). The balance of income remaining (net income for non-housing costs) was then compared with the fixed assistance standard for non-housing costs (line 13, Tables 1, 2, 5, 6). This identified those families whose initial resources fell short of the official poverty line—the *initially poor* of the first column of Tables 13 to 16. Some of these families were, however, having their defective initial incomes supplemented by assistance and thus were lifted out of official poverty (second column). The rest remained in poverty because they were not entitled to assistance or had not asked for it (third column).

The tables show the survey's own findings about families with more than one child and about one-child families of fully employed fathers. For completeness they also include the writer's own estimates (or guesses) about other one-child families and about the numbers of adults (parents) in poor families.

The numbers of families and children estimated to be in old-standard initial poverty in 1966—about a million children in more than a third of a million families (with about 600,000 adults) (Table 13)—was larger than many people expected. More than a decade of marked growth in the general standard of living and of improving social services had left a wide-spread impression that, in an emerging affluent society, child poverty had been reduced to trifling dimensions. And the discovery that less than half of this unexpectedly large amount of family poverty was being removed by the assistance service (Table 13, col. 2) damaged the complacent belief that the 'welfare state's' social services could be relied upon to remove all hardship.

Only 3 per cent of families (including one-child families), with 4 per cent of children, lived in *unrelieved* old-standard poverty (col. 3) — a vast

---

* e.g. Families' statements about their incomes were not verified and are believed to have involved some understatement.

improvement by the criteria of 1919-39. But they amounted to over half a million children with over a third of a million parents—large numbers to discover after two decades of a fully employed and economically progressing welfare state. Moreover the welfare state had not removed the relationship between poverty and family size. The proportion in unrelieved poverty rose from 2 per cent of children in one- or two-child families to 11 per cent

TABLE 13. FAMILIES IN POVERTY, 1966: SUMMARY

		Old Standard			New Standard
		Initially Poor	Assisted	Not Assisted	Initially Poor
One-Child Families	'000				
Families		85	35	50	105
Children		85	35	50	105
Parents		155	65	90	190
Larger Families	'000				
Families		280	135[(i)]	145	345
Children		910	400	510	1,110
Parents		460	190	270	590
All Families	'000				
Families		365	170	195	450
Children		995	435	560	1,215
Parents		615	255	360	780
Percentage of All Families of Each Size					
Children: 1		3	1	2	4
2		5	3	2	
3		7	3	4	
4		11	5	6	
5		19	9	10	
6+		25	6	19	
All		5	2	3	6
All 2+		7	3½	3½	8½
Percentage of All Children in Each Family Size Group:					
Children: 1		3	1	2	4
2		5	3	2	
3		7	3	4	
4		11	5	6	
5		20	9	11	
6+		28	8	20	
All		7	3	4	9
2+		9	4	5	10½

Note:
(i) Including 15,000 wage-stopped families.

of those in five-child families and to 20 per cent of those in larger families (col. 3). Nevertheless, the idea that poverty was largely confined to those with excessively large families was shown to be untrue. Nearly one-half of all poor children were in families with one, two or three children, and nearly two-thirds were in families with fewer than five. And of course the survey's old-standard measure of poverty was obsolete. Applying the new assistance standard of late 1966 resulted in estimates of about 1,200,000 children with nearly 800,000 parents in *initial* poverty (col. 4).*

Table 14 shows one reason why the assistance service cannot remove all officially defined poverty. One-third of all families and children in new-standard poverty (col. 4 : 150,000 families with 435,000 children) depended on very low-earning fathers who were in full employment; and they were not entitled to assistance. Among such families about one in eight (in old-standard poverty) was poor despite the fact that the mother added earnings of her own to the father's earnings. And twice as many would have been poor (old standard) had the mother been unable to earn.

Although, again, this group of poor low earners was a very small minority—only 4 per cent of fully employed fathers with more than one child—yet 9 per cent of low-earning families with five children were officially poor (new standard) and an even greater fraction of larger families. All this fits in well with, and confirms, the conclusions drawn from Table 5. And it reflects not only the fact of the low earnings of a minority but also the small contribution which family allowances were making in 1966 to the removal of poverty associated with family size. (For the two-thirds earner with five children in 1966 disposable income was only $7\frac{1}{2}$ per cent larger than gross earnings, but in 1968 this had been raised to an addition of $18\frac{1}{2}$ per cent—Table 8).

Low-earning men are widely distributed in small numbers in most of Britain's industries. Concentrations of them are found only in a few industries like agriculture (a small industry) and central and local government services (a large industry with considerable numbers of menial but secure jobs). There is also some concentration in certain of the less prosperous areas of the UK.[8] There is some evidence that ill-health is a factor, though not probably the main factor, limiting the earning capacity of low earners. This possibility was mentioned by 14 per cent of the low-earning poverty group in the survey, but by only 4 per cent of better-off fathers; and appreciably more actual ill-health was reported among low-earning than among other fathers.†

---

* On this revised standard assistance would of course remove rather more of this group out of official poverty, but the survey report did not estimate the effects of this change.

† The interviewers' own observations suggest that ill-health impaired the earning power of 20,000 of the 125,000 fully employed fathers of more than one child judged to be in new-standard poverty (cf. Table 14).

TABLE 14. POOR FAMILIES WITH FULLY EMPLOYED FATHERS   1966

		Old Standard		New Standard
		Initially Poor	Assisted	Not Assisted	Initially Poor
One-Child Families	'000				
Families		15		15	25
Children		15		15	25
Parents		30		30	50
Larger Families	'000				
Families		70		70	125
Children		255		255	410
Parents		140		140	250
All Families	'000				
Families		85		85	150
Children		270		270	435
Parents		170		170	300
Percentage of All Families of Each Size					
Children : 2		1		1	3
3		2		2	3
4		4		4	7
5		7		7	9
6+		14		14	21
All 2+		2½		2½	4
Percentage of All Children in Each Family Size Group:					
Children : 2		1		1	3
3		2		2	3
4		4		4	7
5		8		8	10
6+		14		14	22
All 2+		3		3	5

Table 14 gives a 'snapshot' view of the circumstances and earnings of men who were in full-time work in the week preceding the survey. It does not show their circumstances over a whole year. These in fact differed substantially from those of the hypothetical low earners of Table 5, who were assumed to have fifty-two weeks' wages in a year. In the poverty group two-thirds of the fathers had been absent from work (sick, injured or unemployed) at least once during the past twelve months, including no less than 43 per cent with absences exceeding four weeks. Among the non-poor fathers these proportions were one-third and 14 per cent, respectively.

A second poverty group of about the same size comprised the families of fathers who were sick or unemployed (Table 15). Among those with more than one child nearly two-thirds were initially poor (old standard). In this group about a half of all families were receiving sickness or injury benefits from social insurance, while another eighth were receiving unemployment benefit.* Although all these poor families were entitled to supplementary assistance, about 40 per cent were *not* being assisted. In the unassisted families the fathers had mainly been sick only for a very short time or had only very recently become unemployed; others were relying on help from the earnings of wives and other adult family members. If their incapacity or unemployment were to be prolonged probably the majority would eventually apply for assistance.

Most of the families receiving assistance were by that very fact lifted out of their initial poverty, but some were not. Some 15,000 low earners' families could not be given full assistance owing to wage-stop restrictions; and on the new assistance standard this group would have amounted to 20,000.

The remaining large poverty group comprised fatherless families of all kinds (Table 16). Among single-handed mothers with more than one child nearly a half were able to take paid work, although they averaged only twenty-six hours' work a week. About a half were separated, divorced or unmarried mothers receiving payments from the fathers of their children, while a quarter were widows with social insurance or war pensions. Half of all single-handed mothers were *not* officially poor, chiefly because of their earnings or widows' pensions. Among them 75 per cent were working and 47 per cent had pensions. Among the half who were poor only 17 per cent worked and only 2 per cent had pensions. In the poor group initial poverty increased with family size (which tended to prevent mothers from working), but the great majority were rescued from official poverty by the assistance service. Moreover, for fatherless families alone assistance went beyond its primary function of relieving official poverty. It also helped a significant number of families whose initial resources placed them above the official poverty line (line 9, Table 17).

Of all those in old-standard poverty shown in Table 13 only the families of fully employed fathers (Table 14) were not entitled to assistance. Some 280,000 families with 725,000 children could have had assistance, but of these 110,000 families, with 290,000 children, did not ask for it. If their financial difficulties persisted for more than a week or two a fair proportion of these unaided families (e.g. among the 70,000 poor but unaided sick or unemployed fathers) would no doubt eventually obtain assistance. But

---

* Others who were unemployed did not qualify for social insurance benefits owing to their poor working records.

TABLE 15. POOR FAMILIES WITH SICK OR UNEMPLOYED FATHERS   1966

| | | Old Standard | | New Standard |
		Initially Poor	Assisted	Not Assisted	Initially Poor
One-Child Families	'000				
Families		60	30	30	65
Children		60	30	30	65
Parents		120	60	60	130
Larger Families	'000				
Families[i]		95	55	40	100
Children		345			350
Parents		190	110	80	200
All Families	'000				
Families		155	85	70	165
Children		405			415
Parents		310	170	140	330

Percentage of All Families of Each Size				
Children : 2	46		
3	62		
4	85		
5	87		
6+	84		
All 2+	63	37	26

Percentage of All Children in Each Family Size Group:			
Children : 2	46	38	8
3	62	29	33
4	85	54	31
5	87	48	39
6+	84	25	59
All 2+	70	38	32

Note:
(i) Wage-stopped families
     (included above)   '000   15   20

ignorance and feelings of shame seem also to have deterred some families from applying. Such was certainly the government's own conclusion.

By concentrating on the state of affairs during one summer week in 1966, the 'snapshot' approach of Tables 13 to 16 understates the amount of insecurity, fluctuating fortunes and deprivation which over a period affect people at the lower levels of British society. This is shown by the one 'film' the survey provides—of the extent to which people not assisted or not in poverty at the time of the survey had received assistance at some time

TABLE 16. POOR FATHERLESS FAMILIES

		Old Standard		1966 New Standard
		Initially Poor	Assisted	Not Assisted	Initially Poor
One-Child Families	'000				
Families		25	12	13	30
Children		25	12	13	30
Mothers		25	12	13	30
Larger Families	'000				
Families		75	65	10	75
Children		205	170	35	215
Mothers		75	65	10	75
All Families	'000				
Families		100	77	23	110
Children		230	182	48	245
Mothers		100	77	23	105
Percentage of All Families of Each Size					
Children : 2		44	41	3	44
3		61	52	9	61
4		60	40	20	60
5		60	40	20	60
6+		67	67	—	67
All 2+		50	43	7	50
Percentage of All Children in Each Family Size Group:					
Children : 2		44	41	3	
3		61	52	9	
4		60	40	20	
5		60	40	20	
6+		67	67	—	
All 2+		52	44	8	

during the preceding twelve months. Among families with more than one child, 7 per cent were initially poor (old standard) on the survey date (line 5, Table 17), but during the preceding year another 6 per cent had also been both poor and assisted (line 7).* Nearly twice as many families had been assisted for a time during the preceding year as were being assisted on the survey date (line 7 compared with line 4). Among fully employed men

* The survey does not state how far these recent experiences of income deprivation were short-lived or prolonged.

at the survey, 2½ per cent of whom were officially poor despite their earnings and family allowances, during the preceding year 5½ per cent had been both poor and assisted (presumably during sickness or unemployment). Thus the experience of income deprivation, even in a single year and even if shortlived, extends much beyond those affected by it at one moment in time. As with influenza, the prevalence of income deprivation over a period exceeds its incidence at a given moment.

TABLE 17.   FAMILIES ASSISTED AT ANY TIME DURING YEAR   1965-1966

| | | *Family Type* | | |
	All Types	*Fully Employed* Fathers	*Sick or Unemployed* Fathers	*Father-less*
All Families	100	100	100	100
Families Poor at Survey				
1. Never assisted during year	2½	2	14	6
2. Previously assisted during year	1	½	12	—
3. Not assisted at survey date	3½	2½	26	6
4. Assisted at survey date	3½	—	37	42
5. Total	7	2½	63	48
Families Not Poor at Survey				
6. Never assisted during year	86½	92	31	33
7. Previously assisted during year	6	5½	6	15
8. Not assisted at survey date	92½	97½	37	48
9. Assisted at survey date	½	—	—	4
10. Total	93	97½	37	52
Total Assisted During Year				
11. Previously (2+7)	7	6	18	15
12. At survey date (4+9)	4	—	37	46

Notes:
  (i) Period: twelve months preceding 1966 survey.
  (ii) Family type at survey date.
  (iii) Poor: in initial old-standard poverty.

ANCILLARY ANTI-POVERTY MEASURES

Britain's main anti-poverty services are those of the social security system. But a wide array of other social facilities are available to poor families on specially favourable terms or entirely free—*if* they know how to obtain them and have the initiative to apply.

Non-profit housing is provided almost exclusively by local authorities ('councils'). They accommodate about 30 per cent of all households, including some 39 per cent of manual workers' households.[9] Among its other purposes public housing is intended to provide decent homes for families unable to afford the full cost. In choosing tenants councils are therefore expected to show some preference for low-income families. And they have power, and very large funds provided by central government, to subsidise their rents so as to vary housing charges according to tenants' means and needs. The 1966 survey did in fact establish that above-average proportions of the poverty groups were in council dwellings—54 per cent of all poor families, including 45 per cent of those with fully employed fathers, 60 per cent of sick or unemployed fathers, and 56 per cent of the fatherless.

Unfortunately, it did not investigate the extent to which local authorities concentrate *rent subsidies* on their poorest tenants. But it is notable that among the whole group of poor fathers (whether housed by councils or otherwise) who were fully employed, and so could not look to the assistance service for help with housing costs, nearly one-third had housing costs of at least £208 and another 15 per cent had costs between £156 and £207—compared with the AMW average cost of £94 assumed in Table 1. In England and Wales alone some 1,450 local authorities provide dwellings. Each council has its own ideas and standards for subsidising poor tenants. Probably no two of their rent-aid schemes are alike, and there is no national information about their effectiveness in relieving poverty among public tenants.*

Housing costs include a universal but locally levied and widely varying *tax on the value of dwellings* which is highly regressive. This local 'rate' can be a heavy burden on a low income. In 1966, regardless of family size, the married AMW was paying £32 to £34 a year for rates and the very low earner about £28 to £31.[10] In 1966 the Wilson government introduced a *partial remission of local rates* for low-income families, the relief varying with income.† To obtain this new tax relief people have to know it exists, to apply twice a year and to fill in forms giving fairly detailed information about their incomes and circumstances. Until the government engaged— and pressed local authorities to engage—in determined publicity (especially in 1968), response to the new relief was sluggish except among old people who are the main beneficiaries (about 80 per cent in the first year). In the summer of 1968 the government estimated that about one and a half

---

* It is not unknown for a council, which has greatly reduced the rent of a low-income tenant, to withdraw the whole subsidy if the family eventually obtains help from the assistance service. In that eventuality, the council argues, the government's assistance service should meet the family's full housing costs. The assistance service disagrees. In the argument between the two public authorities it is sometimes the family which suffers.

† In 1968 a family qualifies for maximum relief if its annual income is below £572 (married couple) plus £104 for each child. Thus a couple with four children and an income of £988, and paying rates of £50 a year, could be relieved of £28 of this tax.

million households in England and Wales were eligible for the relief but doubted whether, despite their publicity, more than a million would apply.* The number of poor families with children receiving rate relief is not known. The proportions of households of all types who apply and qualify vary widely from place to place.

All families are entitled to a daily pint of milk at a heavily subsidised price† for every child under five years old; and the 1966 survey found that virtually all eligible families, poor or not, were obtaining their *welfare milk*. (The scheme is very well known, having originated during the 1939-45 war.) Poor families—broadly as defined by the assistance standard—are not expected to pay for this milk. But the survey found some evidence that a great many poor families were in fact paying; and this has since been confirmed by much incidental evidence. Orange juice and vitamin preparations are also available for young children generally through the public welfare services, the charge for them being waived for poor families. In March 1967 these *welfare foods* were being received free by 195,000 out of 215,000 eligible children who were supported by assistance. But fewer than 5,000 children not on assistance were getting their vitamins without payment,[12] although perhaps 120,000 other young children in poor but unassisted homes were eligible.

More important and better documented is the partial failure of the *school meals service* to reach all poor families whom it could help. For the general convenience, as well as for nutritional and anti-poverty reasons, midday meals can be obtained by nearly all children at nearly all schools in the public system. The price is heavily subsidised,‡ and can be reduced or waived for families at or near the official poverty line.

Not all children take the school meal, although the 'dining rate' is

---

* In 1967-68 (fiscal year) rate relief was granted to 5 per cent of households in England and Wales, in addition to 12½ per cent of households having their housing costs (including rates) paid partly or wholly by the assistance service. A large majority of households relieved by these two methods of part or all of their local taxes were retired old people, among whom about 50 per cent are believed to be helped. (Ref. 11.)

† 4d. a pint in 1966. Welfare milk is also supplied to older handicapped children unable to attend school and to expectant and nursing mothers. Early in 1968 the standard charge was raised to 6d. But, in addition to remission for low income, the new charge was automatically waived for children in excess of two in any family with three or more children under five years old. In England and Wales at the end of 1968 about 200,000 young children were getting milk automatically free under this arrangement. Until 1968 all older children could drink milk at school free of charge. Free provision in secondary schools is now discontinued.

‡ In 1966 1s. for a meal costing about 2s. 3d.; in 1968 1s. 6d. (cost about 2s. 6d.).

rising* If the mother is not working and the school is nearby the family may prefer to feed a school child at home; or, if the child dislikes the school food or the family dislikes the cost, the parents may give the child food to take and eat at school. Some of the failure to use school meal facilities seems to derive from cultural deprivation in the home—as when children from very poor homes with restricted diets dislike the strange dishes offered at school, or have never sat as a family at table for meals at home. More frequently, perhaps, a family which cannot afford the school dinner charge refrains from applying for remission because in many schools, owing to their methods of collecting dinner money, their children might be identified to their classmates as 'poor' or 'charity' children.

The 1966 survey in fact found that only 18 per cent of children from poor families were not taking school dinners when they could, against 33 per cent of children in non-poor families. But of the 400,000 poor children who dined at school, 150,000 were paying the full charge although they could have been spared payment. On the other hand about 150,000 children in the non-poor group—presumably in families only marginally above the assistance standard—were paying no charge (100,000) or a reduced charge (50,000). Thus of 500,000 children eating at school and poor enough to qualify for free meals, nearly one-third were paying the full rate. Among the 90,000 poor pupils who did not eat at school, 40,000 or 50,000 may have refrained owing to the indignity their parents expected if they applied for remission.

When family allowances were first introduced at the end of the second world war, their extremely low level was justified by the government's declared intention to add a substantial 'allowance in kind' by making school dinners universally available and free of charge. Family allowances remained at very low levels until the improvements of 1968. But school dinners have not been made free. The failure of a large fraction of poor families to obtain this important benefit, in a situation where family allowances are too small to remove them from poverty, is a matter of obvious concern. In November 1967, impatient with the reluctance of some local education authorities to make free dinner facilities for poor families widely known and to avoid humiliating methods of remitting charges,† the government itself engaged in publicity. In England and Wales a leaflet from the education ministry went to all parents and had a large impact. In addition, from April 1968 dinner charges were automatically waived for

---

* In England and Wales from 46 per cent of pupils in 1957 to 70 per cent in 1967; in Scotland from 29 to 42 per cent; in Northern Ireland from 27 to 54 per cent.

† The rules about dinner charges and their remission are national and central government bears the cost of school meals. But management of the service, including collection of parents' payments, is in the hands of the larger local authorities which provide the schools.

children in excess of three in any family. These two changes dramatically increased the number of 'free dinner' school children—in England and Wales from 404,000 to 841,000 between September 1967 and September 1968 (from 8·3 to 16·8 per cent of all children dining at school). 'It is estimated that in September 1968 between 250,000 and 300,000 children were having free meals, because they were members of large families, who would not have had them on grounds of financial hardship.'[13] By November 1968, however, the Wilson government had second thoughts, and the concession of free dinners, regardless of means, for children from large families was withdrawn from April 1969.

Independently of central government local authorities may *financially assist pupils* from poor homes in other ways—grants for shoes, clothing, school uniforms, special expenses (expeditions, subsidised holidays), and for support of pupils remaining at school beyond compulsory age ('education maintenance allowances'). In these matters most local authorities go their own separate ways—in all, 141 separate ways in England and Wales. No national rules or standards apply, and the range between the best and the worst provision is wide. In their financial aid to pupils—as distinct from support for university students, for whom generous national standards are enforced—local authorities generally seem secretive, unencouraging and often mean.

A study[14] of a sample of London families with at least five children in 1966 (eighty-six families, 617 children) found nearly one in four to be in (old-standard) official poverty. Of aid to pupils the investigator reported:

'Compulsory school uniform posed enormous problems for some families. The child without full uniform could be made to feel very inferior and was labelled "poor" in the same way as the child getting free meals . . . The grants, worth at most £12, did not cover the full cost of the uniform . . . The ease with which clothing problems could be solved depended less on need and more on the mother's knowledge of her rights, her persistence, and her ability to call on the support of a social worker.

'Shoes and clothing, apart from uniform, could be provided either by the education authority or, if the family was drawing assistance, by the National Assistance Board. Sometimes there would be a demarcation dispute, each authority maintaining that a child's shoes were the responsibility of the other . . .

'Education maintenance grants were rarely received . . . Only one mother had heard of them. Apart from those getting maintenance allowances all the oldest children of the lowest income families either had already left at fifteen or their mothers expected them to. These decisions were made without the knowledge that financial assistance was available for children staying on.

'Whether a child had a subsidised holiday depended more on the initiative of teachers, school care committee workers or the family doctor than on the mother . . . Free or substantially subsidised holidays had been provided for forty-two school children (10 per cent) from twenty-one families; 29 per cent (116) of the school children had never had a holiday away in their lives . . . Only one mother out of eighty-six had had a free holiday with the children in the previous year. One-third of the mothers had not had a holiday since their marriage.'

The support of children remaining at school beyond fifteen is of particular concern to a nation which wants to prevent the premature dropping out of education of boys and girls with untrained abilities. *Education maintenance allowances* are not intended to compensate parents for loss of earnings by their children. But standards of support and the family income level above which support is denied vary arbitrarily from place to place, and are not uncommonly below the minimum support standards of the assistance service. Late in 1966 Reddin[15] ascertained from the eighty-two cities in England and Wales what allowances they would pay for a pupil of sixteen in each of three hypothetical families of identical composition but differing incomes. Their answers ranged for the very low earning family from £40 to £115 a year, for the intermediate family from £0 to £105, for the AMW family from £0 to £65. 'Is it logical that a family with an income of some £700 per annum is judged "affluent" and ineligible for award by most local education authorities, if they should apply for an educational maintenance allowance to keep their child at school? Yet if that same child gets to a university his parents are judged "poor" and will receive the maximum rate of grant?'

Much the same picture of variety of provision and under-use by poor families emerges from the little that is known about *other local authority services* which normally charge users but remit charges in cases of hardship. These include day nurseries, domestic help during family emergencies, contraceptives, recuperative holidays, support of children in public care or in special residential schools (physical handicap, maladjustment), aid to foster parents and much else. All told, according to Reddin,[15] local authorities in England and Wales must be operating over 3,000 separate systems for assessing families' resources and needs for particular purposes (including council house rents and aid to pupils)—a labyrinth of rules, forms and offices in which the average poor, ill-informed and inarticulate family, without a social worker to help, readily gets lost.

Britain's nationally financed *medical care services* charge adults, but not children, for care of teeth and eyes (including dentures and spectacles) and

for prescribed medicaments.* Thus, while all the health care of children in
a poor family (as in others) is free, the parents may be charged if they use
certain services. Reimbursement of charges is readily available to families
supported by assistance. Reimbursement is also provided for low-income
families who are not assisted and may be depending on a father's earnings,
provided the family's income does not much exceed the assistance stand-
dard.† Obtaining reimbursement is, however, less simple, and it is fairly
certain that the majority of those entitled do not bother to claim. The
Child Poverty Action Group believes that among low earners only one in
every five of those who could be reimbursed actually apply.[16]

In sum: far too little is known about the contribution made to reducing
child poverty by all the social services and remission systems discussed in
this section. But it is fairly clear that, even as they stand, they could make
an appreciable impact on income deprivation if all their potential beneficiaries were fully aware of their rights and made adequate use of them.

DISCUSSION

How many and who were officially poor at the end of 1968? We do not
precisely know. Britain's official definition of poverty is in real terms more
generous than it was in 1966. This change alone could markedly raise the
numbers judged to be initially poor. Among fully employed fathers with
more than one child 70,000 families were poor by the old 1966 yardstick,
but 125,000 when the new yardstick was applied (Table 14). Had that new
yardstick in turn been raised by a further £52 a year per family—an overall
average increase of 9 per cent in the assistance scale for non-housing costs
—this total would have swollen to 200,000.

From the end of 1966 to the end of 1968, however, the real improvement
in assistance for non-housing costs was greater than this—about 12-13 per
cent.‡ Must we conclude that the number of fully employed families with
more than one child who are officially poor by the latest definition has
grown to perhaps 250,000 or more? We cannot, for improvements in
family allowances, rate reliefs, low earners' own wages and direct taxes

---

* Adults over sixty-five and expectant and nursing mothers are also exempt from
  prescription charges. The Wilson government abolished prescription charges in
  1965 but reintroduced them in 1968.
† An unemployed man on assistance may have net earnings of £1 a week without
  reducing the amount of his assistance. But for the fully employed low earner
  claiming reimbursement of a health service charge £2 of his net earnings is disregarded and also £2 of his wife's earnings. The same applies to a man on sickness
  benefit. He may also have £1 disregarded of any private sick pay or £2 of a disablement pension (but not more than £2 of these two combined).
‡ From 1966 last quarter to 1968 last quarter prices rose by 8 per cent. Tables 3 and 7
  show generally more modest real increases in levels of total assistance (general and
  housing costs combined) because they measure changes from 1966 *first* quarter to
  1968 *last* quarter (price rise of 11 per cent).

have tended in the direction of reducing income deprivation. For fully employed low earners with more than one child Table 7 suggests a genuine enlargement of real disposable income. The doubling of family allowances (in money terms) at the end of 1968 was sufficient to remove from initial poverty more than half the families (working and non-working) found to be poor at the end of 1966 by the poverty standard then applied. Over the next two years prices rose by 8 per cent and the assistance standard in real terms by even more. Without a fresh survey the present dimensions of child poverty, applying present poverty standards, cannot be precisely delineated.*

What can be said is that the volume of poverty as measured by the yardstick of late 1966 must have been markedly reduced. Whatever the dimensions of relative improvement, the absolute improvement must have been large. No other conclusion can be drawn from the tables in this paper. Applying the present assistance standard, the tables suggest that

(A) No family with a *fully employed father* is now in poverty unless he earns only 60 per cent of the AMW's wage and has more than one child, or is a two-thirds earner with more than four or five children. (With five children the 60 per cent earner's disposable income would be about 5 per cent below the poverty line, on the assumptions of Table 6).

(B) The *pensioned widowed mother who is employed*, even though earning only a quarter of the AMW's wage, should normally be well above the poverty line during her first two years and usually above thereafter. Much the same is true of *other single-handed mothers in employment*, though they are less well placed than widows.

(C) During most *sickness or unemployment* (under twenty-nine weeks), thanks to the new earnings-related insurance benefit, it would be very exceptional for an AMW to find himself in poverty, especially when account is taken of wages continued or sick pay received during illness, and of possible tax refunds. Total benefits for low earners are, however, still at sub-poverty levels—for the two-thirds earner only slightly so (falling short by 1 per cent with one child, by 5 per cent with five children), for the 60 per cent earner more markedly (with five children 9 per cent below and restricted by the wage stop).

(D) The *60 per cent earner on assistance* is likely to have his assistance restricted to sub-poverty levels if he has more than two children, because his normally low earnings impose a wage stop.

(E) For the minority experiencing *very prolonged illness or unemployment*, beyond the twenty-eighth week when earnings-related benefit ceases, basic flat benefit income is very much below the poverty line

* The government intends to make a second child poverty survey in 1970.

for all workers. (Even for the lowest earning father 20 per cent below
with one child, 17 per cent below with five.)

(F) The *pensioned widow who is not employed* is well protected during
her first six months. Even if her deceased husband was only a two-
thirds earner, she could stand 30 per cent above the poverty line with
one child, 25 per cent above with five. Thereafter, with only her flat
benefits,* she falls below the line if she has fewer than five children
but may rise a little above with six or more. (On the enhanced
assistance standard applied after two years' widowhood she would
need seven children to rise above the line.) Other *single-handed
mothers* are always likely to be in initial poverty, since the maintenance payments (if any) they get from husbands, ex-husbands, or
the fathers of their children are generally at sub-poverty rates.

This analysis pinpoints the main policy issues under debate in 1968 and
1969. In (F) above all initial poverty among single-handed mothers could
be removed if all would accept the public assistance to which they are
entitled, unless they are in full-time work, and which the great majority
already claim and receive (cf. Table 16). The same applies to certain other
poverty groups. British sentiment would, however, prefer to enable people
to keep out of poverty without recourse to assistance. The Wilson government's social security plan[18] issued in January and July 1969 and intended
to start operating in April 1972, seeks to achieve this by gearing to normal
earnings almost all social insurance payments made during working life.
The plan is primarily concerned with the reform of retirement pensions.
But it also proposes:

(i)   To continue the existing combination of flat and earnings-related pay-
      ments as short-term benefits for the sick, the unemployed and widowed
      mothers (as described on pp. 10 and 21).

(ii) To replace the present flat benefits for long-term contingencies by
      earnings-related benefits — except for the long unemployed. These,
      after exhausting their first six months' higher benefits under (i), would
      continue as now on the basic benefit for a further six months.

Short-term benefits under (i) would be determined by a man's earnings
during the preceding year. Long-term payments under (ii) — invalidity
pensions (replacing sickness benefit) and widowed mothers' pensions —
would be determined, as retirement pensions are to be determined, by
reference to a man's 'life average' earnings. Applying this approach to the
long-term sick and to widowed mothers involves combining (a) actual

---

* A minority of widowed mothers have occupational pensions in addition to their
insurance pensions. Of some 15·3m. adult male workers in the UK, about 5m. are
covered in the event of premature death for occupational widows' pensions (ref. 17).
How many widowed mothers are actually benefiting is not known.

average earnings during the years when the man was working, with (b) notional future earnings for the unexpired period up to retirement at sixty-five.

Combining (a) and (b), the plan's benefit formula would yield a payment consisting of (i) 60 per cent of the man's life average earnings (actual plus notional) up to half the level of the AMW wage *plus* (ii) 25 per cent of his actual past earnings above that level up to a ceiling of one and a half times the AMW wage. Working-age benefits so calculated would be adjusted every two years to move in line with current trends at least in prices and possibly in the national average wage. For men who earn more than half of the national average wage—that is, for virtually all men—this formula in effect guarantees for forty-five years' work (actual or notional) a flat benefit equal to 30 per cent of the AMW wage, *plus* a supplement varying with actual earnings in the half to one and a half AMW wage band, *plus* flat additions for dependent wives and children at current levels.*

If the new system had been operating in 1968, the change it implies for the long-term sick and for widowed mothers is shown in Table 18. In all cases it is there assumed that benefit is being paid to men who have worked twenty years before claiming (or to their widows); but the rates payable after ten years' work are not markedly lower. The table also assumes that additional insurance payments for dependants, family allowances and assistance standards remain at the 1968 rates.

The intended amelioration is impressive. For the widowed mother the difficulties mentioned under (F) above are removed. None remains below the poverty line, even though the assistance standard for widowed mothers is more generous and is raised after two years. Indeed, for the widow with a large family benefits would be larger than for the married man with the same number of children (lines 11-13 compared with lines 2, 4, 6), because insurance provision for children is more generous in the case of widows.†

For the AMW in long illness most of the difficulties under (E) above are removed, though his invalidity pension (line 2) comes very close to the assistance standard (line 8) if he has more than three children, and could fall below the standard if his family were large, his children all older than assumed or his housing costs unduly high. If ill for more than two years,

---

* The government has not committed itself also to protecting family allowances—as distinct from insurance payments for dependent children—against erosion by rising living costs.

† The government resists suggestions that social insurance payments analogous with widowed mothers' pensions might be provided for divorced, separated or unmarried mothers. It is to make a special survey of the financial circumstances of one-parent families (though not apparently before 1970), and to appoint a committee 'to consider the general position of one-parent families in our society and whether there are further methods by which they should be helped'.

possibly a permanent invalid, a more generous assistance standard applies. His benefit could fall below this higher poverty line if he has more than three, or possibly two, children.

The proposed benefits for low earners would lift them above the poverty line if they have no more than three, possibly four, children (two-thirds earner), or two or three children (60 per cent earner). But with very prolonged invalidity their situation would be less favourable. Moreover, although for cases of illness extending beyond three months the assistance wage stop has been abandoned (hence line 9 shows the unrestricted assistance standard), it seems that the government intends to retain something like the present wage stop in insurance benefits. If that restriction remains as now, then benefits for the larger families of low earners would be limited as shown in the table (lines 4 and 6, figures with asterisk). Even without this restriction, however, the families concerned would have benefits a little below the assistance standard.

Thus, despite the projected massive raising of benefit levels, not all the difficulties under (E) would be removed during prolonged incapacity, and none would be removed during prolonged employment. Low earners' difficulties during shorter sickness or unemployment, under (C), would remain. Restriction of assistance to sub-standard levels on account of low earnings, mentioned in (D), although it now spares men in long illness, still affects low-earner employed fathers having only benefit to live on, sick fathers whose illness is not expected to run beyond three months, and the families of men imprisoned for not more than three months. Finally, the government's social insurance plan does not touch the poverty of low earners in full-time work.

All these difficulties, confined very largely to the low-earning minority in or out of work, require other measures if official child poverty is to be abolished. At the level mainly of the lowest 10 or 15 per cent of earners, an improvement has to be engineered in the balance between disposable income and the official poverty standard. Disposable income can be improved (i) by reducing direct taxation on low incomes, (ii) by raising the level of the lowest earnings, and (iii) by enlarging family allowances (not included in the government's social insurance plan and still, by European standards, rather modest).

Though enlarging the gross and disposable incomes of most low earners in real terms (chiefly by the doubling of family allowances), changes since 1966 have also enlarged the proportion of gross income taken away by direct taxes.* The government's social insurance proposals would afford a small relief. Replacement of flat by proportional contributions would reduce

---

* e.g., even for the 60 per cent earner direct taxes took 12½ per cent of gross income in 1968, against 8 per cent in 1966, if he had one child, though the proportion remained at 6 per cent for both years if he had five children.

TABLE 18. PROJECTED LONG-TERM SICKNESS AND WIDOWED MOTHERS'
BENEFITS

Government Proposals (1969) if operating in 1968
(Benefit claimed after twenty years' work)

	Family with Children:				
	1	2	3	4	5
SICK FATHER	£	£	£	£	£
1. Present Total Benefit	452	525	598	671	744
AMW					
2. Proposed Total Benefit	635	708	781	855	926
3. Disposable Income, 1968	946	1,010	1,078	1,147	1,214
Two-Thirds Earner					
4. Proposed Total Benefit	592	665	738	811	866*
5. Disposable Income, 1968	691	751	812	872	930
60 per cent Earner					
6. Proposed Total Benefit	583	656	729	748*	800*
7. Disposable Income, 1968	620	682	742	803	857
Total Assistance Standards					
8. AMW	586	669	752	836	919
9. Low Earners	563	646	729	813	896
WIDOWED MOTHER					
10. Present Total Benefit	353	471	589	708	826
Proposed Total Benefit:					
11. Husband: AMW	535	653	771	890	1,008
12. Two-thirds Earner	492	610	728	847	965
13. 60 per cent Earner	483	601	719	838	956
Full Assistance Standards					
14. First two years	432	534	633	730	827
15. Thereafter	458	560	659	756	853

* Figures with asterisk restricted by wage stop. Full amounts would be:

4. Two-thirds Earner					883
6. 60 per cent Earner				802	874

the two-thirds earner's annual tax bill by £6 and the 60 per cent earner's by £7. But the bulk of direct taxes paid by the smaller low-income families would remain, and a raising of the tax floor (which is overdue) would be needed to help them.* Whatever may be done in these respects, it is clear

* Postscript, July 1969: For the fiscal year 1969-70 (beginning April 1969) the tax floor was raised. For widowed mothers £77 was added in every case to the levels of annual income not subject to income taxation as shown in the last line of Table 11. For fathers of families income free of tax was raised above the figures at line 16 of Table 2 by varying amounts—£45 for a one-child family, falling to £15 for a five-child family.

from Table 6 that the scope for help by tax reductions is very limited. This is true also of the reduction of low earners' housing costs by the new relief from local taxes on dwellings.

One big current argument concerns the possibility of forcing up very low earners' wages—by trade union action or legal measures—without sparking off a chain reaction of claims to maintain wage differentials at higher levels, so undermining the national policy of restraining growth in money incomes unless it flows from growth in productivity. Trade unions generally are not much interested in raising the lowest wages unless they can use this as a means of raising wages also at all higher levels. And the government is dubious about using extended minimum wage legislation as an instrument for abolishing child poverty.

Mr Crossman, the minister responsible for social security, has expressed these doubts: [19]

'The elimination of intolerably low earnings depends largely on two factors, the trade unions and public opinion. It is a delusion to believe that low wages can be got rid of simply by passing an Act of Parliament and introducing a national minimum wage. From the experience of those countries with a national minimum wage two deductions can be drawn. In the first place the reduction of differentials at the bottom of the scale is gradually cancelled out over a period of years, so that the legislation has to be repeated at intervals. In the second place, even though it does narrow the differential, a national minimum wage can never protect the unskilled labourer with a large family against the threat of family poverty. Eliminating intolerably low wages helps, but it can never remove the need for social security measures to deal with the problem of the low wage earner with a large family.'

Mr Crossman was in no doubt that family allowances must constitute 'our main instrument for the attack on family poverty', both because no feasible raising of low wages would suffice and because 'it is surely obvious that the levels of family assistance to those out of work and to those in work must be kept in step'. Additionally, the wage-stop difficulties previously mentioned stand in the way of further improvement of assistance standards — unless this improvement is associated with an equivalent raising of family allowances.

During 1968 the main public argument was not about minimum wages but about how to use family allowances to abolish child poverty. Since want affecting children is largely confined to the minority of low earners, it would be needlessly costly—as well as generally unpopular*—to increase family allowances massively for all families simply in order to help the

---

* There is ample evidence that a large majority of the British people are unenthusiastic about family allowances and regard pensions as much more important.

lowest tenth or fifth. Of various possible ways of providing additional income support only to the poorer families, the Wilson government then decided (i) to double family allowances, payable to all families regardless of need, and (ii) to 'claw back' from families with average or higher incomes the whole of the increase, by countervailing reductions in the remissions of income tax granted in respect of children.

But the increase in family allowances (which Mr Crossman was explaining) sufficed to remove only about half of officially defined family poverty. And the opportunity was not taken to vary allowances with a child's age as income tax reliefs and assistance payments are varied.*

Had the government not decided to initiate a major reform of social insurance, it seems likely that it would have given more attention to the possibility of a further raising of family allowances accompanied by an extension of 'clawing back' the increase—or the whole family allowance—through income taxation, with the aim of tapering off the net gain for families above one income level and cutting it off completely at a higher level.† Disregarding the new social insurance plans, if insurance and assistance standards were to be kept (in real terms) as they were in 1968, child poverty could be very largely eliminated (including all the wage-stop impediments to full relief) by raising family allowances to about £52 a year for the first eligible child and to £78 for each other child (against current rates of £47 and £52).‡

This would be the case provided in addition (i) the whole increase were recouped (by tax adjustments) from families at or above the AMW income level, without (ii) increasing direct taxation at or below that level but only higher up.

While these provisos are plausible, this estimate also assumes that the assistance standards of 1968 are the 'right' measure, if not of income deprivation in a wider sense, at least of the kind of poverty that public policy should strive to remove. As to the proper measure and definition of poverty, opinions of course differ and agreement is hardly to be expected. But as economic advance continues there can be no doubt that the

* As the Beveridge plan (1942) had proposed and as the Labour Party also proposed when fighting the 1964 election which installed the Wilson government.

† A more radical reform would require (i) a recasting of the whole system of tax remissions for children and of the progressive steps by which tax rates rise with rising income; (ii) a recasting of family allowances, varied by age, to replace or fit in with a refashioned system of education maintenance allowances and a new system of housing allowances (in place of subsidies to council tenants and other haphazard measures); and (iii) the integration of (i) with (ii); possibly by giving a family either family allowance (unrelated to income) or tax relief (related to income), whichever is the greater but not both, possibly by replacing child tax reliefs altogether by untaxed family allowances.

‡ Author's own estimates.

assistance standard will eventually be further improved. Early in 1966 the standard for a couple with two young children was about 60 per cent of the AMW's disposable income. Late in 1968 it was set at about 66 per cent. To raise it further to 70 per cent would require no more than a 10 per cent improvement in the real level of assistance payments for non-housing costs. Yet even so modest a change in the official definition of poverty would greatly increase the numbers of low earners caught by wage-stop rules when drawing benefit or assistance—unless family allowances were put up correspondingly.*

This handicapping of the anti-poverty services in fulfilling their intended purpose is of course an argument against setting the official definition of poverty at an unrealistically high level in the context of the prevailing distribution of incomes. But equally it is a powerful argument for altering the distribution of incomes by appreciably extending redistribution through family allowances — enlarging the element of child-related social income included in the total resources on which families can rely whether in or out of work. To remove family poverty in the 1968 situation, while *also* re-defining it by a 10 per cent raising of the level of (non-housing) assistance, would require family allowances on present lines of £91 a year for every eligible child (80 to 90 per cent more than now)—as well as a large extra tax bill for assistance.

A change of this magnitude would involve tax increases and difficulties over 'clawing back' arrangements probably too large for any British government to contemplate during the next few years, particularly a government planning a big and costly improvement in social insurance. On the other hand that improvement cannot materialise in less than three years. Its good working will almost certainly require revision and improvement of standards of provision for dependants on benefit, as to which the government's plan is silent. Any such revision could not be confined to insurance payments for children, which exist in their present form chiefly because of the long-standing inadequacy of family allowances. It would have to extend to family allowances, and it may be doubted whether some further, even though modest, reconsideration of family allowances can be deferred until 1972.

---

* Even a 10 per cent raising of the assistance standard for general costs would involve wage-stopping all two-thirds earners with more than two children. But a 40 per cent increase would not put AMW families in this situation unless they had five or more children.

NOTES ON TABLES

General

For convenience items in these tables have uniform *reference numbers.*
Annual rates for all items except income tax are fifty-two times the weekly rates from which they are derived.
Children: All assumed aged between five and ten.

Numbered Items

1. *Earnings:* For the AMW the mean of the average earnings (including receipts in kind) found for adult male manual workers during one spring and one autumn week by the Ministry of Labour's half-yearly earnings census, which covers the main range of British employments. Chief omitted groups: agricultural workers, coalminers, railway transport workers, dockers. 1968 figures partly estimated.

2. *Family allowances* (Tables 2, 6): 1968 rates as raised in autumn.

5. *Social security contributions* at higher rates introduced in October 1966 and May 1968.

8. *Work expenses* (Tables 1, 2, 5, 6): Weekly rates assumed for 1966 are 5s. for travel, 7s. 6d. for other costs; for 1968 7s. for travel, 7s. 6d. for other costs. Weekly rates multiplied by fifty-two.

10. *Basic minimum benefit:* Social insurance payments plus the family allowances in item 2. All at flat rates unrelated to earnings or children's ages.

11. *Earnings-related benefit:* Introduced in autumn 1966. Payable from third week of sickness or unemployment for following six months. Related to annual earnings during *preceding* fiscal year (April to March) at rate of one-third of earnings between £450 and £1,500. Total *insurance* payment (flat plus earnings-related) limited to 85 per cent of relevant *total earnings,* but any reduction involved applies only to earnings-related benefit.

13. *Assistance for general costs* (Tables 1, 2. Included in item 15 in Tables 5 and 6): For 1966 two rates shown, for 1968 only the higher rate introduced in autumn.

14. *Housing costs:* Average actual costs incurred by manual workers' households with household incomes in the AMW range (Tables 1, 2) and in lower ranges (Tables 5, 6). Data from ref. 6 and estimated for 1968.

18. *Restricted assistance* (Tables 5 to 8): In 1966 this corresponded to net income as in item 9. In 1968 it could be somewhat higher, since it was no longer obligatory for assistance to take account of expenses other than travel costs.

General

Where possible items numbered uniformly with Tables 1 to 8.
Same conventions used about annual incomes and children's ages.
Appropriate comments on Tables 1 to 8 apply to items 1-7, 10, 11 and 13 of these tables.

Numbered Items

3. *Gross income:* Earnings plus family allowances plus widow's insurance benefits. Family allowances as item 2, Tables 1 and 2.

6. *Direct taxes:* Assuming the pensioned widow in employment exercises her option *not* to pay the main flat national insurance contribution.

8. *Work expenses:* Normal expenses assumed to be 80 per cent of the AMW's (widowed mother, more than others, tends not to work full-time or to make long journeys to work). Costs attributable to child-minding or use of nurseries added at rates of 3s. (1966) and 4s. (1968) a day per child for 240 days a year; but it is assumed that not more than two children would generate costs on this scale, with any others attending school.

10. *Basic minimum benefit:* Long-term rates after expiry of short-term additions (items 20 and 11).

11. *Earnings-related benefit:* Not wage-stopped for widowed mothers.

13 and 14. *Assistance rates:* These apply to all single-handed mothers.

14. *Housing costs:* There is no information about widowed mothers' average housing costs. They are here arbitrarily assumed to be 80 per cent of the AMW's costs, as with low-earning men. An AMW widow inheriting a dwelling with AMW average costs might reasonably be assumed to cut costs by letting rooms or sharing, obtaining rate remission, or moving to cheaper accommodation.

19. *Disregarded benefit:* Since autumn 1966 part of a widowed mother's pension is not counted as income when determining her level of assistance. The *full assistance standard* for her, but not for other single-handed mothers, is therefore item 15 plus item 19.

20. *Extra flat benefit:* Special additional short-term payment for first three months till autumn 1966, thereafter for first six months.

TABLES 13 TO 17

Estimates for *one-child families*, save in Table 14, and for numbers of *parents* are author's informed guesses. All other data derived from official survey—ref. 2.

Old-standard poverty: As measured by National Assistance scales before November 1966.

New-standard poverty: As measured by Supplementary Benefit Scales then introduced.

Per cent distributions of families and children partly estimated; and in Table 16 open to wide margin of error owing to smallness of sample and rounding of published figures.

TABLE 18

Total benefit: Insurance payments plus family allowances.

1. 10. *Present total benefit:* Flat basic minimum—item 10 in Tables 2, 6, 10.

2, 4, 6, 11, 12, 13. *Proposed total benefit:* Amounts if claimed after *twenty years'* employment. If claimed after ten years the rates would be lower by £33 (AMW, items 2, 11), £11 (two-thirds earner, items 4, 12), or £7 (60 per cent earner, items 6, 13).

3, 5, 7. *Disposable income* figures taken from Tables 2 and 6 but adjusted to allow for the government's proposed new insurance contributions (increased charge of £13 for AMW, reductions of £6 for two-thirds earner and of £7 for 60 per cent earner).

8, 9. *Total assistance* for sick fathers: rates are increased by £26 after two years' assistance (cf. items 14 and 15).

14, 15. *Full assistance* for widowed mother allows for disregarded element in her pension (cf. note to item 19 in Tables 9 to 12).

2. Housing and Socially Deprived Families

Kenneth Spencer

The theme to be developed here is that of housing deprivation amongst British families. Housing deprivation must be seen in its relative national context, for what might be thought of as deprivation in one country may be quite an acceptable situation in another. Hence national housing standards are of prime importance, particularly when national studies of housing deprivation are being compared.

There are basically two approaches to this study, both incorporated into this chapter. These arise out of a consideration of how one ought to define deprived families in relation to the provision of housing accommodation. One way is simply to take those of our minimum national housing standards relevant to this discussion, and then assess to what extent these are not achieved. The fundamental problem of this approach is that Britain's minimum housing standards are linked primarily with the physical condition of dwellings, for which various statutory definitions are applicable. The second approach relates to another group of standards, mainly of a social and economic nature. These standards are rarely statutory but arise from social justice considerations. It must be emphasised that the two groups are not mutually exclusive; indeed it is often their inter-relationships which provide interesting focal points, and each helps to illuminate the other.

These housing standards, of whatever kind, are dynamic. They are constantly subject to change as they represent measures of levels of acceptability at a specific point in time and within a specific locality, in the context of cultural, technological and economic conditions. Standards established at a national scale provide a common denominator, but local interpretation can vary. This is so because some areas suffer from certain housing problems more than others, and the general character of the housing stock differs from area to area. Local government housing policies can thus vary considerably, depending upon local circumstances of housing condition and the practicabilities of what can be achieved to improve the local situation. The local authorities, of course, essentially work within a nationally set framework of standards and legislation, but in many instances this is quite flexible—for example, in the interpretation of the statutory standard of dwellings unfit for human habitation; in relation to local governmental decisions whether to adopt certain available powers or not; and in relation to some level of discretion in the use of public funds, both national and local, in assisting local housing policies.

The fact that this discussion is concerned with housing deprivation in Britain presents several problems. Scotland has different housing legislation from that of England and Wales, partially reflecting the marked differences between housing conditions in Scotland and the rest of Britain. National housing surveys are produced separately for Scotland and the problem thus arises of evidence on certain issues existing for different points in time, while some evidence might not be available at all for Scotland though it is for England and Wales, and vice versa. This discussion therefore concentrates on England and Wales, with scattered but specific reference to Scotland where it is felt that the Scottish evidence is illuminating to the general picture.

Though this paper is sectionalised under various headings this is merely a guide to the principal points being discussed within that section. It cannot be assumed that each section is self-contained. Economic and tenure issues in British housing are discussed, and it will be made evident how the evidence presented there is vital to an understanding of both physical housing deprivation and deprivation found amongst specific groups of the population.

TERMINOLOGY

Generally speaking, British housing statistics do not refer specifically to family units but instead to *households* or *dwellings*. It has been the practice in the census reports and other housing surveys to define households in terms of their eating arrangements. Generally a household is defined as that group of people who eat meals together. All families would thus be included under this definition, but there would be other groups who would also qualify as households. The 1966 sample census defines a household as:
'(a) any group of persons, whether related or not, who live together and benefit from a common housekeeping; or
(b) any person living alone who is responsible for providing his or her own meals.'

Thus the great majority of housing surveys and housing statistics do not refer to families but to households, and so it is necessary for this report to be written in terms of households, rather than families.

The second problem of definition arises in relation to the term *dwelling*. Usually an appropriate definition is one of a structurally separate accommodation unit, but problems arise in relation to residential buildings in which several households live, particularly those which have not been purpose-built for multi-household accommodation. The problems of defining a dwelling in these circumstances are crucial. The first guiding principle is that an accommodation unit can only be regarded as a dwelling if it has a separate front door of its own; furthermore this front door must be reached without passing through any part of the accommodation of another household; while it is also necessary to be able to move between all the rooms of a dwelling without having to use a hall, landing, or staircase used by people in other households. These are the basic criteria for the determination of whether an accommodation unit qualifies as a dwelling or not. Most housing statistics refer to dwelling units when physical issues are involved, and to household units when social and economic issues are under consideration. This situation can cause complications in some instances. Usually one household will occupy one dwelling; but there are cases, not uncommon, where several households will occupy one dwelling, and this will generally introduce further complications in the sharing of certain facilities and amenities. Most of these cases arise where a building has been converted from single household occupation to multi-household occupation, with an inadequate level of conversion to separate each household's accommodation unit to the dwelling criteria specified above.

The definitions of household and dwelling are the two most important in terms of analysing the material which is available on deprivation in housing. Basically, therefore, this chapter is about socially deprived households and dwellings which are lacking in certain facilities and amenities.

DEPRIVED HOUSEHOLDS IN RELATION TO HOUSING ACCOMMODATION

As mentioned briefly in the introduction, the operational definition of deprived households is twofold. The first group is defined in terms of the relative obsolescence of the physical structure of the dwellings they inhabit, of the unavailability or sharing of basic amenities, and also of the standard of the environment of the dwelling. This latter point has received very little attention until quite recently, yet it is obviously of importance in terms of housing deprivation.

The second group of deprived households, amongst which many correlations exist with physical conditions, is defined by means of a general consensus of opinion in the literature available. These groups of households are in some cases overlapping categories: for example, there is a high correlation amongst large families, overcrowding, and the poor.

Besides the high incidence of overlap of these socially deprived groups, which are defined essentially on the basis of social and economic considerations, it is important to bear in mind that the relative incidence of deprivation amongst these groups varies. At one end of the scale are the homeless, all of whom, by definition, must be considered to be deprived, while at the other end of the scale might be placed the large households.

Before surveying the groups which are defined as being deprived in terms of their housing accommodation, it is necessary to discuss a few features of the state of housing in Britain, and to elucidate a little the background to the current situation, as it helps to explain many of the problems and aspects of housing policy which will arise later. Besides this general background it is useful at this stage to discuss the sources available in Britain for this type of study, and this logically comes first.

SOURCES OF INFORMATION

Two points ought to be made concerning the availability and production of statistics and surveys concerned with various issues in the field of housing in Britain. The first point is that the late 1950s saw the beginning of a period of concern for housing surveys and statistics, while housing issues began to attract the attention of research workers in universities and in the Ministry of Housing and Local Government itself. To some extent this has been undoubtedly due to the growth in British universities of the popularity of social administration and sociology courses, as well as in the number of statisticians and economists with an interest in housing issues.

D. V. Donnison's views on the change in attitude to housing research in the later 1950s are worth recording:

'Less than a decade ago the Ministry of Housing and Local Government did virtually no research on the questions discussed in this book (though a decade before that its record had been a good deal better). The statistics it published were scanty, being confined mainly to data on the building of new houses and other figures that recorded the extent of the government's efforts rather than clarifying the problems to be solved . . . Independent research workers outside government had little to say about housing, and academic studies in this field were fewer and poorer than those of the pre-war period . . .

'Times have changed. The Ministry now has a small but competent statistical staff, a Sociological Survey Unit, and a consultant economist; its architects are conducting experimental work in several parts of the country and the outcome of their projects is being published and evaluated; town planners and others in the Ministry are collaborating with an expanding circle of research workers in universities and elsewhere, a growing number of whom are supported by government funds. Many more questions on housing have been squeezed into the Census. The Building Research Station has extended the scope of its work to include the economics of building, and various social, administrative and economic aspects of urban development. The Social Survey made its first housing inquiry for the Ministry in 1958 and now seems likely to make regular inter-censal investigations of the housing situation . . . The Milner Holland Committee made the first comprehensive study of housing problems to be carried out by an independent committee since the Royal Commission on the Housing of the

Working Classes in 1885—although, unlike the Royal Commission, it dealt only with London.'[1]

Donnison also goes on to explain this change of attitude:

'In housing, as in other fields, the crucial change in the climate for research arose from the acceptance by government of more comprehensive responsibilities for meeting the nation's needs—a commitment which compelled Ministers (sometimes in advance of their administrators) to .call for more information and advice, and encouraged them to shed inhibitions about inquiring into social problems and publishing the results.'[1]

The second point is that despite this great increase in the research being carried out, and in the wide range of statistics being published, there are still criticisms of governmental records.

'The records of neither local nor central government are adequate for a thorough appraisal of the standard and condition of London housing, and we think it is important that further research should be undertaken to make good this gap in our knowledge.'[2]

The need for accurate data is acknowledged as a preliminary to the establishment of constructive housing policies, as recently indicated by a Scottish White Paper on housing which states:

'Constructive thinking has often been inhibited by the absence of accurate information; much of the information we have had—based for instance on local authority returns of houses which were classified as unfit for human habitation—is now seen to have been misleading.'[3]

This changed attitude of the Ministry of Housing and Local Government towards research has enabled much to be done. Indeed, it is only with the aid of research publications, issued mainly by government and university staffs, that it has been possible to identify those groups who are regarded as deprived in terms of their housing. It must also be remembered that the primary objective of housing appraisal is not just to collect information but to provide means to encourage action which will improve housing and environmental conditions.[4]

The main source materials may be classified into three groups, namely, regular statistical publications; housing surveys, physical, social and economic; and books and articles concerned with various housing themes which are particularly significant in terms of housing deprivation, but which do not necessarily contain this as their main theme.

The best known of the regular statistical publications are the housing statistics presented in the census volumes. Since the second world war there have been three of these—the 1951 census, the 1961 census, and the

1966 sample census. The introduction of the sample census in 1966 is an encouraging sign, as a ten-year period is far too infrequent a time span. Furthermore, inevitable delays arise between the completing of census forms and the publication of results. During this period of post-war censuses there has been a significant increase in the questions asked about housing. At the same time, however, there have been various changes of definition, some minor, others more significant; changes which can hinder inter-censal comparison. For example, in the 1966 sample census the kitchen was counted as a separate room, whereas in the 1961 census it was only counted as such if meals were eaten there. The definition of the term 'dwelling' has also been defined successively in each of these three censuses. The significance of the census data is not simply in its published form, as since 1961 census information on the basis of enumeration districts has been made available to research workers, thus allowing a more microscopic study of housing conditions which can be linked with other census variables.[5] In the 1966 sample census each electoral ward area in Birmingham, for example, is divided into about twelve to fourteen enumeration districts, each of which has its own schedule of census data. The basic housing material in the census is concerned with occupancy levels and the availability of amenities. Statistics are provided of the number of rooms in a dwelling in relation to the number of persons in the household; the census also provides density figures of persons per room. In terms of amenities data are provided on the number of households and number of persons in households in relation to the availability to that household of certain basic amenities—hot water, fixed bath and water closet. These data on amenities also differentiate between sole household use, shared use, and unavailability.

The second group of regularly produced statistics are those of the Ministry of Housing and Local Government. The ministry's quarterly *Housing Statistics* provides data on a great variety of topics, ranging over new construction, improvement grants, slum clearance, housing loans and rent regulation, together with various miscellaneous statistical tables. This report is also used to publish certain of the statistics relating to special surveys which the ministry carries out from time to time—for example, the results of the national and conurbation house condition surveys. These data generally relate to the national level. In some cases they are based on the economic planning regions of the country, and in others on the different types of local authorities. These statistics also often include parallel figures for Scotland where available.

The other main series of housing statistics are the series of *Local Housing Statistics* which relate only to England and Wales, but provide comparative data, at local authority level, on various aspects of housing including the numbers of new houses built and under construction, differentiating private from local authority, and the number of unfit houses demolished. This is a recently introduced quarterly publication, first issued in January 1967. The Institute of Municipal Treasurers and Accountants publishes annually their *Housing Statistics*, incorporating a variety of statistical data, much of it financial and relating to local authority housing, by local authority areas. The institute also publishes a variety of other, mainly financial, data relating to various facets of local government responsibilities.

The Department of Employment and Productivity publishes its *Family Expenditure Survey* annually, which provides evidence on the housing costs of families, as well as other forms of family expenditure. Similarly in the later 1950s the Government Social Survey published several consumer expenditure surveys which, in part, related to housing costs.

Many special housing surveys have been carried out by government departments or have been commissioned by them, while others have been produced by various academic research workers. The Government Social Survey has produced several valuable reports relating to housing. The most important of these are the two housing survey reports for England and Wales: *The Housing Situation in 1960* by P. G. Gray and R. Russell was published in 1962; this was followed by *The Housing Survey in England and Wales, 1964* by M. Woolf, published in 1967. It is hoped that these housing surveys will be regular publications as they are extremely valuable in monitoring housing change in the country, and they throw much light on issues not dealt with by the census or other regular statistical publications. The 1964 survey deals with a variety of issues including household tenure patterns, accommodation size and the living space of households, the standard of accommodation, the mobility of households, the formation of new households, and the rateable units. The production of such surveys at regular intervals is vital if information about a nation's housing conditions is to be kept up-to-date.

A similar housing survey was produced for Scotland in 1965. In this case the Scottish Development Department commissioned J. B. Cullingworth to carry out the survey on their behalf, an example of the growing co-operation between government departments responsible for housing matters and university research workers. This report, *Scottish Housing in 1965*, was published by the Scottish Development Department in 1967. At the same time as the national Scottish survey was being undertaken Cullingworth was also carrying out a survey of housing in the city of Glasgow, commissioned by Glasgow corporation and published in 1968.[6] This is one of the best examples of a local housing survey, as opposed to the national surveys.

Housing conditions in Greater London were similarly surveyed by a committee under the chairmanship of Sir Milner Holland which was convened in 1963. The *Report of the Committee on Housing in Greater London* was published in 1965, and discusses in considerable depth London's housing problems. The committee was appointed by the Minister of

Housing and Local Government with the following terms of reference: 'To survey the housing situation in Greater London (as defined in the London Government Act, 1963) with particular reference to the use, maintenance and management of rented accommodation, whether privately or publicly owned, and to the relations between the occupiers of rented accommodation and private landlords,'[2] In fact the committee went much further than its terms of reference, and the report constitutes the most valuable piece of research on London's housing conditions and its problems. However, though the committee make specific mention of the fact that they were concerned with London only, there are nevertheless particular aspects and sections of the report which are valid as criticisms of, or comments on, the national housing scene.

In 1959 P. G. Gray and E. A. Parr, of the Government Social Survey, produced a report entitled A *Survey of Residential Caravan Life*. This was followed by the Consumer Council's *Living in a Caravan*, published in 1967. Again in 1967 the Ministry of Housing and Local Government's own Sociological Research Unit published a report dealing with the problems of gypsies and other itinerant persons, *Gypsies and Other Travellers*. This provided, for the first time in many years, data on this group of people which indicated how they were generally extremely ill-catered for in terms of the availability, quantity and quality of sites. Some local authorities provided adequate sites, but these were the exceptions rather than the rule.

The Ministry of Social Security is involved in the problem of housing costs, as social security payments are made to low income households, particularly the elderly or families suffering unemployment, and such payments include housing cost allowances. In 1966 the Ministry's National Assistance Board published its report *Homeless Single Persons*.

The physical condition of the nation's housing stock was the subject of an inquiry undertaken early in 1967; this was the Ministry of Housing and Local Government's national house condition survey carried out on the basis of a sample of some 6,000 dwellings in England and Wales. It was felt that insufficient data were available about the physical condition of dwellings, while the number of unfit dwellings was ascertained by adding all the local authority returns. This practice, however, presented several problems, the most significant being that each local authority was using its own interpretation of the statutory definition of a dwelling unfit for human habitation. It was felt that many discrepancies were arising as a result, and hence very little reliance could be placed on the national total of unfit dwellings. This extreme caution was shown to be amply justified by the findings of the national sample house condition survey. The statistics relating to this national survey have been presented in several publications. Some have been provided in the quarterly series of *Housing Statistics* mentioned previously; others were published as an appendix to the White Paper on older housing in England and Wales.[7] The most comprehensive report on the survey is to be found in *Economic Trends* for May, 1968.[8] In addition to the national house condition survey, similar surveys have been carried out in several conurbation areas and are planned for others. Besides the conurbation surveys of dwelling condition, there have also been several household surveys carried out in the conurbations. Thus besides data on the national scale based on dwelling and household conditions there are also data at conurbation level in several instances.

A variety of other housing surveys have been carried out by academic research workers. A large proportion, published in the early 1960s, were supported with research funds from the Joseph Rowntree Memorial Trust. The whole group of these studies are collectively referred to as the Rowntree Trust Housing Study. Several have been published in the series of Occasional Papers on Social Administration published by Bell and Son. The main ones are: D. V. Donnison, *Housing policy since the war*, 1960; D. V. Donnison, C. Cockburn and T. Corlett, *Housing since the Rent Act*, 1961; D. V. Donnison, C. Cockburn, J. B. Cullingworth and D. A. Nevitt, *Essays on housing*, 1964; J. B. Cullingworth, *English housing trends*, 1965; J. Greve, *Private landlords in England*, 1965.

Other books have also been published on subjects arising from the Rowntree Trust Housing Study, which was really a series of studies at both national and local level. J. B. Cullingworth's *Housing in Transition*, published in 1963, was a study of housing in the town of Lancaster between 1958 and 1962. The study began as an inquiry into the operation of the 1957 Rent Act, but, 'It then developed into a study, first, of private landlords and, secondly, of owner-occupiers who were taking over previously rented houses'.[9] The same author's *Housing and Local Government*, 1966, is concerned essentially with the role of the local authority as a provider of social housing.*

Another housing survey is the study by J. Greve of London's homeless families. In 1961 the then London County Council faced a growing problem in the number of families who were becoming homeless, and consequently invited J. Greve to undertake a study on their behalf. The report of this research is one of the very few pieces of evidence available about homeless families, though it was obviously restricted to London's problems. J. Greve's report, *London's Homeless*, was published in 1964 and also published in the Occasional Papers on Social Administration series. Another

---

* In Britain the term 'social housing' is not used very much but it is used extensively in the rest of Europe. Social housing refers to the provision of dwellings of at least an approved minimum standard, and intended for renting or purchase by families whose income is insufficient to enable them to obtain accommodation in the private market without the direct or indirect help of public authorities or social institutions. Social housing thus encompasses other types of housing as well as local authority housing provision, though local authorities provide by far the bulk of Britain's social housing.

valuable paper in this series is R. H. Parker's *The Rents of Council Houses* published in 1968, which deals with the financing of local authority housing in England and Wales. Finally, a comparative house condition survey of urban areas in England and Wales was written by F. T. Burnett and S. Scott and published in 1962.[10]

Other useful publications include L. Needleman's *The Economics of Housing*, 1965, which is not so restricted in the topics it deals with as its title might suggest; whereas A. A. Nevitt's *Housing, Taxation and Subsidies*, 1966, is concerned essentially with the whole basis of housing costs for different types of dwelling, for different types of households, and for different tenure groups. The problems of predicting housing needs were not really adequately understood in Britain until 1960 when J. B. Cullingworth's book *Housing Needs and Planning Policy* was published. This dealt with predicting housing needs by considering the dynamics of population structure, and determining those factors which were most likely to provide useful indicators of future housing needs.

Two books dealing with the problems of housing immigrants, with special reference to coloured immigrants, were published in 1967. Both were concerned, amongst other things, with local authority housing policies in relation to immigrants. That by J. Rex and R. Moore, *Race, Community and Conflict*, is a study of the Sparkbrook area of Birmingham. E. Burney's *Housing on Trial* deals with general issues and with the particular problems of immigrant housing in several English towns. At the small study area level are two publications on housing in Nottingham. K. Coates and R. Silburn's *St. Ann's—Poverty, Deprivation and Morale in a Nottingham Community*, 1967, is a study of conditions and attitudes in a twilight housing area; *The Morale of the Poor*, 1968, edited by K. Coates and R. Silburn, is a study of poverty on a Nottingham council housing estate. Both were published by the Adult Education Department of Nottingham University.

Two other useful books dealing with the housing scene in totality are S. Alderson's *Britain in the Sixties: Housing*, a Penguin special published in 1962; and D. V. Donnison's *The Government of Housing*, Penguin, 1967. The latter is an invaluable textbook and general reference book for the study of housing, not just in Britain but in the countries of western and eastern Europe.

THE BACKGROUND TO HOUSING IN BRITAIN

Before proceeding to the study of deprived households a few points must be made about the current state of housing in Britain, and some of the underlying trends. This aids an understanding of the nature of housing deprivation and its links with current trends in housing.

The first point concerns the age of the housing stock. Britain's housing stock is relatively old compared with countries such as Sweden, the Netherlands, West Germany, and the Soviet Union. On the other hand the housing stock is older in Ireland, France, Belgium and East Germany. Table 1 provides the basic data on dwelling ages in England and Wales, while Table 2 presents similar data for Scotland.

TABLE 1*

The year in which accommodation units were built, as of 1964,
Greater London and England and Wales

Year built	Greater London	England and Wales
	%	%
Before 1919	46	39
1919 - 1944	34	29
1945 - 1960	14	22
After 1960	4	9
No information	1	1

* M. Woolf, *The Housing Survey in England and Wales.* Government Social Survey, 1967.

TABLE 2*

The year in which dwellings were built, as of 1965,
Glasgow and Scotland

Year built	Glasgow	Scotland
	%	%
Before 1861	—	4
1861 - 1880	7	11
1881 - 1900	36	19
1901 - 1918	14	10
1919 - 1944	22	22
1945 or later	21	34

* J. B. Cullingworth, *Scottish Housing in 1965,* Scottish Development Department, Edinburgh, 1967; and *Profile of Glasgow Housing, 1965.*

Thus a greater proportion of Scottish housing was built after 1945 than in England and Wales, 34 per cent compared with 31 per cent, but Scotland possessed more dwellings which had been built before 1918, 44 per cent compared with 39 per cent for England and Wales. In the two conurbation areas the dwelling stocks were significantly older than their respective national figures. Age of the dwelling stock is highly correlated with levels of obsolescence. It is amongst the older dwellings that the basic amenities are most lacking, while these also contain virtually all the unfit dwellings. Furthermore, most of the older dwellings are privately rented. Tables 3 and 4 demonstrate this situation respectively for England and Wales in 1964, and for Scotland in 1965.

TABLE 3*

The year in which accommodation units were built according to tenure types, England and Wales

Year built	Owner Occupied	Local Authority rented	Privately rented Unfurnished		Furnished	Other types
			controlled	not controlled		
	%	%	%	%	%	%
Before 1919	40	7	77	74	75	52
1919 - 1944	35	29	19	15	20	14
1945 - 1960	14	52	3	6	3	20
After 1960	10	12	—	3	2	10
No information	1	—	1	2	—	4

* M. Woolf, *The Housing Survey in England and Wales.* Government Social Survey, 1967.

TABLE 4*

The year in which dwellings were built according to tenure type, Scotland

Year built	Owns/is buying	Rents from council	Rents privately, etc.
	%	%	%
Before 1861	7	—	6
1861 - 1880	15	1	22
1881 - 1900	26	2	48
1901 - 1918	17	1	15
1919 - 1944	22	32	8
1945 or later	12	64	1

* J. B. Cullingworth, *Scottish Housing in 1965.*

In Scotland only 12 per cent of owner-occupied dwellings were built after 1945, whereas in England and Wales the figure was much higher at 24 per cent. The comparative newness of the local authority housing stock is only to be expected, since it was not until 1919 that local authority housing programmes really became effective, primarily because of the subsidy arrangements made in that year. Also the emphasis on local authority housing construction is particularly marked in Scotland, where some 80 per cent of all dwellings built since 1918 are council dwellings.[12]

Certain changes have been taking place in the structure of national tenure patterns, which in England and Wales have resulted in a decline in the privately rented sector, and increases in the owner-occupied and local authority sectors. D. V. Donnison sums up this situation in the following words:

'The two growing sectors are the owner-occupied houses (many of them large, and scarcely any of them really small; mostly well equipped but with an appreciable fringe of poor quality) and council houses (a uniform group well equipped, with few really small units and even fewer large ones). The shrinking sector consists of private houses, rented unfurnished; most of them are old and obsolete, but they offer a greater type of variety and sizes, including most of the country's smaller and cheaper dwellings. Furnished accommodation appears to be retaining its very small place in the market; concentrated in the south and in the cities, it consists of small units, and its tenants share much essential equipment with their neighbours.'[1]

In 1964 the situation in England and Wales was that 46 per cent of the accommodation units were owner-occupied, 25 per cent rented from local authorities, 22 per cent rented privately unfurnished, 3 per cent rented privately furnished, and 3 per cent other forms of tenure.[11] In Scotland, on the other hand, the growth in owner-occupation is small compared with that of local authority housing, which represents 49 per cent of Scottish dwellings with only 27 per cent owner-occupied. Hence the relative significance of owner-occupied and local authority housing is reversed in Scotland. The remaining 24 per cent of Scottish dwellings are rented privately in most cases; a few of them are in other forms of tenure.[12]

The scale of the decline in the privately rented sector is indicated by the fact that in England and Wales between 1960 and 1964 the number of accommodation units occupied by private tenants decreased by 15 per cent. A principal reason was that many of these accommodation units were demolished, and the tenants transferred in most cases to local authority housing. A second reason was that many of the privately rented accommodation units were being sold to owner-occupiers, and in a few instances they were being bought by local authorities ahead of demolition.

Briefly summarised, the main features of households in different tenure categories were:

'The heads of owner-occupying households tended to have above average incomes; local authority tenants tended to be larger households with dependants; those in controlled accommodation were more likely to be older, smaller households, either pensioner households or with working adults; while those renting uncontrolled accommodation appeared most likely to be either pensioner households or younger households with dependants. Tenants in furnished accommodation in the country as a whole appeared to be individuals or small adult households; in Greater London there is evidence to suggest that proportionately more of these households were small families.'[11]

Controlled, uncontrolled and furnished accommodation is, of course, by definition, privately rented. However, the situation in controlled and uncontrolled tenancies requires clarification. Rent control has been a basic principle of British housing policy, and was first introduced during the first world war with the aim of freezing the rent market at a particular point in time. Between 1939 and 1957 nearly all privately rented dwellings

were subject to rent control, the effect of which, generally, was to freeze
rents at their 1939 level, or for lettings made after that date at a fixed level.
After 1954 landlords were entitled to small rent increases if they carried
out repair and maintenance work. These rents were thus artificially low,
and there were often inadequate rent resources to carry out repair works.
The 1957 Rent Act exempted from control all dwellings with rateable value
exceeding £40 a year in London and Scotland, and £30 a year elsewhere.
Additionally, when tenancies of lower rateable values than those specified
became vacant, the new tenancy arrangement was freed from rent control.
The Rent Act also established new rent levels for houses remaining in
control. Obviously this led to increases in rent levels, and to the harassment
and eviction of tenants in some areas in order to render the tenancy vacant
so that rents could be increased, despite the various tenant protection
clauses of the Rent Acts.

In the 1965 Rent Act a 'fair rent' system for rent regulation was introduced. Its aim was initially to deal with decontrolled unfurnished tenancies, excepting the more expensive ones, with the purpose of keeping rents
down when severe shortage in some areas would have otherwise led to
rapid increases in rents. Rent regulation aims at creating a market where
the pattern of rents changes in relation to supply and demand, while local
impacts of severe or abnormal scarcities are kept within reasonable levels
of rent values. It basically provides a cushioning effect against short-term
high rent increases. However, as D. V. Donnison points out, 'At the time
the 1965 Rent Act was passed, few commentators grasped that it is in the
longer run a measure for the raising rather than the lowering of rents.'[1] In
England and Wales, between January 1966 and March 1968, of the 47,576
tenancies which were referred to the Rent Assessment Panels, some 54 per
cent had their rents increased, while 36 per cent had rents decreased.[13] In
the financial year 1967/68 increases occurred in 60 per cent of the cases,
and the levels of increase were of the magnitude as indicated in Table 5,
which refers to England and Wales during the period April 1967 to March
1968.

Thus privately rented housing areas with cheap rents are being reduced
by rent increases, by transfer to other types of tenure especially to owner-
occupation, and also by slum clearance. Despite the subsidies which are
available to local authorities for slum clearance and redevelopment the
rents of new council housing are often considerably higher than those of
council tenants' previous accommodation, especially where tenants previously occupied controlled tenancies. This leads on to a consideration of
housing costs related to levels of income, and to government taxation and
subsidy policies. The financial issues are a basic recurrent theme throughout
the study of virtually all the deprived groups which are dealt with in this
paper. It is necessary, therefore, to consider certain aspects of housing
finance which are tied in closely with tenure considerations. This is a

TABLE 5*

Rent assessment panels, increases in annual rent levels

Annual rent increases (£s)	England and Wales (%)
1 - 25	14·3
26 - 50	16·1
51 - 75	10·9
76 - 100	8·1
101 - 150	7·2
151 - 200	2·3
201 and over	1·1
All increases	60·0
All rents registered	100·0
Number of rents registered	28,906

* Ministry of Housing and Local Government, *Housing Statistics No. 10*, 1968.

highly complex and involved field, particularly in Britain, and it is only possible here to present a brief outline.

HOUSING FINANCE AND TENURE

There is a general awareness amongst many researchers and commentators in the field of housing finance that a review of the whole situation is required, and not just in relation to local authority rents. R. A. Parker has the following·to say:

'In the last resort, however, the problem of council rents will only be solved satisfactorily within the much wider context of general policies which clarify the processes and objectives of income redistribution. This will involve the comprehensive treatment of such disparate issues as interest rates; land prices; family allowances; housing subsidies; social security payments, and taxation.'[14]

D. V. Donnison states:

'The fundamental dilemma underlying most of our housing problems arises from a willing acceptance of great inequalities in the distribution of personal incomes, coupled with a rejection of similar inequalities in the distribution of housing. Britain appears to be gradually incorporating a concern about bad housing conditions into its collective social conscience, alongside the concerns for unemployment and medical care incorporated there a generation earlier. But a determination to provide decent housing for people now deprived of it cannot bear fruit unless they are enabled to pay for what they need. The present "system" of government contributions to housing, if it can be called that, includes housing subsidies, improvement grants, tax reliefs and Social Security rent allowances. It is quite inadequate for this purpose, though it brings about redistributions of income that are large enough, if effectively deployed, to go a long way towards achieving it.'[1]

This would appear to form the crux of the problem of housing deprivation in Britain, though one would also require to eradicate the worst housing conditions by demolition and redevelopment, or by improving dwellings to a reasonably acceptable standard. The issue cannot, therefore, be seen in terms of income redistribution alone, but must also be related to improving the condition of the existing dwelling stock and to increasing the dwelling stock in those sectors where need is greatest.

The Milner Holland Committee was very concerned about the whole question of housing finance and its relation to particular tenure categories. Its report concludes that with present fiscal arrangements, private landlords and housing associations* are unable to develop a full contribution to the housing problems of London. Both suffer from tax disadvantages, which the committee felt ought to be reviewed to encourage the improvement of older housing. The committee also felt that the 1965 subsidy arrangements amongst different local authorities appeared to be 'a haphazard and somewhat irrational pattern'. Council housing subsidies were changed as a result of the 1967 Housing Subsidies Act, but one would feel that the committee's criticism still remains valid. The fact that private landlords' tenants are the only group who received no type of financial or fiscal aid towards their housing costs was felt by the committee to present certain problems, especially as these people were amongst the lowest income groups, and were found in the worst condition dwellings.[2] The London report contains a table which usefully summarises the differences in weekly accommodation costs in the London area for two dwellings whose costs and local authority location varied. This is reproduced as Table 6.

These costs were calculated in 1965 and thus cannot be taken as truly representative of present-day comparative costs, as there have been some changes, for example new subsidy arrangements for local authorities, higher rates of interest on capital borrowed, and other changes. The general level of differences, however, remain valid, and similar patterns at lower cost could be duplicated for other areas of the country.

---

* Housing associations are charitable bodies which provide housing, often in the form of dwellings converted from large houses, though also by buying older houses, and by constructing their own dwellings. Rents are not necessarily low, despite there being no profit motive involved. Some of the associations provide accommodation for special groups of people, e.g., the elderly, single persons, unmarried mothers, etc. Others do not specialise in their selection of tenants to the same degree.

TABLE 6*

Weekly costs of accommodation under various types of owner

Dwelling cost including land	Local Authority[1]	Landlord (rent per week) Housing association[2]	Private landlord[3]	Owner-occupier (per week[4]) Before tax relief	After tax relief
£5,500	£3 3 8	£7 14 1	£10 1 8	£8 13 1	£6 7 6
£3,750	£2 7 0	£5 19 0	£7 1 6	£5 18 4	£4 7 0

[1] Local authority rent set by the local authority owning the dwellings in the examples.
[2] Rents calculated on a sixty-year loan at 6½ per cent interest. £30 a year has been allowed for repairs and management.
[3] The rent has been calculated on a 9 per cent gross return. No allowance has been made for the costs of repairs.
[4] Calculated on the basis of a twenty-five-year mortgage at 6½ per cent interest. No allowance has been made for the costs of repairs.

* *Report of the Committee on Housing in Greater London.* HMSO, 1965.

TABLE 7*

Effects of taxation on private landlords' improvements, 1965

Assuming the dwelling will last for a further twenty years.
£100 spent on improvements.
Annual sum required to be set aside at 2½ per cent compound interest
to recover £100 in twenty years, £3·91 = £3 18s. 2d. £3·91 grossed
up for Income Tax and Profits Tax at 10s. 9d. = £8 9s. 1d.

Gross Income per annum	£12 10 0
Less: Sinking Fund provision grossed up for Income Tax and Profits Tax	£8 9 1
	£4 0 11

Return £4 0s. 11d. on £100 = 4·05 per cent.

* *Report of the Committee on Housing in Greater London.* HMSO, 1965.

One of the main housing problems in Britain which relates to financial issues, and whose effect is felt throughout practically the whole spectrum of housing deprivation, is that of the relative disadvantaged tax position of the private landlord, whose ability to improve the older dwelling stock is thus hindered. An example will suffice to demonstrate this situation, and is given in Table 7.

This calculation assumes that the property had a controlled rent, hence the gross annual increase of rent allowed was £12 10s. for each £100 spent on improvement. With a similar calculation over a fifteen-year period the return would be 0·43 per cent, and over twenty-five years it would have been 6·2 per cent. Thus when capital can only be borrowed at interest rates of 6½ per cent or more, then each of these three specified levels of return would mean that a landlord would not be able to undertake this form of investment without suffering financial loss. Yet landlords can in fact be compelled to carry out improvement and repair work. The Milner Holland committee felt that the tax position of the private landlord was such that many landlords could be expected to turn to other forms of investment. Many landlords felt that their income from rents since 1945 had been too low to allow them to maintain and repair their properties adequately.[2]

Generally, therefore, with the exception of those providing furnished accommodation, private landlords can be regarded as a decaying element in housing provision in England and Wales.

'Privately rented housing in the city of Lancaster is a dying institution. Between 1948 and 1960 the number of privately rented houses declined by over 50 per cent—mostly because of sales to owner-occupiers. The typical landlord is an old-age pensioner owning a single nineteenth-century house of low value, let at a weekly rent of 14s. 9d. He—or more usually she—has little interest in sound property management or even in continuing to remain an owner. On the contrary: only 6 per cent of owners stated that they intend to re-let when their houses become vacant or decontrolled.'[9]

Privately rented accommodation, especially unfurnished, is very important in terms of housing the poor, the elderly, small adult households, and persons in the lowest of the Registrar General's social class groupings. Furthermore, the greater part of privately rented accommodation was built before 1919, and, as will be indicated in the section dealing with deprivation in terms of amenities and housing condition, these are the dwellings where the incidence of bad conditions is particularly acute. Table 8 presents data on age of household head, type of household, income of head of household, and household size in relation to the various housing tenure groups.

The net incomes of household heads show that though in 35 per cent of council tenancies the head of household's income was under £10 a week, the similar proportion in privately rented controlled tenancies was much higher at 53 per cent. Thus the privately rented market is extremely important as a provider of housing for the lowest income households, and in proportion to the stock of dwellings in each sector relatively more poorer households are found in controlled tenancies, while even in uncontrolled tenancies the proportion of household heads with incomes of less than £10 is the same as in council housing. The prime reason for this situation in controlled tenancies is that the relative incidence of elderly one and two person households is considerably higher here than in any other tenure category, and elderly households, living in the main on pensions, have low incomes.

The owner-occupiers are usually the higher income groups, though most of the low income owner-occupiers can be explained by the fact that they are outright owners, that is they have finished repaying their mortgages, or they bought outright. The growth of this tenure category has been particularly noticeable in the last fifteen years or so. Several brief comments upon this are relevant. In England and Wales in 1967 the total sum of housing loan advances from the main institutional sources was £1,762,000,000 of which 84 per cent was lent by building societies, 9 per cent by local authorities (this was a major source for loans on older properties) and 7 per cent by insurance companies. Of building society mortgages some 32 per cent went to buyers of newly constructed dwellings, and the average mortgage as a proportion of the average house price was 72·5 per cent, while the average price paid for a house with a building society mortgage was 2·6 times the average annual income of their mortgagees (£1,565). Over three-quarters of the mortgages were over repayment periods of twenty or twenty-five years, and as a corollary to this 40 per cent of building society mortgages were granted to persons aged twenty-five to thirty-four years, while persons under forty-four years of age accounted for 84 per cent of the mortgages issued. Furthermore as mentioned above, though nearly one-third of all building society mortgages went to newly constructed houses, only 18 per cent were issued for the purchase of dwellings built before 1919. Thus owner-occupation with the aid of a mortgage becomes more difficult the older the purchaser is, and also if the dwelling to be purchased was built before 1919. Despite this, however, many older rented dwellings are being purchased for owner-occupation, often with the aid of local authority mortgages. Local authorities also generally lend to lower income households than building societies and insurance companies.[13] Between 1960 and 1964 evidence shows that the median net weekly level for unfurnished uncontrolled rents outside London had risen by 28 per cent, while the rents of local authority accommodation had risen by 32 per cent. The rents of local authority housing in Greater London averaged £1 8s. 10d. in October 1961 and by October 1967 this had risen to £2 7s. 7d. In the rest of England and Wales the average council rent over this period rose from £1 1s. 1d. to £1 13s. 6d. Table 9 indicates rent levels in England and Wales in 1964, excluding Greater London, by types of tenancy.

Since 1964 however there have been significant increases in local authority rent levels, as new local authority housing is built to a high standard—some would argue, possibly too high a standard. The costs of house construction are also rising and the rents of many new council tenancies are relatively high. One of the long standing criticisms of local authority subsidy systems is that they subsidise the dwelling, whereas in the case of owner-occupiers it is the household which is subsidised through income tax relief, assuming that this has sufficient income to pay tax. There has been in many local authority areas a swing towards charging more economic rents and then subsidising those in real need who cannot afford these rents. This is done in different ways by local authorities who operate

TABLE 8*

Characteristics of households occupying their accommodation under different forms of tenure, England and Wales, 1964 (percentage values)

	Owner occupied	Local authority	Privately rented Unfurnished Con-trolled	Privately rented Unfurnished Uncon-trolled	Furnished	Other types	All types
1. Age of household head							
Up to 29 years	7	6	2	19	48	13	9
30 - 39 years	19	18	6	18	22	27	18
40 - 49 years	20	26	16	14	10	31	20
50 - 59 years	22	20	25	18	11	12	21
60 - 69 years	17	18	29	13	5	7	18
70 years and over	14	12	22	17	4	10	14
No information	1	—	—	1	—	—	—
2. Household type (a)							
Individual under 60	3	2	4	6	30	2	4
Small adult households	14	7	11	17	28	14	13
Small families	22	22	10	24	25	26	21
Large families	10	19	5	11	4	20	12
Large adult households	23	26	28	15	3	19	23
Older small households	27	23	41	27	10	19	27
Unclassified	1	1	—	—	—	—	—
3. Income of head of household (per week) (b)							
Up to £5	10	13	23	16	6	10	13
£5 to £7 10s.	7	13	17	12	11	4	10
£7 10s. to £10	6	9	13	7	19	15	9
£10 to £12 10s.	10	16	16	19	17	20	14
£12 10s. to £15	16	24	16	18	14	12	18
£15 to £20	24	20	11	19	19	22	20
Over £20	27	5	5	12	12	17	16
4. Household size							
1	11	11	21	19	35	9	14
2	33	22	36	32	32	24	30
3	24	24	21	22	20	18	23
4	19	21	13	16	9	27	18
5	9	13	6	7	2	14	10
6 or more	4	9	3	4	2	8	5
No. of persons per household	2·95	3·47	2·58	2·76	2·18	3·39	3·0

(a) Household types are based on the following classification :

		Persons under 16 years	Persons 16 years and over
(i)	Individuals under 60 years	—	1 ⎱ none aged 60
(ii)	Small adult households	—	2 ⎰ or over
(iii)	Small families	1 or 2	1 or 2
(vi)	Large families	3 or more	any number
	OR	2	3 or more
(v)	Larger adult households	0 to 1	3 or more
(vi)	Older small households	—	1 or 2 (at least one aged 60 or over)

(b This is income per week, less deductions, plus overtime, bonuses, etc.

* Woolf, *Housing Survey in England and Wales.*

TABLE 9*
Net weekly rent by type of tenancy, England and Wales, 1964, excluding
Greater London (percentage values)

Net weekly rent	Privately rented		Furnished	Local authority	All tenancies
	Unfurnished				
	Controlled	Uncontrolled			
Less than 10s.	20	15	7	2	9
10s. but less than £1	55	30	14	15	26
£1 but less than £1 10s.	20	25	7	45	35
£1 10s. but less than £2	4	8	5	30	20
£2 but less than £2 10s.	1	8	12	5	5
£2 10s. but less than £3	—	4	12	2	2
£3 but less than £3 10s.	—	3	2	1	1
£3 10s. but less than £4	—	3	5	—	1
£4 but less than £4 10s.	—	—	21	—	1
£4 10s. but less than £5	—	2	—	—	—
£5 but less than £6	—	—	14	—	1
£6 or more	—	2	2	—	—
Median net weekly rent	14s. 7d.	£1 0s. 7d.	£2 16s. 10d.	£1 7s. 7d.	£1 4s. 0d.

* Woolf, *Housing Survey in England and Wales.*

differential rent schemes. Many authorities operate such schemes but not all.

As R. A. Parker points out there are two main types of differential rent arrangements plus a subsidiary third but minor one. The first, and most commonly used, is based on the assumption that tenants ought to pay a certain proportion of their income in rent. Often however this disregards family size. A seventh of gross income is often the criterion used, but it varies between one-fifth and one-ninth. Rebates are given to ensure that not more than the specified proportion of income is charged as rent. However this system presents many problems: a fixed proportion of income as rent, regardless of family size, means that large families suffer, while a fixed proportion of a lower income is a greater burden than in the case of a higher income. Some authorities have introduced sliding scales to compensate for this, others vary the proportion not on an income basis but by the type of accommodation provided. It would appear that these rent determination systems require much more rational thought.

The second type of scheme is based on the assumption that families of different sizes require a 'certain minimum disposable income', and that the rents payable ought not to make families live below this level. However, relatively high minimum rents frequently blunt their more discriminating features. The third system is that of setting rent or rebate levels for specific household income ranges. This is becoming less popular. Many anomalies and problems arise through these differential rent systems.[14]

Despite these schemes it still appears that many poorer tenants are finding difficulty in paying their rents. That some of the poorer families find rents high is suggested by two studies. Harbert's in Southampton showed that 76 per cent of council households in arrears contained three or more children whereas in the country as a whole only 8 per cent of households contain as many children.[15] Hilary Land's pilot enquiry into the problems of large families in London (those with five or more children) showed that whereas forty-four of those in her sample lived in the property of councils operating differential rent schemes, only five were in fact getting rebates, and these were by no means the poorest.[16]

Parker says:

'We started this chapter asking how local authorities identify their poorest tenants. There seems a reasonable possibility that many do not; that rebates are not received by some of the poorest families largely because income is measured in crude terms and little attention is paid to income per head. Just as some of the poorest families tend not to be in council houses, so those who are stand in some danger of not receiving the benefits which differential rent schemes appear to offer.

'The field of council rents is frankly chaotic. They are surrounded by untested assumptions, expediency, convention and lack of basic data . . . Even more disturbing is the national uncertainty about the role which local housing authorities should be expected to play in the process of redistribution of incomes, and how far they can really be expected to assume responsibilities which may more appropriately be those of the Ministry of Social Security.'[14]

It should be stressed that differential rent schemes operate only in relation to council tenancies; however, assistance with housing costs is also given by the Supplementary Benefits Commission, a section of the Ministry of Social Security. These benefits can apply to the housing costs of private tenants as well as council tenants. The Ministry of Social Security supplementary rent payments largely go to retired tenants on small pensions. Generally about half a local authority's retired tenants will receive supplementary rent payments, thus to some extent relieving the local authority of the problems of the elderly in relation to high or increased rents. A further 4 to 5 per cent of council tenants also receive such assistance but are not retired. These include the long-term unemployed, fatherless families, the handicapped and the long-term sick.[14] Similar assistance is provided for such people in other renting categories.

In Scotland the main difference in rents is that those of the local authorities are lower than their counterparts in England and Wales. The data for Scotland relates to 1965 when the average weekly net rent paid by all renters was 13s. 7d. Council tenants paid an average of 15s. 5d. while tenants of unfurnished private rented property paid 10s., and in the case of furnished tenancies the rent was £1 12s. a week. The same situation is revealed as in England and Wales where the older the household the less rent is paid, and the higher the income the higher is the rent. The Scottish rent figures are given in terms of averages while the figures relating to England and Wales are indicated by median values rather than averages and are found in Table 9.

In comparing the relative rent levels one must also consider income levels, as lower rent levels might relate to lower household head incomes. In fact this is the case in Scotland, yet the rent levels themselves, particularly in the case of council housing, appear to be considerably below the level in England and Wales (see Table 8, part 3) even taking account of the lower level of Scottish incomes. There is also a strong tradition in Scotland of a much heavier subsidy of local authority housing costs from the local rate fund than in England and Wales. The Scottish income situation is as indicated in Table 10.

TABLE 10*

Net income of head of household by tenure, Scotland, 1965

Weekly net income	Owns/is buying %	Rents from council %	Rents privately, etc. %	Total %
Up to £5	15	16	17	16
More than £5, to £7 10s.	7	11	10	10
More than £7 10s. to £10	8	11	13	11
More than £10 to £12 10s.	10	21	24	19
More than £12 10s. to £15	14	21	15	18
More than £15 to £20	18	15	12	15
More than £20 to £25	10	4	5	5
More than £25	17	1	4	6

* Cullingworth, *Scottish Housing in 1965*

Thus while 56 per cent of Scottish heads of households earned up to £12 10s. net per week in 1965, the figure for England and Wales in 1964 was lower at 46 per cent. Other points to arise from comparison with England and Wales are that lower proportions of owner-occupiers in Scotland were in the income range £12 10s. to £20 (32 per cent compared with 40 per cent), but 15 per cent of owner-occupiers in Scotland had incomes under £5 (compared with 10 per cent). There was no significant difference in terms of council tenants' incomes, though there is some reflection of the general Scottish situation of slightly lower incomes.

The average household size in Scotland is slightly higher than in England and Wales, 3·17 and 3·0 persons respectively. However Scottish owner-occupiers had an average household size of 2·87 compared with 2·95 in England and Wales. This is the only significant difference in average household sizes by tenure groups, and is probably related to the higher cost of owner-occupied dwellings in Scotland, partly because of their scarcity and the fact that families with children will find it harder to become owner-occupiers in the fringe income range, which as indicated above is the range £12 10s. to £20 a week. These Scottish figures relate to data collected in April-May 1965 and since then there has been a general rise in local authority rents as in England and Wales but incomes have also risen.

In the last few years the government has introduced two new measures to encourage the growth of owner-occupation. The first was the introduction of the option mortgage scheme. Under this system an owner-occupier buying with the aid of a mortgage can opt to obtain his mortgage at an interest rate of 2 per cent less than the current building society rate if he relinquishes his right to income tax relief on that part of his mortgage payments which represents the interest sum. This is aimed at the lower fringe income groups of those who can just about afford to buy their dwelling. Basically, this scheme is better for those people who pay less than about £70 a year in income tax, and who will continue to do so for many years ahead. The second scheme to be introduced, both being financed by central government funds, was the 100 per cent mortgage scheme, which was aimed at overcoming the problem of saving up for a house purchase deposit, often 10 per cent or more of the purchase price. The problem here is that the 100 per cent loan relates to the mortgagor's valuation of the property, which tends to underestimate value, and not to the purchase price, while in addition the legal fees, etc. must be paid. Both measures have however done a little to encourage the growth of owner-occupation amongst households with lower incomes.

This section dealing with housing finance and tenure has set the scene for the study of deprivation in terms of both the physical condition of dwellings and of the special groups of deprived persons. In relation to physical condition the discussion of privately rented accommodation and the problems imposed by rent control and regulation, by taxation policies, and the difficulties of getting a reasonable return on repair costs over short-life periods, provide ample indication of the importance of financial problems. The tenure survey has also supplied evidence on the types and characteristics of households occupying dwellings under different tenure arrangements.

THE PHYSICAL CONDITION OF THE HOUSING STOCK

The most recent data concerning the physical characteristics of dwellings are derived from the national sample house condition survey of 1967. Two criteria are adopted here to indicate deprivation. The first concerns housing unfit for human occupation, a statutory standard though one open to wide interpretation by local authorities. Before the survey the national estimate had been derived from local authorities' own returns, which as shown earlier were unreliable. In a 1965 return from local authorities the estimate of unfit dwellings in England and Wales was placed at 820,000 while the house condition survey of 1967 placed the estimate at 1,800,000. The second criterion is concerned with the availability of the standard amenities in dwellings. The four standard amenities to be considered are an internal water closet; a fixed bath or shower; a wash-hand basin; and a hot and cold water supply linked to a bath, a wash-hand basin and a kitchen sink.

Unfit dwellings in England and Wales are determined by the criteria set out in the Housing Act of 1957. These are specified as follows:

'In determining for any of the purposes of this Act whether a house is unfit for human habitation, regard shall be had to its condition in respect of the following matters that is to say—(a) repair; (b) stability; (c) freedom from damp; (d) natural lighting; (e) ventilation; (f) water supply; (g) drainage and sanitary conveniences; (h) facilities for storage, preparation and cooking of food and for the disposal of waste water; and the house shall be deemed to be unfit for human habitation if and only if it is so far defective in one or more of the said matters that it is not reasonably suitable for occupation in that condition.'[17]

A committee investigating these criteria concluded that an additional three points ought to be added.[18] The White Paper on older housing, and the 1969 Housing Act, however, include only one of these three extra points, that the dwelling be free from internal bad arrangement. The committee also felt that the term to be used in relation to the unfitness criteria ought to be *dwelling* and not *house* (see section on terminology). The report on older houses in Scotland recommends the adoption of two standards: a satisfactory standard, representing a target at which policy ought to be directed (similar to the present discretionary grant standard, see later); and a tolerability standard, below which houses should not be allowed to exist.[19] The Scottish Development Department, under the Minister of State for Scotland, intend to develop these standards.

Furthermore the Scottish criteria for unfit dwellings are slightly different from those applying in England and Wales.[20] Again, however, too much reliance cannot be placed on these returns of unfit housing, and no similar survey to the national house condition survey has yet been carried out in Scotland. Thus a latest estimate of Scottish unfit housing is 100,000 houses, 6 per cent of the total housing stock (this compares with 5 per cent for England and Wales from local authority returns in 1965).

The total of unfit houses demolished or closed in England and Wales in 1968 was 72,000, and 67,000 families comprising 189,000 persons were moved as a result of slum clearance. The figure refers to houses not dwellings, though usually these would be synonymous. The term house 'refers to a building and not to the separate dwellings which may be contained within it, and the figures do not, therefore, indicate the total number of dwellings which have to be dealt with.'[21] Included in the 72,000 are 743 dwellings which were closed as being unfit but which were situated in buildings which otherwise continued to be occupied. The 72,000 demolitions or closures also include some 6,250 houses demolished in clearance areas by reason of their bad arrangement or by the need to demolish them in order to free land for the redevelopment of the cleared site.[21] In Scotland the number of houses demolished or closed under slum clearance procedures in 1967 was 19,000.[21] In this case the term house is used to mean a separate dwelling, and thus direct comparison with the figure for England and Wales is not possible.

One must also point out, however, that not all unfit houses are closed or demolished. In 1968 72,000 houses were dealt with in this way in England and Wales, but a further 85,000 were rendered fit as a result of formal procedure under various Acts, or as a result of informal action. Thus significantly more unfit houses were rendered fit than were demolished or closed.[21]

The national house condition survey estimated the number of unfit dwellings to be 1,800,000 of which all but 700,000 were in potential clearance areas and could be dealt with by the normal channels of redevelopment. The 700,000 dwellings required individual treatment by repair, closure or demolition, as appropriate. The proportion of unfit dwellings in the rural areas was 13 per cent compared with 11 per cent in the conurbations and urban areas. The survey also indicated that some 42 per cent of unfit dwellings were located in the three northern economic planning regions of England and Wales, that is the area including and north of Lancashire, the West Riding of Yorkshire and the northern parts of Lincolnshire, Lindsey and Kesteven. Also included is a part of north Derbyshire. Local authority returns of unfit dwellings gave no indication of tenure. The 1967 survey did, and this showed that about 30 per cent of the unfit dwellings were owner-occupied but that this only represented 7 per cent of all the owner-occupied dwellings; secondly, privately rented housing accounted for about 60 per cent of unfit housing, while 33 per cent of all privately rented housing was unfit.

Unfitness is correlated with lack of amenities, with the older dwelling stock of which 97 per cent were built before 1919, with households living on low incomes, and with elderly households. Many of the privately rented unfit dwellings are subject to rent control as they possess low rateable values. Eighty-three per cent of unfit dwellings lacked a hot and cold water supply at three points, 79 per cent lacked a hand-wash basin, 77 per cent lacked an internal water closet and 72 per cent lacked a fixed bath. Unfit dwellings by definition have short future spans of life unless the dwelling is outside a clearance area and the owner undertakes to render the dwelling fit. This would only normally be done where the sum of money needed to achieve fitness was not too great in relation to the value of the dwelling and to the ability of the owner to pay for improvement. Standard grants are available to assist financially with the installation of basic amenities for the first time and discretionary grants cover much wider improvement. These grants are for half the cost of carrying out the necessary works, and are dealt with in the next section.

In order to speed up the process of clearing unfit housing the government has defined 135 local authorities in England as 'priority areas'; there are separate programmes for Wales and for Scotland. These authorities are those in greatest need because of housing shortages, problems of overcrowding and of large numbers of unfit dwellings. The increase in local authority housing construction in those areas averaged 25 per cent in 1966, compared with a fall of 9 per cent in the case of other English local authorities.[22]

The city of Birmingham operates a system whereby areas of unfit housing which are to be demolished and redeveloped in several years' time are bought by the city, improved to make them habitable for the period they will remain occupied before demolition and subsequently managed as part of the city's housing stock. This 'patching' policy, as it is sometimes referred to, is possibly more socially than economically justifiable. It ameliorates the housing conditions of those whose dwellings await demolition. Salford is another authority which operates such a system, and there are several London boroughs with similar acquisition policies but which do not improve such properties on a scale as significant as that in Birmingham.

At present there are many local authority areas nearing the end of their slum clearance programmes, and it is the aim of the government to encourage such authorities to utilise powers for the improvement of housing conditions and of the environments in which these dwellings are found.[7] Unfit dwellings have a high incidence of lack of amenities, but lack of and sharing of amenities are also found in fit housing.

The national house condition survey found that 75 per cent of the dwellings in England and Wales possessed all the four amenities for the exclusive use of the occupier for which grant aid is given. Thus 25 per cent lacked one or more of these amenities. A fixed bath or shower was lacked by 13·4 per cent of dwellings (for the exclusive use of the occupiers), 19·4 per cent lacked a hand-wash basin, 21·7 per cent lacked a hot and cold water supply at three points and 18·6 per cent had no internal water closet. Some 12 per cent of all dwellings lacked all four amenities.

Housing in the south-east was found to be better than elsewhere as regards amenities. Here only 11 per cent of dwellings lacked internal water closets compared with 25 per cent of those in the three northern economic regions, and 20 per cent in the rest of England and Wales. In all these cases data relate to the availability for the sole use of the occupiers of a dwelling, hence dwellings sharing facilities are included with those lacking them. Table 11 presents data on the lack of basic amenities and their relationship to tenure patterns. The main points to emerge are that dwellings of owner-occupiers and public authorities were far better equipped than were privately rented dwellings. The 20 per cent of the housing stock which was privately rented included 65 per cent of all the dwellings without a fixed bath, and over 50 per cent of all the dwellings lacking each of the other basic amenities.[8]

TABLE 11
Lack of basic amenities by tenure, England and Wales, 1967 (percentages)

	Owner occupied	Rented from L.A.s or new towns	Other tenures[1]	Closed[2]
Total stock	50·8	27·1	21·4	0·7
Amenities lacked				
Internal water closet	32·6	12·4	52·2	2·8
Fixed bath	26·8	4·4	65·1	3·7
Wash basin	27·9	15·8	53·7	2·6
Hot and cold water at three points	30·0	15·3	52·3	2·4
One or more of the amenities	32·7	17·1	48·1	2·1

[1] Virtually all are privately rented.
[2] Dwellings closed under Housing or Planning Act powers.

Once again the relatively deprived position of many private tenants is indicated. The Milner Holland committee made their views on this issue felt when they stated, 'the houses most deficient in domestic amenities, most inadequately maintained and most in need of clearance are found among those which are privately rented, and our enquiries give us little confidence that their present owners would be able to prevent their further deterioration, even if they are willing to attempt it'.[2]

In terms of the sharing of amenities the 1964 housing survey provides evidence of its significance in respect of different amenities. Water closets in or attached to buildings were the most frequent of the shared amenities with 6·3 per cent of households in England and Wales sharing, fixed baths or showers were shared by 5·1 per cent of households, 3·5 per cent shared the use of a hand-wash basin, while about 2 per cent in both cases shared a sink and a water closet not in or attached to the building.[11]

Another point to emerge from the 1964 housing survey of England and Wales was that the older the dwelling the less likely it is to possess the four specified amenities: only 40 per cent of dwellings built before 1919 had the exclusive use of these amenities (78 per cent for dwellings built between 1919 and 1944 and 98 per cent for those built between 1945 and 1960). The likelihood of having the exclusive use of the four amenities was also greater outside London than within it. Similarly the less sound the structural fitness and the nearer the likelihood of demolition of a dwelling then the less likely was it that it would possess the exclusive use of the four amenities for its household. Tenants in furnished accommodation were more likely to share, but tenants in controlled accommodation (often the elderly with their small incomes) were more likely to be without access to these amenities.

The higher the head of household income the more likely that the exclusive use of the amenities would be available, while in terms of head of household ages it was the young (in uncontrolled and furnished dwellings) and the elderly (in controlled dwellings) who were most likely to suffer from lack of amenities. Those in the middle-age ranges fared best, partly no doubt due to better earning power. It is also the large families rather than the small families who are more likely to have the use of the amenities, a reflection of the high proportion of large families in council housing with its associated high amenity provision levels.[11] Thus the private tenants, especially in unfurnished accommodation, tend to suffer from a high incidence of amenity deprivation. This again reflects the economic position of the landlord and his tenant.[23]

A national system of improvement grants has been in operation since the late 1940s to provide amenities for dwellings lacking them and to issue grants to bring dwellings up to a reasonable state of repair. There are two types of grants, standard grants and discretionary grants. Standard grants were first introduced in the House Purchase and Housing Act of 1959, and subsequently amended in the 1961, 1964 and 1969 Housing Acts. These grants are for providing the five standard amenities in dwellings which lack any number of them. These standard amenities are the four listed in Table 11 plus a satisfactory food store. Once provided with grant aid the amenities are for the sole use of the dwelling's inhabitants. Where a local authority feels costs would be too high for improvement to the five point standard, it is empowered to make a grant towards a reduced amenity standard often referred to as the three point standard. This three point standard excludes the wash-hand basin and a fixed bath or shower. Before issuing a standard grant the local authority must be satisfied that the dwelling will have a future life of about fifteen years, and that it will continue in use as a private dwelling. The maximum grant to an owner, whether owner-occupier or landlord, is half the cost of installing the amenities, subject to a normal grant limit of £200, which is only payable if all five amenities are installed for the first time. Where dwellings already contain several of the amenities then the grant is still payable, but the maximum grant is reduced by specific amounts for each amenity already existing. If a tenant or owner can show that their dwelling complies with the regulations for the issue of a standard grant the local authority must make the grant. This grant is a legal entitlement.

In the case of discretionary grants, as the name suggests, they are issued at the discretion of the local authority. These grants are now referred to as improvement grants in the 1969 Housing Act. They are not normally given unless the dwelling has a future life of about thirty years, and it must continue in use as a private dwelling. These grants were first introduced in the Housing Act of 1949. The current enactment relating to these grants is the Housing Act, 1969. This Act establishes a twelve point standard which is to be achieved by a dwelling after improvement or conversion with the aid of an improvement grant. Note that this grant is also payable for conversion as well as improvement. The twelve points are:

1. be in a good state of repair and substantially free from damp;
2. have each room properly lighted and ventilated;
3. have an adequate supply of wholesome water laid on inside the dwelling;
4. be provided with efficient and adequate means of supplying hot water for domestic purposes;
5. have an internal or otherwise readily accessible water closet;
6. have a fixed bath, or shower, in a separate room;
7. be provided with a sink or sinks with suitable arrangements for the disposal of waste water;
8. have a proper drainage system;
9. be provided in each room with adequate points for gas or electric lighting;
10. be provided with adequate facilities for heating;
11. have satisfactory facilities for storing, preparing and cooking food;
12. have proper provision for the storage of fuel (where required).

Again the amount of grant is half the cost of approved improvement works. The financial ceiling for approved improvement works, to qualify for grant, is £2,000, thus the maximum grant obtainable is £1,000 per dwelling. There are slight variations for blocks of dwellings of three or more storeys in height. In 1968 the total number of improvement grants issued in England and Wales was 114,216 of which 60 per cent were standard grants and 40 per cent discretionary grants. Local authorities received for themselves about 27 per cent of all these grants, two-thirds of which were discretionary grants for improvement; another 49 per cent went to owner-occupiers, nearly three-quarters of which were standard grants; and the remaining 24 per cent went to private landlords in the main. Several other points ought to be made regarding these grants. The maximum rent increase allowed on a controlled rent property after improvement with grant aid was 12½ per cent of the landlord's capital expenditure of one half the cost of approved improvement works. As shown in the section on housing finance and tenure, the landlord's return on investment would only be 0·43 per cent if the dwelling had a future life of only fifteen years and the money was available without having to borrow it at current interest rates. In other words, if the landlord had put this money in a building society at 4·5 per cent interest, he would have been a much wiser investor. However landlords can be compelled to undertake improvements with grant aid if this is desired by a tenant who is willing to pay the increased rent. In some instances with dwellings qualifying on a minimum future life span this can cause hardship to landlords, especially as many of them own only one dwelling to let, and are often elderly with insufficient capital. These types of landlords are quite common.

Housing associations receive special consideration and can obtain grants covering both acquisition and improvement costs up to £2,500 per dwelling. This new grant aid is also available to local authorities. This generally encourages housing associations to provide small units of accommodation, thus maximising their grant income. It therefore makes them largely ineffective as providers of housing for large families or large adult households. Several local authorities operate a system whereby they do not normally issue discretionary grants, which can only be deplored.

The 1964 Housing Act first contained powers enabling local authorities to declare improvement areas, and to compel landlords to improve to the standard amenity level. In relation to owner-occupiers in these areas the council can only 'encourage' them to make use of the grants. This act states, 'If a local authority are satisfied that any area in their district contains dwellings lacking one or more of the standard amenities and that, of the dwellings in that area which are so lacking, at least one-half:

(a) are so constructed that it is practicable to improve them to the full standard, and

(b) will, after they have been improved to the full standard, be in such condition as to be fit for human habitation, and will be likely, subject to normal maintenance, to remain in that condition for a period of not less than fifteen years, the local authority may cause the area to be defined on a map and may pass a resolution declaring the area to be so defined to be an improvement area for the purposes of this Part of the Act.' [24]

Besides these powers for compulsory improvement of tenanted properties in improvement areas, there are also compulsory powers relating to dwellings in tenanted tenement blocks and to individual tenanted dwellings where the tenant applies to the council in order to ensure that the landlord brings the dwelling up to standard amenity level.

The improvement area powers of local authorities have not been used as much as they might have been; many authorities felt the procedure was too protracted and cumbersome. The city of Leeds has declared about one hundred improvement areas under Housing Act powers other than those of the 1964 Act, but few other authorities have made much headway.

It is recognised that not simply the dwellings require to be improved, but also the environment in which they are situated. Several studies have been carried out by, on behalf of or with the co-operation of the Ministry of Housing and Local Government. The most important of these, as a result of which a pilot housing and environmental improvement scheme has been effected, is the Ministry's *The Deeplish study, improvement possibilities in a district of Rochdale*, 1966. Other such studies have been carried out in Fulham, the Halliwell district of Bolton and the Barnsbury district of Islington, while many local authorities are examining the potential for housing and environmental improvements within some of their older residential areas.

In order to facilitate matters and to direct local authorities into housing and environmental improvement, on the basis of general improvement areas, the government passed the 1969 Housing Act. The main points in the Housing Act, which have not been mentioned so far, can be summarised as follows. Local authorities ought to be concerned with all unsatisfactory residential areas and not only with slum clearance areas and council housing estates. The 1964 Housing Act improvement area provisions are thus repealed and replaced by more effective powers which will enable local authorities to declare 'general improvement areas'. For the first time a grant for environmental improvement is to be paid: an exchequer grant of one-half the costs of environmental improvement, up to a maximum claimable expenditure of £100 per dwelling in the general improvement area. Thus the maximum amount of grant will be £50 per dwelling, which is felt by many to be too small a sum. The problem of future life spans of dwellings with statutory levels at fifteen and thirty years is to be made more flexible. The rents of dwellings achieving a certain standard of amenity and condition will be assessed by rent tribunals under the 1965 Rent Act; this will mean possibly significant rent increases especially in previously controlled tenancies, though there will be some phasing of rent increases. Local authorities will be given powers to regulate or prevent proposed multiple occupation of houses in certain defined localities. Finally landlords and owner-occupiers of unfit housing subject to slum clearance will be paid higher compensation, especially in the case of owner-occupiers where compensation will be the equivalent of market value.

There has thus been a definite shift of housing policy towards more concern for those dwellings which are not unfit but are unsatisfactory, and whose environments require an injection of capital to bring them up to a more reasonable standard for residential properties. The clearance of unfit dwellings in Britain is one of the most rapid clearance and redevelopment programmes in Europe, and thus at this end of the house condition spectrum relatively rapid progress has been made, though it needs to be sustained longer in the 135 priority housing areas. It is hoped that by investing national and local public funds in housing improvement, as well as private funds, dwellings will be given a longer useful life at a reasonable standard of accommodation. Without this improvement to the dwelling stock the process of obsolescence would be unhindered, and many dwellings would become slums prematurely. In one sense it is possible to solve the slum problem, by clearing all those dwellings falling short of the unfitness criteria of the 1957 Housing Act as amended and improving others. Though at any one time there is a static set of unfitness criteria, the essential point about slums is their relation to the total housing stock. As one era demolishes its slums so another set of criteria will be devised for that group of existing dwellings which are felt to fall below newly defined acceptable standards, standards which are constantly rising at an ever-accelerating pace. There will thus never be a solution to the slum problem in the foreseeable future. This problem is therefore a continuous one whose scale and character is subject to gradual change.

SPECIAL GROUPS OF DEPRIVED HOUSEHOLDS

There were no specific criteria to determine those groups suffering relative housing deprivation, rather did the groups suggest themselves from the general consensus of opinion and publications on housing and related studies. The groups are: the overcrowded; the homeless; the large family; the poor; the disabled and handicapped; the coloured immigrants; and the travellers and caravan dwellers.

(i) *The Overcrowded.* The measurement of overcrowding entails a consideration of the sizes and character of households seen in relation to their existing accommodation. It is necessary therefore to adopt certain measurement criteria which can be used to assess not only the extent of overcrowding but also its relative degrees. In Britain there are three measures of the space available to households: the statutory overcrowding standard, the number of persons per room and the bedroom standard.

The space standards for statutory overcrowding are contained in the

1957 Housing Act and are accepted as representing an extremely low standard. The Act specifies the number of persons permitted to live in a dwelling before it is considered overcrowded on the basis of the number of habitable rooms. However, the standard contains a second table based upon the floor area of rooms and the permitted number of persons. The number of occupants permitted to live in a dwelling is assessed from these two tables; the relevant table for use (number of rooms or room floor area) is whichever results in the lower figure of occupants.

TABLE 12

The statutory overcrowding standard

Number of rooms	Permitted number of persons
1	2
2	3
3	5
4	7·5
5 or more	10 with an additional 2 for each room in excess of 5

Floor Area of Room	Permitted number of persons
110 sq. ft. or more	2
90 sq. ft. to 110 sq. ft.	1·5
70 sq. ft. to 90 sq. ft.	1
50 sq. ft. to 70 sq. ft.	0·5
Under 50 sq. ft.	nil

For the purpose of the statutory overcrowding tables, children under the age of one are not counted, while those aged one but under ten count as a half; all other persons count as one. From a practical point of view it is much easier to consider the number of rooms in relation to the number of persons, as this saves having to measure floor areas.

The second measure of overcrowding is known as the census room standard because it is a measure of the number of persons per room and the only overcrowding measure derivable from census data. It is found by dividing the total household size by the number of habitable rooms which are for the sole use of the particular household. In this case each person is assessed as one unit. Habitable rooms exclude entrance halls, cloakrooms and bathrooms and until the 1966 sample census excluded kitchens which were not used as a room in which meals were regularly eaten. In the 1966 sample census, however, all kitchens were counted as a room irrespective of eating habits.

The statutory overcrowding standard is generally regarded as being too low for modern needs, while the census room standard fails to consider the type of family occupying the accommodation. Thus when the Government Social Survey were conducting a study of housing in England and Wales in 1960 it was felt that a new overcrowding measure ought to be used. Hence in 1960 the Social Survey adopted a bedroom standard. Not only is this a measure of overcrowding, it can also be used as a measure of under-occupancy, which is the difference between the household's bedroom space needs and the excess of bedrooms over that need. Under this Social Survey bedroom standard, a specific number of bedrooms is allocated to each household on the basis of the following criteria:

(i)   each married couple, one bedroom;
(ii) other persons aged twenty-one or over, one bedroom each;
(iii) persons aged ten to twenty inclusive and of the same sex, one bedroom per pair;
(iv) any person aged ten to twenty, left over after pairing, paired with a child of the same sex aged under ten years with a bedroom to the pair. If no pairing possible with a younger child, a separate bedroom for that person;
(v)   any remaining children under ten years of age paired, with a bedroom for each pair. Any child remaining after this pairing, had a separate bedroom.

This standard, of course, makes no allowance for the needs of expanding families which might be expected to require at least one spare bedroom. Nor does it take into account the possible need for a spare bedroom for visiting friends and relatives.

In considering levels of overcrowding one must necessarily also consider the size distribution of the existing stock of dwellings. Furthermore, the problems of overcrowding and under-occupancy are related to the mal-distribution of fit between households and household spaces: many of the problems of overcrowding could be overcome with a much more rational distribution of the housing stock amongst family units of different sizes. Unfortunately, however, it is often the larger families which are least able to afford the higher housing costs usually associated with larger accommodation units.

In 1964 in England and Wales 6·6 per cent of accommodation units consisted of two rooms or less, 11·1 per cent had three rooms, 26·3 per cent had four rooms, 35·1 per cent had five rooms, while 15·2 per cent had six rooms and only 5·8 per cent had seven rooms or more. These figures include kitchens only where they were used for eating meals. In terms of the number of bedrooms available in accommodation units in 1964 some 50 per cent had three bedrooms, 31·3 per cent had two bedrooms, 10·5 per cent had one or no bedrooms, 6·2 per cent had four bedrooms and 1·9 per cent had five or more bedrooms. The most common type of accommodation unit was one of two living rooms and three bedrooms (34 per cent of accommodation units in England and Wales, though only 23 per cent in Greater London where accommodation units tended to be smaller than nationally).[11]

In 1960 the Social Survey estimated that 0·6 per cent of households in England and Wales fell below the statutory overcrowding standard, and by 1964 the figure was 0·5 per cent. Its incidence was found to be higher in Greater London. In 1964 the number of persons per room where households contained at least one person per room was 6·9 per cent of all households. In 1960 some 11 per cent of all households fell below the bedroom standard, 1·75 per cent having two or more bedrooms less than the standard while 9·25 per cent had one bedroom less than the standard. By 1964 this had fallen slightly to 9·4 per cent of households falling below this standard, 1·3 per cent had two bedrooms or more less than the standard and 8·1 per cent had one bedroom less than the standard. The 1964 Social Survey data for England and Wales on levels of overcrowding are given in Table 13. This also provides some measure of under-occupancy.

TABLE 13*

Households living at different density standards, 1964

No. of persons per room	Greater London %	Rest of England and Wales %	All England and Wales %
over 2	1·1	0·3	0·4
over 1·5 and up to 2	3·3	1·4	1·7
over 1 up to 1·5	5·6	4·6	4·8
no. of persons = no. of rooms	19·0	13·9	14·8
0·66 up to 0·99	29·5	26·9	27·4
0·5 up to 0·65	21·0	26·1	25·2
less than 0·5	20·3	26·7	25·5
unclassifiable	—	0·3	0·2
Bedroom standard			
2 or more below standard	1·7	1·2	1·3
1 below standard	10·6	7·6	8·1
equal to standard	47·1	35·7	37·8
1 more than standard	28·2	37·3	35·7
2 or more in excess of standard	12·2	18·2	17·1
unclassifiable	0·3	—	0·1
Statutory overcrowding (persons per room measure only)			
accommodation units overcrowded	1·0	0·4	0·5
accommodation units not overcrowded	98·7	99·4	99·3
unclassifiable	0·4	0·1	0·2

* Woolf, *Housing Survey in England and Wales.*

The above discussion has related to overcrowding in relation to all households, but one must also consider overcrowding in relation to specific types of households, for example, by family size, tenure, socio-economic grouping and so on. The housing survey of 1964 showed in terms of the census room standard, as one would expect, that large families (not large adult families) were the households most likely to be overcrowded, and particularly so in the case of such families occupying parts of rateable units in Greater London. Also small families living in parts of rateable units were more overcrowded than other household types with the exception of large families. Similarly the large families had the highest incidence of bedroom standard deficiencies, particularly if the family occupied part of a rateable value unit in Greater London. In terms of social class differentiation those more likely to be overcrowded were in the semi-skilled and unskilled occupations.[11] Tenure was also significant as an overcrowding variable. 'Less than 1 per cent of owner occupiers in England and Wales (apart from those occupying only part of their rateable unit) were living at a density of more than 1·5 persons per room, compared with 3 per cent of local authority tenants, 4 per cent of tenants in uncontrolled accommodation and 19 per cent of tenants in furnished accommodation. As with owner occupiers, proportionately fewer of the tenants in controlled accommodation were living at higher densities. On both measures of density—persons per room and the bedroom standard—tenants in furnished accommodation were the group most likely to be overcrowded while in terms of the bedroom standard there is evidence to suggest that proportionately more of the tenants in uncontrolled accommodation (particularly in Greater London) were below the standard.'[11]

The problem of overcrowding in Greater London is particularly acute and the committee reporting on housing there was aware of the relationship between overcrowding and coloured immigrants. 'There is no doubt that, for reasons inherent in the situation, housing accommodation occupied by coloured immigrants is, in general, too heavily overcrowded. . . . Overcrowding is worst in single furnished rooms; and we ourselves have seen, on our visits, large families of coloured immigrants living in single rooms in conditions of extreme difficulty and discomfort.'[2] There is also reason to suspect that this relationship is not purely a Greater London phenomena, though one would expect its incidence there to be higher.

Another survey has indicated that overcrowding is of high incidence in the cases of fatherless families and of families where the father is sick or unemployed. It was also found that this incidence increased quite markedly the higher the number of children in the family.[25]

In Scotland overcrowding is more common than in England and Wales. Some 3 per cent of Scottish households were overcrowded in 1965 on the basis of the persons per room table in the statutory overcrowding criteria. Glasgow showed a particularly high level of overcrowding. There the pro-

portion was 6 per cent (1965). Similarly in relation to the census room
standard 2 per cent of households in England and Wales had over 1·5
persons per room. For Scotland the proportion was 8 per cent, but 9 per
cent in the case of Glasgow. It is not possible to compare the bedroom
standard as in the Scottish context multi-purpose rooms (one purpose of
which is to provide bed space) are much more frequent than south of the
border, and the Scottish data included as bedrooms all rooms which were
used for sleeping in. Thus kitchens used for sleeping in, and living rooms
with bed-recesses, were counted as bedrooms.[12] In Scotland it was also the
private tenants who suffered most overcrowding, though it was particularly the unfurnished tenancies which had the highest incidence (in
England and Wales the highest incidence was found amongst furnished
tenancies).[12]

Despite the fact that one of the purposes of a local authority providing
council houses is to relieve overcrowding, its incidence in some areas is
still relatively high. Households which are particularly vulnerable to overcrowding are found in houses in multiple occupancy, where sharing of
amenities and facilities is also common. Local authorities are empowered to
control houses in multiple occupancy by limiting the number of tenants
and by making landlords improve amenities. However, the regulations governing multi-occupation are not easily enforced and where they are enforced,
local authorities often accept no responsibility for the rehousing of dis-
placed tenants. This arises because of local council house allocation systems,
which are highly variable, but which often exclude persons who are single
and of working age, and persons who have not resided in the local authority
area for a specified number of years.* Thus the fact that a family is overcrowded does not necessarily mean that it will be allocated a council house.
Indeed it has been argued that the rigorous application of anti-overcrowding
regulations, particularly in Greater London and Glasgow, would render
many people homeless as local authority housing would not be available in
sufficient numbers.[26] Overcrowding is thus generally symptomatic of areas
where there is a high degree of housing pressure, where the available
housing stock is, because of the demand, relatively highly priced. Thus
families and persons in the lower income ranges have to accept smaller
units of accommodation than is desirable, or have to share housing to
reduce their costs.

Overcrowding can thus lead to homelessness, while the threat of homelessness can lead to overcrowding. Overcrowding and homelessness,
whether they be incipient or a reality, are often closely connected and
interchangeable.

---

* The Ministry of Housing and Local Government has now appointed a committee
under Professor J. B. Cullingworth to investigate council housing allocation policies.
This committee reported in November 1969.

(ii) *Homelessness.* There has been extremely little study of the problem of homelessness in Britain despite the fact that in recent years the numbers of homeless people in local authority accommodation for homeless families has been increasing. By the end of 1967 there were over 15,500 persons in such accommodation in England and Wales. This figure represented an increase of about 2,500 persons over the previous year. In 1967 some 45 per cent of homeless families in this type of accommodation were found in Greater London (that is about 1,350 families). At the end of 1968, 2,029 families (9,791 persons) were in local authority temporary accommodation in Greater London. Essentially homelessness is only a problem of significant magnitude in Greater London and Birmingham according to official statistics of persons in local authority accommodation for the homeless.*

Under the 1948 National Assistance Act local authorities have a duty to provide emergency temporary accommodation for families which become homeless through no fault of their own. The exact interpretation of this part of the Act is left to individual local authorities and as will be shown later, many injustices can arise as a result of this situation. The 1948 Act also requires local authorities to provide accommodation for those people who lead an unsettled way of life, this generally being interpreted as including tramps, vagrants, itinerants, casuals and wayfarers, etc., but once again the Act is not specific. The Act also places a duty on local authorities to provide homes for old people and others in need of care and attention. Gypsies, though leading unsettled lives, move about with their own accommodation and in family groups. They are not considered as homeless by official statistics, and this group of people are discussed separately later.

Local authorities operate their own, often differing definitions of whom they regard as homeless: unmarried mothers, single persons, non-residents of a local authority area, or new arrivals in the area, may often find it difficult to be accepted as homeless persons by some local authorities. In the Greater London area, rejections by local authorities are currently about 75 per cent of applications for homeless accommodation. In other parts of the country the rejection rate was generally lower than this. Thus official statistics are rendered relatively meaningless by a range of various definitions of people local authorities will accept as being homeless. There is thus a difference between the actual state of homelessness and of administratively qualifying as homeless in the views of very many local authorities. Furthermore, besides differences in local authority definitions, many authorities regard the problem of homelessness as being simply as large as the local authority provision to cope with it. Thus, if a local authority has emergency accommodation for thirty families it may reject homelessness applications once its accommodation is filled. Also affecting official statistics

---

* The annual reports of the Ministry of Health and Social Security give brief statistical summaries.

is the fact that a few families when applying for homeless accommodation are immediately rehoused in council houses. These families never appear in the statistics as homeless together with those who are turned away to fend for themselves before an application is made. The official statistics of families in local authority homeless accommodation thus represent under-estimates of the true levels of homelessness. Immediate council rehousing depends of course on the local housing situation, and tends to be more common where there is less demand for council housing, in other words in the non-housing pressure areas.

Probably the greatest impact on homeless family policy has arisen from a documentary play called *Cathy Come Home*, written by Jeremy Sandford in 1963 and shown on BBC television in 1966. The play concerned the plight of a homeless family and did much to arouse public concern and indignation over the manner in which homeless families were being treated by local authorities. Before the mid 1960s it was not uncommon for home-less accommodation to be provided for the mother, children under sixteen years of age and usually daughters up to a few years over sixteen years of age. Fathers and sons over sixteen (irrespective of whether still at school or working) were boarded out as lodgers. Thus the father had two sets of accommodation costs to pay and was required at the same time to look for alternative accommodation. In other instances, fathers were separated from mothers, who in turn were separated from their children who were placed in the care of the local authority. Such action undoubtedly did much to destroy any cohesion of family life. Even when families (or reduced families) were accepted into the temporary communal accommodation there was little privacy, and several families might be required to occupy one room, possibly fitted with curtain partitions. The standard of amenity provision was sometimes exceptionally low. While it is not being claimed that this picture was generally applicable to all communal accommodation for homeless families, it was far too common, particularly in those areas of greater housing pressure.

A joint circular of the Ministry of Health, Home Office, and Ministry of Local Government of 1966 recommended that families ought not to be split up at reception centres, and that more family privacy was desirable.[27] The great majority of local authorities incorporated these suggestions into their policies. Despite a rethinking of local authority homelessness policies, there still appear to exist great discrepancies amongst policies, together with several apparent injustices.[28]

The problem of homelessness is most acute in Greater London where low cost accommodation units are difficult to obtain, particularly for fami-lies with children against whom landlords often discriminate. The gradual reduction in the availability of low-cost rented accommodation makes it more and more difficult for those on low incomes who lose their accommodation to find somewhere to live. The result can be homelessness or overcrowding.

In 1961-62, J. Greve carried out a survey of London's homeless on behalf of the then London County Council.[29] Its information is now out of date and has been affected by the reorganisation of local government in Greater London in 1965. However some of the points made in this study are presented below. The main causes of homelessness amongst families in temporary accommodation towards the end of 1961 were as follows: landlord required accommodation (18·5 per cent); domestic friction (17 per cent); new to London (15 per cent); rent arrears (13·5 per cent); house sold (12·5 per cent). The term 'temporary accommodation' is used by Greve for the welfare institutions or reception centres in which many homeless families are initially placed. Some of the people from temporary accommodation are then transferred to 'short-stay' accommodation which might be in old institutions which have been adapted or in council acquired properties, usually built before 1914 and of a low housing standard. Greve states, 'People in short-stay housing formed the hard core of the homeless. It was a large, expanding core which indicated that homelessness was growing in size and persistence as a social problem.' Of the families in short-stay accommodation their main reasons for becoming homeless were, in 1961, landlord required accommodation (22·5 per cent), house sold (19 per cent), overcrowding (13 per cent), domestic friction (10·5 per cent) and rent arrears (6 per cent).[29]

The study also found that most homeless families admitted to the temporary accommodation of the London County Council were couples aged between twenty and forty years with two or three children under sixteen. Younger couples were increasingly likely to become homeless compared with middle-aged or elderly couples. The principal family wage earner was in unskilled or semi-skilled manual work earning £10 - £14 a week (average manual earnings in London at this time were £16 a week). Amongst homeless families, a much higher figure than average fail to conform to the norms of society. Thus high proportions were separated women, unmarried mothers, or women living with men to whom they were not married. Homeless families immediately before becoming homeless lived in privately rented accommodation in 85 per cent of the cases, 10 per cent had been owner-occupiers and some 5 per cent were in council housing.

The 1967 Ministry of Health annual report indicates that the largest group applying for temporary accommodation in Greater London consisted of those evicted by court order after a landlord had taken legal action. This was often done because of rent arrears. Very little is known about the current problems of homelessness in Greater London, and because of the growing number of official homeless families the Minister of Health and Social Security has recently commissioned a study of the problem in

London, which it is hoped to follow up by studies in other areas.*

In most local authorities the problem of homeless families is dealt with by welfare departments. In Birmingham this responsibility was transferred to the housing department in 1957 and this situation is in accordance with the Seebohm Committee's recommendations. 'The full range of housing responsibilities should be placed upon housing departments. To relieve them of responsibility for dependant or unreliable tenants would discourage them from looking at the housing needs of their area as a whole and create or reinforce degrading stigmas and social distinctions. We recommend that housing departments should, as a few already do, assume responsibility for providing accommodation for homeless families. Since their basic need is for housing we see considerable advantage in this.'[30]

A report of the Housing Management Committee to Birmingham City Council contains a brief section dealing with homeless families.[31] The number of applicants seeking assistance on grounds of homelessness rose from 1,279 cases in 1960 to 1,496 cases in 1966. In 1965 there was a significant decline to 988 cases, felt to be due to the passing of the 1965 Rent Act with its anti-eviction clauses. However, by 1966 the figure had risen once again to a high level. Of the 1,496 cases in 1966 the Housing Management Committee felt that 50·6 per cent of the cases did not warrant help, or the applicants refused the accommodation offered to them. A further 22 per cent were allocated council houses, usually sub-standard ones, which were shared with another family, 15·7 per cent were placed in hostels and later rehoused in halfway or sub-standard accommodation, 9·6 per cent were placed in hostels and later found their own accommodation and 1·9 per cent were still in hostels or in a miscellaneous category. The houses were usually those in clearance areas which were due for demolition in several years time.

The report also contains a table of statistical information about the families housed in hostels in 1966. It is a miscellany of data which is given in Table 14.

The report then goes on to point to one of the principal dilemmas facing a local authority with a substantial waiting list for council housing. 'While homelessness is a great problem, the committee still has duties to families who have lived in sub-standard accommodation for many years, and those living in rooms or with parents who have been on the waiting list many years. It is emphasised that where homeless families are given shelter, they can only be given a municipal tenancy in their turn on the waiting list. Homelessness cannot be allowed as a short cut to a council house'.[31]

It has been shown that homeless families often progress from one type

---

* The study is being undertaken by members of the Centre for Urban and Regional Studies of the University of Birmingham under the direction of Professor J. Greve of the University of Southampton.

TABLE 14*

City of Birmingham, families accommodated in hostels for the homeless in 1966

1. 35 per cent of the families had been in receipt of National Assistance money for some time.
2. 28 per cent of families consisted of parents who were previously cohabiting or where the marriage had broken down.
3. 20 per cent of mothers admitted were pregnant.
4. 36 per cent were locally born families.
5. 39 per cent were Irish born families.
6. 19 per cent were immigrant families other than Irish.
7. 30 per cent of families were evicted from multi-occupied houses.
8. 19 per cent were evicted by relations.
9. 24 per cent had either or both parents aged under twenty-one years.
10. 47 per cent had been paying £2 10s. or more weekly rent prior to eviction, usually from furnished accommodation.
11. 32 per cent had been evicted for non-payment of rent or mortgage repayments.
12. Pressure by the Public Health authorities was responsible for 4 per cent of the families.
13. 15 per cent were unmarried mothers.

* City of Birmingham, City Council Summons, February 1967, Housing Management Committee Report.

of homeless family accommodation to another. The first stage is often, though not always, placement in a hostel or communal temporary accommodation unit. This is followed where necessary by a move to short-stay accommodation which is usually in the form of a local authority owned dwelling of considerable age and lacking in basic amenities. In some cases this might be followed by a move to a permanent council tenancy in a council built, rather than council acquired, house. During either of the first two stages the family may leave and find its own alternative accommodation. In London this would be particularly difficult because of high rents. Other families may be fortunate and be provided with decent housing supplied by a housing association: in this context 'Shelter' (the national campaign for the homeless) has played an important role in providing finance from charitable collections. The Ministry of Health and Social Security via its Supplementary Benefits Commission may assist in providing money towards the cost of the rent where alternative accommodation is offered. This very fact, particularly in London, may well be a cause in the general increases of low level rents, as landlords might feel that even if the tenant cannot quite afford the rent, the state will assist with the cost. The state provides subsidies for housing associations and for local authorities' own housing besides which rent rebates and differential rent policies are often operated by local authorities while housing allowances are also payable by the Supplementary Benefits Commission.

The National Assistance Board in 1966 published a study of homeless single persons following a survey carried out between October 1965 and March 1966.[32] This comprehensive fact-finding survey is concerned with data in four fields, namely: persons sleeping rough; persons using reception centres administered by a few local authorities though most are financed by central government; persons using lodging-houses, hostels and shelters, provided by local authorities, voluntary bodies and for commercial gain; and persons seeking financial help from the Board's local offices when they were without accommodation.

A census of single homeless people was held on the night of 6th December 1966 which indicated that about one thousand persons (nearly all men) were sleeping rough. There may of course have been many who were not discovered and thus not enumerated. The figure, therefore, represents an underestimate but how much of an underestimate it is impossible to say. The census was also in winter and it might be expected that more people would sleep rough in summer. A further 1,262 persons were enumerated in reception centre accommodation, by far the largest of which is one at Camberwell in London. Persons applying to the National Assistance Board offices who were homeless at the time numbered 1,350. Adding to these figures the number of people in lodging-houses and hostels who stated they sometimes slept rough or in reception centres, it was found that a total of about 13,500 persons, almost all of whom were men, either sometimes slept rough or used reception centres.

In answer to questions about why they slept rough, the most frequent reason given was one of preference. 29·3 per cent of those who were found sleeping rough and who answered the question gave this as their reason. On the other hand, of the users of reception centres and persons asking assistance at a Board's local office who said they sometimes slept rough, the primary reason given was lack of money in 52·6 per cent and 55 per cent respectively of the interviewed persons. The main statistical findings of the report are summarised in Table 15. All the data in the report relate to England, Wales and Scotland.

Of the hostels and lodging-houses provided by bodies other than local government, the Salvation Army and the Church Army had respectively sixty-two establishments with 7,395 beds for men and 652 for women and twenty-six establishments with 1,831 beds for men and 252 for women. Of the 567 establishments (59·4 per cent of which were run by private owners on a commercial basis) some 84·7 per cent were in county or London boroughs. Most of the managers of the establishments said that they sometimes had to turn people away because their accommodation was full.[32]

Besides the accommodation provided for homeless families which has been outlined above, there are also rehabilitation or recuperative units which take families for a temporary period, and provide accommodation,

TABLE 15*

Homeless single persons census, 6th December 1965

	1	2	3	4
		Percentages		
1. no close relatives or not in touch for over one year	62	53	68	50
2. aged over forty years	—	80	65	47
3. single persons	—	67	71	66
4. of working age but not working	57	40	—	—
5. had worked for less than six months in previous year	—	—	60	46
6. had received national assistance in past	90	—	92	92
7. had received national assistance in previous month	—	50	—	51
8. sometimes slept rough	100	28	70	78
9. sometimes used reception centres	21	23	100	43
10. sometimes used lodging-houses	41	100	73	62
11. felt they needed help or advice	20	22	—	—
12. were thought to be physically or mentally handicapped	—	18	21	16
13. had been in prison	—	28	60	56
14. had been in prison in previous two months	9	—	—	—
15. were heavy drinkers or suspected alcoholics	—	—	28	—

Key to columns:

1. Those sleeping rough who gave information.
2. Persons in lodging-houses.
3. People in reception centres.
4. Homeless persons applying for national assistance.

* National Assistance Board, *Homeless Single Persons*. HMSO, 1966.

support and any training in managing their own affairs which is felt to be necessary. This may include subsequent follow-up work by the personal social services.

Preventive measures might well significantly reduce the incidence of homelessness, especially where local authority and housing association housing stock could be used. Evictions from council housing are problems which local authorities ought to face squarely and develop some form of early warning system, so that families at risk can be identified early on and remedial measures taken as necessary. There will still remain the problem of the bad rent payer, but the local authority must decide upon the line to take in relation to family composition, especially where children are concerned, and family circumstances in the light of any alternative form of action.*

The main problems arise from tenants of privately owned accommodation, but even here an early warning system for evictions (legal or illegal)

* Cost benefit analyses of eviction from council houses and of the problem of homeless families are found in the Institute of Municipal Treasurers and Accountants, *Cost Benefit Analysis* (1969), pp. 115-122 and pp. 71-78.

could be instituted together with a similar system for families at risk from other causes. The relevant local and central government organisations should be contacted, together with voluntary societies where this is felt desirable.

In addition the Seebohm committee felt that the problem of homelessness amongst families in privately rented accommodation could be combated in three ways. 'First, if local authorities knew more about the private sector, negotiation and liaison might forestall some evictions, as they do now in some areas. If an advice service existed on the lines we suggest, it could accumulate a wide variety of useful information in this respect. Second, if local authorities take increased responsibility for housing the most vulnerable families, fewer of them will have to depend on the private sector. These are the families least able to make arrangements and negotiate with private landlords. Third, the courts and rent tribunals should (as some already do) work in close collaboration with the local authority as soon as they know of proceedings which might lead to eviction. More effective advice, assistance, and sometimes, prevention would then be possible.'[30] Similarly better co-ordination of policies relating to homelessness amongst neighbouring local authorities, particularly in the conurbation areas, is required.

In the Greater London area the acute problem of the lack of an adequate low cost housing stock is a major reason for homelessness. In other areas its significance is less important and there the problem revolves more around the concept of the socially inadequate family that finds it difficult to cope, in a variety of ways, with modern society. The problem is further exacerbated in those areas where there is a housing shortage and where local authority housing waiting lists are long, and where it will be several or many years before the council house building programme can meet the demand.

(iii) *The Large Family.* Many of the points about housing deprivation amongst large families have already been made. The higher than average incidence of overcrowding amongst large families has been noted, particularly in the Greater London area. A high proportion of large families are found in the local authority housing stock because points systems for the allocation of council houses usually contain heavy weightings for the number of children in a family, and thus large families have tended to get some priority in rehousing. It is usually the large family in privately rented furnished or unfurnished accommodation, generally uncontrolled, which suffers the highest levels of overcrowding, lack of amenities and often relatively exorbitant rents.

The large family suffers in the privately rented sector from landlords' discrimination against families with children, particularly several children. Again many of the larger families with children at school have household heads whose incomes are average or lower than average and who fall within the unskilled and semi-skilled occupations. It is thus these families which are often in need of additional financial support through social security payments, and through differential rent schemes where these are operated by local authorities. The financial problems of large families are particularly acute where the father has died, has suffered long-term unemployment, or has left the marital home.

The Ministry of Social Security found that, 'Of the families where the father was a householder in full-time work, 28 per cent spent less than £2 a week on housing, about 44 per cent spent between £2 and £4 and 28 per cent spent £4 or more. The smaller the family the higher the proportion spending £4 a week or more; in contrast, the larger the family, the higher the proportion spending less than that amount.'[25]

Housing costs are rising quite markedly and where the earning power of the household head of a large family fails to keep pace with such rises, particularly with local authority rents, then housing costs begin to cut back even more the sum available for other necessities. The housing survey of 1964 indicated that from 1961 outside Greater London unfurnished, uncontrolled rents had risen some 28 per cent while the rents of local authority accommodation had risen about 32 per cent. Rents have continued to rise, at a higher rate in Greater London than outside it. The large family suffers particularly from increases in housing costs, especially when the family has an average or below average income. A study of nutrition in Britain has shown one of the side effects of this problem. During the 1950s, though there had been wage improvements at all income group levels, a noticeable deterioration in the family diet, where there were three or more children, had occurred even amongst those families above the poverty line. Rising housing expenditure was to some extent responsible. On the other hand, old age pensioners, whose housing costs are more restricted in growth by rent control and whose rents are more often paid with the aid of social security payments, had an improved diet over the same period.[33]

Overcrowding amongst coloured immigrants was found to be particularly high in London, and these are often large families with young children. 'Especially amongst West Indians, children originally left behind in their home countries are brought here as soon as a home is established and opportunity offers.'[2] Often these large families find themselves in over-crowded conditions, and they are not the large families who are likely to be rehoused quickly in council properties, often because of lack of residential qualifications or because some housing waiting lists become closed because of pressure.

The problems facing large families of finding adequate housing in a period when two and three bedroomed dwellings, particularly the latter, are being built, and very few four bedroomed houses, is often acute. There has, of course, been a steady decline in average household sizes. In England

and Wales in 1911 it was 4·36 persons, in 1951, 3·19 persons and by 1961, almost 3 persons. This is particularly significant because about half the housing stock was built before 1914 when families were larger than today. Furthermore, while in 1911 16·3 per cent of households contained seven or more persons, in 1961 just over 3 per cent of households were of this size. At the same time there was a trebling of the number of one and two person households. Twentieth century house building, particularly that of local authorities, has thus concentrated on providing more three bedroomed and smaller units of accommodation. This had led to the present situation where the accommodation of large families is largely a responsibility of local authorities, whereas nearly all the large dwellings are in private ownership. Thus in 1958 when over 40 per cent of households of six or more persons were council tenants, only 1 per cent of dwellings with seven or more rooms were owned by local authorities.[34]

(iv) *The Poor.*   The chapter by Professor Lafitte is concerned with income deprivation and discusses the question of the poor in detail. Here it is necessary to make only a few points in relation to housing deprivation. To a large extent the problem of low income levels is a recurrent theme in all the categories of housing deprivation which are discussed in this paper. Hence to discuss housing deprivation because of low incomes at length here would simply be to reiterate what has been said or remains to be said.

Problems of overcrowding are often related to low income levels. Rent arrears and failure to find adequate alternative accommodation at a rent that can be afforded are two of the root causes of homelessness. The problems of the poor in the London housing market lead to much overcrowding and homelessness. The large family often has a low income and can find it difficult to manage. Essentially it is not simply the head of household's income which is the crucial factor but rather income per head. The elderly too are generally poor, because they subsist on state pensions in the main. But the elderly are particularly assisted in several ways, often part or all of their housing cost is met by social security payments, many of them live in controlled tenancies where the rents are kept low and where increases in rent are only permitted for specific improvements, and then the increases are of limited amounts. Coloured immigrants are usually found amongst the lower paid workers and have other housing problems besides that posed by relatively low incomes.

Where poor families live in controlled accommodation their rents are low, but much of this stock of accommodation is lacking in amenities and generally of poor quality. Much is also being demolished under slum clearance programmes and council houses at high rents are offered to those people who lack the ability to pay such rents without some assistance. In other cases the council houses offered to them at lower rents may be pre-1914 acquired properties whose condition is not much better than that of their demolished dwelling. Because of the problems of balancing the housing revenue account each year, many local authorities are unwilling to subsidise heavily these poor tenants by providing them with newly-built housing at a rent which they cannot afford. To a large extent the deprived housing situation of the poor results from the fact that it is the dwelling which is subsidised, whereas a strong case can be made for subsidising the people. Dwellings could then be more realistically allocated according to need, rather than according to the annual state of local authority housing revenue accounts, and to a whole variety of points allocation systems which remain often inflexible and rarely provide a truly objective measure of housing need.

Unfortunately it is usually the case that in housing pressure areas the zones of accommodation let privately at relatively low rents also happen to be in the worst districts. Hence the large, poor family in such an area has inadequate schools, play areas and car parking facilities, run-down shops and so on. Thus not only do the poor suffer from a lack of reasonable housing conditions, but also frequently from the lack of an environment of reasonable standard.

Ministry of Social Security payments including housing allowances and unemployment pay are available, but the former are probably insufficiently utilised by those who could claim them. Furthermore for tenants in local authority housing there is the alternative source of housing cost subsidy through the local authorities' rent rebate and other differential rent schemes. Because there are these two sources for housing allowances, conflict can arise where the local authority feels that the Supplementary Benefits Commission of the Ministry of Health and Social Security ought to help a family with its housing costs rather than itself. If the Ministry of Social Security pays an allowance, it is tantamount to a saving on the housing revenue account where the local authority would otherwise have had to grant a rebate of one kind or another.

The whole question of housing finance is in urgent need of review but until that time the poor will continue to suffer considerably from housing deprivation, despite the supplementary payments and rent rebates, etc., which may be payable to them. The relative housing deprivation of the poor is further emphasised by the decline in privately rented accommodation units. Rent control has kept many rents in check at low levels, and rent regulation also contains rent levels but to a much more limited extent. However, the regulation and control of certain rents does nothing to offset the decline of privately rented accommodation, which becomes more difficult to obtain, particularly in housing pressure areas.

(v) *The Disabled and Handicapped.* One of the essential needs of disabled and handicapped people is to be provided with a dwelling designed around the particular disablement or handicap. At the end of 1967 there were

362,000 persons registered with local authorities as physically handicapped. The total was made up as follows: 103,000 blind; 34,000 partially sighted; 25,000 deaf; 16,000 hard of hearing and 184,000 suffering from other physical handicaps. About two-thirds of the blind and partially sighted were aged over sixty-five years, as were 55 per cent of the registered hard of hearing. Many handicapped people are ill-housed and may have difficulties with finance, particularly those disabled who are not able to work. The Seebohm committee felt it was difficult to justify the distinctions drawn by the Ministry of Social Security, which could mean that a family with a member disabled by chronic illness might be worse off than a similar family where the disablement was a result of war or industrial injury.[30] In terms of housing deprivation the Seebohm committee stated, 'There is generally no lack of sympathy for the special needs of the handicapped for bungalows or ground floor flats close to shops and social facilities and for adaptations, and special aids. Nevertheless, many of them have to live in unsatisfactory conditions, or wait for months or years before a suitable appliance is provided, or adaptations made, or a suitable house provided.'[30]

The committee also felt that much more could be done for disabled and handicapped people in providing them with sheltered housing as is done for the elderly.

The basic problem still remains as one of the adequate design of dwellings for the disabled, one of the most important functions of which must be the elimination of potentially dangerous hazards. In 1961 a conference was held on the topic of architectural design for the disabled, and in 1967 the Royal Institute of British Architects published the second edition of *Designing for the Disabled*, by P. S. Goldsmith. Other studies being carried out on disabled or handicapped persons with reference to housing matters include work by P. G. Gregory of the Department of Social Administration in the University of Hull on planning for the disabled. Goldsmith of the City Architect's Department at Norwich continues with his studies and G. R. Adams of the Department of Town and Regional Planning at Sheffield University is studying the design of buildings for the blind. Finally the Centre for Applied Social Research of the Tavistock Institute of Human Relations is considering the problems of organisation in homes for the physically handicapped and the extent to which they meet their needs.*

(vi) *The Coloured Immigrant.* The 1966 sample census birthplace data indicated there were about 900,000 coloured people living in England and Wales. It showed that about 270,000 people were born in the Caribbean,

* Work commenced or completed during 1964-1967 is recorded in *Planning Research*, third edition, published by the Town Planning Institute (1968).

about 230,000 in India (including white immigrants), about 73,000 in Pakistan, about 89,000 in Africa (including white immigrants) and about 60,000 in Cyprus. About one-third of the coloured population was under fifteen years of age, and a high proportion were under five years. The adults are predominantly of child-bearing age. The census also showed about 840,000 foreign-born immigrants in England and Wales and a further 700,000 born in Eire. Most of the coloured immigrants live in the conurbation areas, particularly in Greater London. The London boroughs with the highest proportions of immigrants born in the Caribbean, India and Pakistan were Brent, Hackney, Lambeth, Haringey, Hammersmith and Islington, where they amounted to about 5.5 to 7.5 per cent of the population. Those areas outside Greater London with high proportions of these immigrants (about 4 to 5 per cent) were in order of magnitude, Wolverhampton, Slough, Bedford, Leamington Spa, Birmingham, Bradford, Derby and Huddersfield.

In terms of the net balance of migration in Britain there have been three distinct periods since 1945. From 1945 to 1958 more people left Britain every year than came into it. From 1959 to 1963 more people entered Britain each year than left it, the peak year being 1961 when the net population gain by migration was 170,000. Since 1964 more people have annually left Britain than have gained entry. To some extent this situation is attributable to the Commonwealth Immigrants Act of 1962 which reduced the flow of immigrants.

Coloured immigrants are undoubtedly amongst the losers in the competition for adequate housing: 'the chief losers in the battle for a fair share of housing are working-class families with young children in big cities, especially if they are newcomers supplying essential labour. Among them are the overseas immigrants, whose plight is unique only in its particular combination of circumstances. Many of those circumstances are shared with, for example: young families; large families; low-paid workers, mobile workers, shift workers; unmarried mothers; and almost any non-English-looking, non-English-speaking, non-conforming people. Any of these features is equivalent to a minus mark in the competition for housing space. Racial discrimination is perhaps the biggest single minus; but even this can generally be overcome unless combined—as it nearly always is—with at least one, if not several, of the other factors listed'.[35]

The report on housing in Greater London devotes a chapter to coloured landlords and coloured tenants. In concluding this chapter the report states: 'The evidence we have received leads us to five broad conclusions.

(1) The basic nature of the difficulties of coloured immigrants is the same in quality as that of all newcomers to London without adequate means, arriving at a time when many local authority housing lists are very overcrowded or even closed, and in conditions where they obtain a

very low priority for allocation of housing.

(2) For coloured immigrants these difficulties are accentuated by a marked degree of reluctance to make rented accommodation available to them.

(3) Their inexperience and their acute need leads them to ill-advised purchases of unsuitable property at high prices, and to involving themselves in expensive mortgages; in these matters they do not receive sufficient reliable professional help and advice, and in a number of respects they are often shamelessly exploited.

(4) The direct results of the combination of all these factors are overcrowding, the unsatisfactory use of large houses for ill-arranged multi-occupation, and high rent levels.

(5) Although coloured immigrants are in great demand in London for manning many of its services, they are one of the groups who have the greatest difficulty in securing satisfactory housing accommodation.'[2]

Several of the other points made by the committee are relevant. It was estimated in 1964 that of the total of immigrants in the United Kingdom from Asian, African and Caribbean Commonwealth countries, some 47 per cent were in Greater London. The total of these immigrants in this country was estimated at about one-third of all immigrants. Rents asked of immigrants appeared to vary. It was felt that in many cases there was a 'newcomers tax'; and on top of that a 'foreigners levy' which was especially high in the case of coloured people. The committee found that there was no exceptionally high incidence of abuses by coloured landlords. The problem of overcrowding has already been noted, and is in part due to large families, low incomes, and the general unavailability of privately rented accommodation. Few coloured people ever declare themselves homeless, and they may well become overcrowded rather than do so. It was found that the difficulties arising from the unsatisfactory housing of coloured immigrants produced much friction between themselves and their neighbours and fellow tenants. The committee also remarked upon the observable feature of the concentration of coloured people in certain areas.[2]

The housing panel of the National Committee for Commonwealth Immigrants published a pamphlet in 1967 entitled *The Housing of Commonwealth Immigrants*. This document repeats much of what the Milner Holland committee had to say about Greater London. It then goes on to discuss the housing problems of coloured immigrants and suggests that local authority residential requirements should be subject to careful scrutiny as they operate against newly arrived persons, including coloured immigrants. It was also suggested that local authorities ought to rehouse all people resident in a slum clearance or redevelopment scheme. Many authorities avoid rehousing particular groups including owner-occupiers, sub-tenants, furnished tenants and single persons. Coloured immigrants, as well as others, often are not rehoused because of such policies. It is suggested that industrial selection schemes can assist with finding suitable accommodation by providing housing and employment in new and expanding towns for all types of immigrant workers. The pamphlet also urges that speedy action be taken to remedy problems of multi-occupation, dilapidated housing and overcrowding. Basically any measures to improve the housing conditions of those most deprived of adequate accommodation will include coloured immigrants along with many other groups of people, most of which have been discussed in this chapter.

A further pamphlet published by the National Committee for Commonwealth Immigrants, entitled *Areas of Special Housing Need*, was also published in 1967. This suggested that the social and economic difficulties facing local authorities with large numbers of immigrant families ought to be recognised as a national responsibility, and proposed that such areas be designated as areas of special housing need. The whole question of priority areas into which the government will inject extra financial resources is dependent upon various criteria, of which such a consideration as suggested by the NCCI is undoubtedly one factor. To date, however, little work has been done upon them.

The Seebohm committee in its discussion of social services for children points out the disadvantaged position of the children of coloured immigrants.[30] This is a particularly significant problem, for about one-third of all coloured Commonwealth residents in Britain are under fifteen years of age. These children may be surrounded by a variety of problems associated with low incomes, bad housing and pressure upon mothers to go out to work, which is strong in many low income families.

A report on racial discrimination undertaken by Political and Economic Planning, and published in 1967, contains a section on housing discrimination. The general conclusion was, 'The enquiry has shown that there is, without any doubt, substantial discrimination in Britain against coloured immigrants in employment, in housing and in relation to the provision of certain services such as motor insurance.'[36]

As to housing it was noted that many coloured immigrants did not expose themselves to possible discrimination by trying to find rented accommodation on the open market. Claims of discrimination were lowest amongst Cypriots and highest amongst West Indians. Asian immigrants would only usually seek accommodation where they knew they would be accepted; 'over two-thirds of them had never applied for rented accommodation to a white landlord who was a stranger.'[36] Of sixty properties advertised to rent which were called on by English, Hungarian and coloured testers, forty-five showed discrimination against the coloured tester, forty of which were cases of refusal and five cases of higher rent being asked. In the case of accommodation bureaux or estate agents with accommodation to let, tests showed discrimination in fourteen out of the eighteen accommodation bureaux and twenty out of the thirty estate agents. In terms of house purchase another forty-two estate agents were tested, twenty-seven of whom discriminated. There were two types of discrimination : first, the coloured immigrant was offered fewer addresses or none at all; and second, there were marked differences in what he was told about the possibility of obtaining a mortgage.

Council housing could not be tested in the same way and interviews with local authority officials were held. The conclusions were that very few coloured immigrants were housed in council property; that the present council house allocation systems usually put immigrants at a disadvantage, and that there is evidence that where coloured immigrants have been housed in council housing it has been mainly in the worst accommodation.

The survey also mentioned the fact that much of the privately rented accommodation occupied by coloured immigrants would become due for clearance and redevelopment in years ahead, when presumably the tenant would fulfil the residential requirement. About a tenth of the West Indians questioned in the survey had placed their names on housing waiting lists. It was felt that the demand for council housing by coloured immigrants will be increased because of the lack of private accommodation open to them.

E. Burney's study also points to racial discrimination in local authority housing policies, as well as indicating the same problems as have been shown above of coloured families trying to rent privately or buy accommodation.[35] J. Rex and R. Moore examined similar issues, this time in the Sparkbrook area of Birmingham.[37] The passing of the 1968 Race Relations Bill will at least reduce the more blatant aspects of racial discrimination. But the problem still remains basically one of human relations.

(vii) *Travellers and Caravan Dwellers.* There are two parts to this section : the first deals with gypsies and other travellers who move about the country with their mobile homes; the second concerns families who live on permanent residential caravan sites. Until a study was carried out in 1965 and 1966 by the Sociological Research Section of the Ministry of Housing and Local Government, no data on the subject of gypsies and other travellers (including tinkers) were available on a national scale for England and Wales.[38] A survey of gypsies in Scotland was begun early in 1969 by the Scottish Development Department.

The survey found the traveller population of England and Wales to be at least 15,000 persons in 3,400 households. Some 43 per cent of the households were found in the south-east of the country. The population was fairly young with larger numbers of children than in the national pattern. Of the traveller households in 1965, 11·3 per cent had five or more children under sixteen years of age, the national proportion in 1961 being 1·2 per cent. This high proportion will probably mean considerable future increases in the numbers of these people.

About 75 per cent of the travellers had always been nomadic and never lived in a house. Very few lived in horse-drawn wagons, the great majority having trailer caravans. Three families out of five said they had been on the road in 1964. This was mainly for economic reasons, but many had been removed from a site by officials. The searching for sites on which to stay is a primary problem for the traveller. Only 20 per cent of families were on licensed or local authority sites, the rest were scattered over various types of makeshift sites, and more than half the families were on sites with no amenities at all. Only one family in three had mains water available. It appears that those with the best living conditions, other than families on specially provided sites, were those on farmland employed as seasonal labourers.

Half the males recorded their occupation as dealers, mainly in scrap metal. It appeared likely that average incomes were below that of a settled manual worker. Most of the people did not wish to move to more settled occupations, and in many instances this would not be possible because of their illiteracy. However, several families have settled down in houses or on permanent caravan sites. There remains a mutual attitude of mistrust between the settled population and the travellers, and this leads to the former not really wishing to improve the travellers' conditions in terms of better sites, more sites, or the education of their children.

In March 1967, there were fourteen sites catering for travelling families over which local authorities had responsibility. On these sites many domestic facilities were available, such as running water, electricity, drainage and sanitary conveniences, as well as schools and health and welfare services. In 1965 at the time of the travellers' census only 143 families were thus catered for. Besides the provision of adequate sites for those who wish to settle, there is a need for transit sites for those on the move. Some families who wish it are housed by local councils. At Bromley and in Hampshire housing in intermediate accommodation is the first step to a proper council tenancy. The answer to the housing problem of these travellers would appear to be a variety of provision; short-stay sites for the travellers who do not wish to settle, permanent sites for those who prefer site life but no longer travel, and housing for those who so desire.

In 1959 the Government Social Survey carried out a statistical survey of permanent residential caravan life.[39] In 1965 the Consumer Council commissioned a study, based on a sample survey of caravan dwellers, designed to discover details about tenure, rents, other recurring charges, conditions on the sites, facilities available, and the attitudes of caravanners towards the caravan.[40]

As with travelling families, most of these caravan dwellers were young, but the families were not as large as in the case of the travellers. The survey indicated that much of the increasing demand to live in caravans is a result of the scarcity of cheap housing to rent privately, particularly so

in and near the Greater London area. The problem ought therefore to be
put in the context of the housing shortage if it is to be fully understood.
Between 1951 and 1961 the number of persons living in caravans increased
from 95,000 to 184,000 and the estimate for 1965 was 300,000 persons.
The survey showed that caravans provided a useful temporary home for
many young couples who were unable to find adequate housing within
their means; most of them, however, would have moved to a house if they
had the chance.

The caravan is thus seen by some as an alternative to becoming homeless. Undoubtedly many families in caravans are overcrowded and one
could justifiably argue that they were homeless, despite the fact that no
official homelessness statistics would indicate this to be the case.

It was found that many of the residential caravan sites, whether owned
by local authorities or privately, lacked adequate facilities. Nearly a quarter
of respondents to the survey's questionnaire complained of having bad
roads or no proper roads on their site. Only 28 per cent had no piped water
in their caravans (compared with 80 per cent in 1959), 61 per cent had their
own toilets, mainly flush toilets. However, there were still cases of
inadequate communal toilet facilities in 1965. The caravanner also suffered
from insecurity of tenure with the threat of eviction rapidly becoming a
reality.

Caravan rents in conjunction with other housing costs have risen quite
rapidly. Between 1959 and 1965 the average site rent paid had doubled to
a sum of £1 10s. a week. Rents on council sites were significantly lower
than those on private sites, though often the standard of the latter was
much higher. Only 4 per cent of caravan dwellers in the sample were
renting their caravans, the rest either owned outright or were in the process of purchasing them. A usual price to pay was between £500-£750.
Eighty per cent of the people had lived on only one caravan site and a
similar proportion had lived on their present site for not more than five
years.

The survey concluded that since the Caravan Sites and Control of
Development Act of 1960, site conditions had greatly improved, but sites
still exist with poor roads, no laundries and unsatisfactory communal
toilets. The Consumer Council urged local authorities to be more vigorous
in carrying out their duties of inspection of residential caravan sites. People
with caravan interests urge local authorities 'to abandon their present
restrictive policy and to license many more sites in areas where they are
needed, as well as giving more long-term planning consents'. This view is
strongly opposed by most local authorities. Apart from their own prejudice
against caravans as sub-standard housing, local councils are under strong
pressure from their ratepayers to preserve local amenities and property
values. Caravans are considered by many local residents to be a threat to
these.[40] This resistance also applies, of course, to provision of more sites for

the gypsies and other travellers. Finally the Consumer Council was alarmed by the fact that local authorities do not appear to intend to license many more new sites. In view of this situation the Council feels that the government have a duty to deal with the effects of artificial shortage thus created. The Consumer Council's recommendations were that there ought to be statutory security of tenure, rent control and the abolition of site premiums. So far, however, nothing along these lines has developed.

CONCLUSION

The problems of housing deprivation are being increasingly recognised in Britain, and are being gradually combated, in some cases with much more success than in others. Much of the difficulty lies in the establishment of the facts of housing deprivation, and many of these have only recently been uncovered, for example via the national house condition survey of 1967, by the Committee on Housing in Greater London, by the study of gypsies and other travellers in 1965-1966. Studies such as these are continuing, for example, the study of homelessness in Greater London, the committee concerned with council housing allocation systems, that considering the future role of housing associations and so on. There has been in the 1960s, and particularly since the mid-1960s, a growing concern with housing policy and with relative housing deprivation, or the underprivileged groups as they are sometimes called. D. V. Donnison concludes his book, *The Government of Housing*, with words which demonstrate the general acceptance of concern for those who are deprived of reasonable housing conditions. He states: 'Homeless families, overcrowding and the more squalid housing conditions have become as intolerable as untreated illness, hunger and lasting unemployment.'[1]

There can be no doubt that a basic common denominator found throughout all the various cases of families suffering from housing deprivation is that of the low income family, despite the massive twentieth century local authority house building programmes. Indeed it has been shown that an inadequate proportion of local authority housing is provided for those in greatest need, and some of the reasons for this have been cited in the preceding sections. This fact, together with the outline of the housing financial situation and how this is affected by different tenure patterns, is sufficient to warrant a complete review of housing expenditure to enable our financial resources to be spent upon those who are in greatest housing need, rather than upon those who qualify for assistance in one form or another, often irrespective of any objective measure of real need. Families rather than dwellings ought to be subsidised.

Housing deprivation correlates with other forms of deprivation, either directly or indirectly. Much of the evidence available on these correlations is associated with educational standards. J. W. B. Douglas summarises relationships between the home and educational achievement as follows: 'For any given level of measured ability, children living on council estates have better chances of going to grammar school than those who live in privately rented dwellings. This appears to be explained by the better provision of grammar school places in these new areas rather than by any special qualities of the children, or the sharpened aspirations of their parents. When housing conditions are unsatisfactory, children make relatively low scores in the tests. This is so in each social class but whereas the middle class children, as they get older, reduce this handicap, the manual working class children from unsatisfactory homes fall even further behind; for them, overcrowding and other deficiencies at home have a progressive and depressive influence on their test performance.'[41]

·The Plowden committee report indicates some of the physical conditions of the home which have an adverse influence upon children's development: overcrowding, lack of play space and of variety of stimulation, insecure tenancies and lack of, or sharing of, basic amenities. The children of manual working class fathers were worst off in having no play area attached to the dwelling.

Other findings of the committee were that family size correlated with the results of intelligence tests. The larger the family, the lower the scores of the children. Family size likewise correlates with nutrition, physical growth, and overcrowding. Overcrowding and sharing of houses are also linked with poor educational achievements. Similarly, the family lacking a parent often suffers from these two defects.[42]

Besides correlation with educational achievement, housing deprivation is associated with health. Thus stress and nervous conditions can be caused by poor housing conditions, while dwellings which are damp, inadequately heated, and lacking sufficient ventilation can give rise to various diseases or exacerbate such illnesses where they exist in embryo form within a particular person. Health can thus deteriorate. Bad housing can also be a hazard because of potential accidents, inadequate means of escape in case of fire, or steep and poorly lighted stairways.

The more significant correlations between income and housing deprivation have already been expressed. Other correlations link delinquency and crime with poor housing conditions. It is also usual to find that an area of poor housing conditions is one of low environmental quality, lacking open space, often containing old noxious industrial premises, with narrow roads and heavy flows of through traffic, inadequate car parking spaces, and so on. Housing deprivation cannot be regarded in isolation; it is caused by and causes other forms of deprivation. It is logical, therefore, to propose that in the future housing policies should not be considered in isolation from other social policies, as has tended to happen in the past.

3. The Socialisation of Children

Harriett Wilson

The present report is concerned with the socialisation of deprived children. The first section deals with the material aspects of deprivation, the second section with the cultural aspects. The third section deals with the available evidence of the malfunctioning of children who are socially deprived. It is divided into (i) educational under-achievement and early school leaving, and (ii) behavioural malfunction in the context of the demands made by an achievement-oriented society. The report concludes with a brief summary.

MATERIAL ASPECTS OF DEPRIVATION

Social deprivation and its effect on children is largely a problem of families on marginal or inadequate incomes. It is a relative concept which must be geared to the standards of living of the community in general, but neither the gross national product nor the average level of incomes of a community can be taken as an indicator of adequacy or inadequacy of provision for the community's children. The level of incomes determines roughly the point at which a community considers the subsistence line to lie at any one time in history. This chapter is not concerned with a definition of such a subsistence line; but as the discussion cannot avoid phenomena of social deprivation which are entirely due to economic circumstances, it will be based on the assumption that the subsistence line is the prevailing level of payments made by the Supplementary Benefit Commission of the Ministry of Social Security. This level cannot be considered unduly generous, but it is widely taken as adequate to meet essential requirements for a limited period. It has officially been referred to as a 'subsistence income'. The scale, as currently in operation, will here be used as a measuring rod or cut-off point in discussion involving inadequacy of income.

The gradually growing literature on poverty in Britain does not examine in detail the effect such a condition has on children. Although some statistical information is now available on the incidence of poverty among families with dependent children, this has been presented as a mere statement of availability of resources in relation to requirements, using the supplementary benefit scale rates as a poverty line. A Ministry of Social Security enquiry of 1967 made a rough estimate of all families with one or more dependent children, of which there were about seven million in all in the summer of 1966.[1] It was stated that of these it seemed probable that approaching half a million families, containing up to one and a quarter million children, had incomes from earnings, insurance benefits, family allowances, or other sources, amounting to less than would be paid to a family which qualified for national assistance (now called supplementary) benefits. Of these, 140,000 could not receive any form of assistance as the fathers were in full-time work, and another 20,000 could not receive assistance in full, although out of work, as this would have brought their income up to a level above that which they were receiving while in work. This rule is known as the wage stop. About 145,000 families were father-less, and 160,000 had sick or unemployed fathers. In families where the father was in full-time work, 3 per cent of those with two or three children, and 7 per cent of those with four or more children, were living at or below the basic assistance level. Only 3 per cent of the total were families who had lived in Britain for less than ten years.

Since the date of this enquiry a number of changes have taken place. In line with previous policy the supplementary benefit scale has been raised to keep in line with rising prices and a general rise of real wages. Family allowances, which are payable to second and subsequent children, have been increased from 8s. and 10s. to 18s. and 20s. per week. This increase was officially admitted to be only sufficient to halve the number of children who grow up in poverty. The increases were also partly offset by increases in the price of school meals and welfare milk. Free milk in all secondary schools was abolished. Contributions to national insurance were increased, and prescription charges were introduced. All these measures impose additional burdens on low-income families. Prescription charges, school meals and welfare milk can be obtained free of charge on a means-tested investigation, but it is known that many families entitled to such assistance do not claim it. In addition, low income families have been hit especially hard by price increases since devaluation, which are estimated to have been 5½ per cent in the year following devaluation. It is not possible to calculate the net effect of all these factors on the size of the population who are now at or beneath the poverty line, but a broad estimate made by the Child Poverty Action Group gives the figures of 400,000 to 500,000 children in poverty at the beginning of 1969.

A glance at typical incomes for various types of families who are at or beneath the subsistence line shows that budgeting is a serious problem which only resourceful and very self-disciplined people would be able to solve. To be exposed to such strain for an extended period is likely to result in the accumulation of debt, as there is no margin for the replacement of major items like household furnishings. The Supplementary Benefits Commission admits that this is so by its willingness to make discretionary allowances from time to time on application to meet these needs. In 1967 over £2 million were spent on such payments. Doubtlessly this sum would have been greater if all those in need of such payment had claimed for it.

A Ministry of Social Security publication concerns itself with actual living conditions of families whose main wage earner is out of work and not in receipt of full supplementary benefit owing to the wage stop regulation.[2] The purpose of the wage stop deduction is to reduce the full supplementary benefit to the level of net earnings while the father was in work. The wage stop results in family income being less than total requirements, taking the scale rate as the subsistence line. It is to be remembered, however, that it is not an initiating cause of family poverty, but merely a reflection that many families live in poverty while the main wage earner is in full-time work. In the course of the enquiry a small sample of families was visited to obtain first-hand information about what living on the wage stop meant. The following is a summary of what was observed:

In most of the families there were three or more children. Most of the fathers had been out of work for a year or more, and the majority had done unskilled work, mostly labouring, in the past. The amounts by which the families fell short of the full supplementary benefits ranged from about 10s. to over £6 per week, with a deduction of £2 10s. or so for the majority of cases in the sample. Only a third of the men said they were in good health, and it was evident that in a number of cases earning capacity was impaired by ill-health. It was found that in some cases the mother was a good manager and the father kept his personal expenditure to the minimum, so that the family could manage without actually getting into debt. Half the families, however, had rent arrears, about two in every five had other debts, and there were some families who lived in real squalor, budgeting on a 'hand to mouth basis and living in a state of constant financial anxiety and crisis'. Diets varied a great deal. Several families said they had difficulty in finding money for food on the last two days before the payment of benefit. Fresh meat was bought only at weekends in many cases, and bread and potatoes were eaten in large quantities. Lack of variety was often commented on, and items like fruit, biscuits and cake were frequently mentioned as unaffordable. The standard of clothing was generally poor, and it was especially difficult to keep the children in shoes. Bedclothes were non-existent in some families, in others very poor. A quarter of the families said that in the winter they commonly ran short of fuel. One of the results of living in poverty which parents felt strongly about was the inability to provide pocket-money for the children, or money for school outings, the cinema, swimming, or watching football matches. Most of them were unable to take their families on holidays: some families said they had never had a holiday and never expected to have one. Television was often

the only source of entertainment. The description ends with these words:
'The general impression . . . was not so much one of grinding poverty in
any absolute sense as one of unrelieved dreariness with, in some cases, little
hope of improvement in the future'. Although the number of families
involved in the sample was small, fifty-two in all, they were representative
of five different areas of England and Scotland. The description of living
conditions has been given in some detail so as to provide a picture of the
style of living of families who have to budget on incomes which are at or
beneath subsistence level. No investigations were made concerning the
effects such economic circumstances have on child development, but it is
obvious that in a household which cannot afford essentials there is no
money to spare for such articles as paper, crayons, picture-books or toys.

In addition to the two above-mentioned government investigations a
number of studies have appeared in the last decade or so which concern
themselves with various aspects of poverty. None deal specifically with the
effect that poverty has on children in terms of impairment of normal
function, nor has any of them successfully tackled the complex problem
of isolating economic factors from cultural factors, as for instance an
ascertainment of the availability of books and toys, parental interest and
understanding of the problems of child development, or cultural stimuli
derived from members of the wider family. Therefore only a short mention
of these investigations will be made here to indicate particularly vulnerable
groups of families in whom social deprivation of children due to extreme
shortage of material resources is likely to occur.

With the exception of the above-mentioned study by the Ministry of
Social Security of families with children, the studies so far published concerning incidence of poverty for the whole population have been based on
data collected for the Ministry of Labour Household Expenditure Survey,
which have been examined by Townsend and Abel-Smith.[3, 4] The National
Assistance scale rate which was in operation at that time was used as the
cut-off point for poverty, including a payment for rent, discretionary additional allowances, and so-called 'disregards' which are frequently made in
assessing income. This brought the poverty line somewhat above the cut-
off point using subsistence income as defined earlier. It was found that by
these criteria poverty in Britain increased between 1953 and 1960 from
7·8 per cent to 14·2 per cent of the total population. The largest single
group was that of families with the head of the household in full-time
work, which contained about three million. The next group of two and a
half million was composed of people of pensionable age. Three-quarters of
a million were fatherless families. Another three-quarters of a million had
one parent disabled or sick for three months or longer. Lastly, half a
million lived in families where the father was unemployed.

Townsend and Abel-Smith are now engaged on the first national study,
and the findings of five preliminary studies are available. Sally Sainsbury

interviewed a sample of 211 men registered as physically handicapped in London, and she concluded that there are few opportunities provided for economic independence and social participation.[5] John Veit Wilson (1967) interviewed a sample of sixty-five chronically sick or disabled men in Colchester, and found that for most material conditions had deteriorated over a long period, often long before final incapacity prevented further work.[6] Reference to last earnings before unemployment was therefore in most cases a misleading guide to the extent of deprivation experienced. Hilary Land interviewed a sample of eighty-six London families with five or more children, and found that over a third had fallen below the Townsend cut-off line of poverty at least once in the course of the previous year, and many had experienced long-term poverty.[7, 8] Dennis Marsden interviewed a sample of 116 fatherless families who were on assistance payments in a northern and a southern town in England, and he found that their living standards were well below those of the general population.[9] Adrian Sinfield in 1967 interviewed ninety-two unemployed men in the north of England, and found that in those cases where there had been recurrent unemployment over five years this had drastically reduced the resources of the families. The unskilled, the disabled, and older workers were most heavily disadvantaged.[10]

A small number of independent studies concerned with specific social problems preceded the national study. Peter Marris investigated the circumstances of widows in East London, and discovered the important function of the wider family in helping the widow in her bereavement emotionally as well as financially.[11] There was a distinct change in style of life due to the deterioration in economic circumstances. In a study of the unmarried mother and her child Virginia Wimperis drew attention to the plight of many such mothers due to inadequate financial resources.[12] Pauline Morris investigated the circumstances of families temporarily without fathers, and found evidence of substantial poverty; she also discovered that there was a good deal of pressure from officials to induce mothers of young children to go out to work rather than receive assistance.[13] Margaret Wynn used official statistics for a study of fatherless families, and stressed the difficulties that women have in collecting maintenance payments.[14]

So far there has only been one investigation of the incidence of poverty in a community. This is a study of two areas of Nottingham, one being an inner city slum area, the other an inter-war housing estate.[15, 16] In the slum area it was found that 15 per cent of the population lived on incomes below the basic supplementary benefit rate. The district is deprived in many ways, including provisions for schooling. Many of the children at school lacked stability: 42 per cent came from broken homes. About 16 per cent are tested annually for educational subnormality. On the estate, in contrast, the incidence of poverty was lower, but due to generally higher standards and social pressures there was some evidence of deprivation in line with Seebohm Rowntree's concept of secondary poverty. The risk of poverty was found to be highest in families where the father is at work, but has a low income; or a large family; or both; in fatherless families; in families where either parent is chronically sick; and in families where the father is unemployed. The old also form a high risk group, but this does not concern us here.

This finding is in line with those of other investigations. While it is known that these are the particularly vulnerable groups, especially in the lower income ranges, there is not much understanding of their overlap as they are obviously not mutually exclusive. Moreover, the circumstances which may create poverty, like chronic illness, disability, widowhood, or an unfavourable ratio of wage to dependants, have not been studied in detail longitudinally, so that it is not possible to define clearly the stages in the life cycles of individual children in which they may experience changes in material circumstances. The study of the chronically sick,[6] for instance, showed clearly that many informants experienced a gradual deterioration over long time spans in which adjustments to lower incomes had to be made in stages. The effect this has on the children is referred to in a later section. Recurrent unemployment among the unskilled[10] showed large fluctuations of income. It is known that in general the greatest stress period economically is that of child-rearing for the low-income earner; but there is no convincing evidence of a 'culture of poverty' which runs through more than one generation.

The incidence of dietary deficiency is hard to determine in low-income households. The National Food Survey seems to see the dietary problems of the 1960s more generally as those related to excess of food intake and consequent obesity than to deficiency. Nevertheless, the Food Survey estimated in 1965 (*Monthly Digest of Statistics*, 1966) that a household with three or more children spent 11s. 1d. a week less per head on food than a family with one child, and this trend had been reported over a number of previous years. Royston Lambert, in *Nutrition in Britain, 1950-1960*, examined the information published by the Food Survey in the light of recommendations of the British Medical Association.[17] He found that the diet of the British people had not improved uniformly. Examining the findings by family size he found that small or childless families had made substantial gains in the decade, whereas the diets of families with three or four children had shown some notable falls in nutritional adequacy. By 1960 the families in all but the top income range were affected, and disparities of intake between families of different sizes and classes were large. Lambert says: 'There is evidence that the financial burden of the large family has increased over the decade and that the nutritional position of these groups suffered as a result of decontrol (of foods) in the middle fifties. Since that time they have been unable to make up what they lost then.' In a small study, *Malnutrition in the 1960s*, the Office of Health Economics states: 'One of the remarkable things about nutrition is that in the area between chronic deficiency and optimum health, more is known about animals than about man'.[18] But there is no doubt that health and physique are directly related to social class. There is evidence that in large families the height of children is less than that for the average, and markedly less than that of only children. Families with three or more children in the lower income groups are likely to be inadequately nourished.[19] The differences in heights and weights of children in good and poor residential districts have been lessening, but they still exist, as is pointed out in *The Health of the School Child, 1964-65*.[20] In Sheffield, for instance, a five-year-old boy in a good district was an inch taller and 1½ lb. heavier, and a fourteen-year-old boy was rather more than an inch taller and 6 lb. heavier than their fellows in poor districts.

J. W. B. Douglas, in a cohort study of children born in one week of 1946, stated that the mothers in families of unskilled and semi-skilled workers are frequently in a low state of health owing to an inadequate diet, lack of rest or relaxation, and the cycle of child-bearing.[21] A reflection of this poor state of health is the high incidence of prematurity, and it is one reason why infant mortality rates remain stubbornly at well over three times that of classes I - III. Bronchitis, pneumonia and whooping-cough are still killers. He found that the condition of infections is also affected. While the incidence was no greater than in other classes, the children in classes IV and V pick up infections when they are much younger, their general state of health is low, and therefore the consequences of infectious diseases are more serious.

In a survey of health services for children in the City of Birmingham Dr Patria Asher found that the number of untreated defects and conditions in primary school children was greatest in a school serving an area of 'many decrepit houses, shifting populations and many problem families'. Dr Asher stated:

'Untreated defects are common among school entrants in a poor neighbourhood because more parents in such a neighbourhood fail to notice the defect or to see that it is treated. Thus there were more squints, and more of them were untreated, among the five-year-olds. . . . Respiratory infections and their complications such as deafness are also common whenever there is much overcrowding. . . . It is disturbing, for instance, to find that an epileptic can go through his school career without anyone being aware of his disability. . . . Another disturbing finding is that potentially serious defects are sometimes diagnosed at the Periodic Medical Inspection (at school), yet apparently neither followed up nor treated. . . . '

Nearly a third of the children in this inner ring area school had untreated conditions or defects.[22, 23]

Perinatal mortality rates also reflect the unfavourable circumstances of the lower socio-economic groups. Butler and Bonham, in a study of children born in one week in 1958, showed that the chances of being born alive and surviving the first week of life are closely related to the number of previous births, and the risk rises steadily from the third baby.[24] While this is true for all social classes, when high birth order is combined with low income the position is considerably worse. J. C. Kincaid, in an investigation of peri-natal mortality, found that mothers of large low-income families had less ante-natal care than the rest. He states that in Scotland, for instance, the stillbirth rate in the unskilled manual group is about two and a half times that experienced by the wives of professional men, the neonatal death rate is twice as high in the unskilled as in the professional group, and the post-neonatal rate is nearly six times as high.[25]

CULTURAL ASPECTS OF DEPRIVATION

The material aspects of deprivation are paralleled by cultural handicaps. Bernstein has drawn attention to the role of speech as a major aspect of culture and as an important means of its transmission from generation to generation.[26] He distinguishes between two essentially different forms of speech, the elaborated and the restricted code, which are commonly used in the upper and the lower socio-economic groups, respectively. A child limited to the restricted form of language, as is normal in families of unskilled manual workers, has little motivation toward increasing vocabu-lary. There is a limited and often rigid use of adjectives, adverbs, etc.; speech is not perceived as a means by which to communicate differences of feelings and experience. Thoughts are often strung together 'like beads on a frame' rather than in a planned sequence. He concludes that the relative back-wardness of children from the lower working class may well be culturally induced through the implications of the linguistic process.

Many other workers have pointed out the importance of language in stimulating the development of cognitive skills. While it is possible for a certain amount of thinking to take place among totally deaf children, most thinking skills depend upon language. A. R. Luria, in a study of a pair of five-year-old twins, has shown how the behaviour of children with limited vocabulary tends to be dominated by sensory stimuli.[27] The twins were intelligent but retarded in speech, being the youngest in a large family. Their actions were guided more by current feelings, wishes or moods than by thought processes. They had difficulties in taking account of the con-sequences of their actions, and this affected their time-perspective and their ability to plan ahead. There is of course a danger in this kind of analysis, and that is to assume that the use of a rich vocabulary, or an elaborated language code, necessarily leads to the development of intelligence and possibly even to the acquisition of wisdom. Language is nothing but a tool, and it is a necessary, but not sufficient, basis for the development of thought processes and the transmission of a culture. It is the content of the culture, the norms and values held by a community, its forms of interaction, institutionalised and informal, which determine the expression of individual potential.

Basically, any society has the task to train its young people to develop the social and occupational skills they will require as adults. In pre-industrialised societies the extended family is the all-important institution in this training; in industrialised societies many of the more specialised skills are acquired in formal educational institutions or at later stages of job training. But basic skills are developed during the early stages of childhood, and very largely while the child is a full-time member of the nuclear family setting. The task of parents in rearing their children has become vastly more complex in the course of this century.

First of all, industrial innovations during this period, especially in auto-mation, have put increasing emphasis on the training of a highly skilled, literate, adaptable and mobile population. There has been an educational explosion, a lengthening of school life, a widening and deepening of curricula, and an extension of systems of higher education to reach wider sections of the community. Although these expansionary trends do not follow the same pattern in all industrialised countries, it is widely recog-nised that a growing supply of highly educated people is a necessary condition for a competitive national economy.

Second, national wealth has grown considerably, and although the share-out of this among the social classes has remained substantially of the same proportions, it has meant a considerable rise in the standard of living of all classes. It is estimated that in Britain at the turn of the century average earnings in industry sufficed merely to meet the essential needs of a two-child family; today average earnings allow the industrial wage-earner to spend a third of his income on things other than basic needs. With a rising standard of living goes a change in the style of life. This is aided by greater educational opportunities, which were introduced in Britain with the Education Act of 1944. Greater equality of educational opportunity has shifted the emphasis to achievement, whereas previously the position of adults in society was more largely determined by their ascribed status as children.

Third, increased social mobility makes for geographical mobility, and this has had an impact on patterns of family life. Old-established communities containing close-knit family networks are gradually disappearing, and are being replaced by neighbourhoods containing nuclear families who live more individuated and more home-centred lives, whose participation in associational life will take them beyond the confines of the neighbourhood, and who are geared to moving from job to job in the course of a career structure.

Fourth, owing to the spread of family planning techniques, the position of women has shifted from that of a largely house-bound person to that of a person who after the completion of her family has some thirty years of relatively independent life to expect, and her freedom is increased by labour-saving devices in the home. (The exceptions to this have been the areas of the wool and cotton industries and the potteries, where working-class wives have traditionally combined child-rearing with work in the mills and factories, and young children had to be fostered out.) The shift in the role of women has brought with it changes in attitude, including a replacement of the traditional segregated role relationship in marriage by greater partnership.

Fifth, there has been a revolution in the understanding and handling of children, which is largely connected with the insights gained in psychology and psychiatry into child development in the course of this century. Paternalistic methods of handling children, which tend to prevail in traditional communities, have to a large extent been replaced by child-centred methods in at least the more educated classes of the western industrialised societies. This process is slow and by no means uniformly observable, but there are indications that in Britain child-centred attitudes are rapidly spreading. J. and E. Newson mention a number of aspects of child-centredness which they have found to be widely followed in a sample of mothers in Nottingham.[28] These are: the mother is responsive to the child's demands; she participates wholeheartedly in the child's play; she is available, if necessary, for the child at night; she accepts the child's statement that he is 'busy' when asked to do something while he is playing; she values the child 'for himself'; and she does not make a moral issue of the child smacking her. The mothers from the upper socio-economic groups had widely adopted these attitudes, and a fair proportion of the wives of manual workers were also positively rated. The main difference lay between the middle and the unskilled working class. The latter show a considerable difference in attitudes exhibited by mothers: for instance, 45 per cent of them would take part in the child's play, compared with 73 per cent of the white-collar families. Nevertheless, the authors sum up:

'The trends at work in this whole area of the mother-child relationship are those general ones of permissiveness and child-centredness which now seem central in our society; the only significant class difference in attitudes towards autonomy is found in so far as the professional class has child-centred behaviour made easier by both education and material conditions.'

In examining child-rearing practices more closely the impact of certain social changes on the social classes has to be taken into account. The middle classes in Britain have had long experience of social mobility and have, in the course of the last century, developed a tradition of child-rearing which prepares for leadership roles, responsibility in social matters, a high degree of self-confident ambition, and the creative use of leisure. The traditional pattern of living in the working class has been group-oriented and based on a close network of kinship relations. Upward mobility has never been, until recently, a reality; ambition was discouraged because it upset the structural balance. Living in crowded and often overcrowded conditions on marginal incomes made essential the inculcation of behaviour which facilitated group relationships in circumstances over which the individual had little if any control. Authoritarian methods of inculcation of obedience were based on physical punishment, rather than verbal explanations or forms of punishment which could be seen by the child as logical consequences of misbehaviour.

While the middle-class family has been seeking to develop internalised standards of conduct which enable the child to understand obligation and to act on his own motivation, traditional working-class patterns of child-rearing relied more heavily on group disapproval of certain kinds of behaviour which were detrimental to the group, such as telling lies, stealing, being disobedient, showing lack of consideration for other people's susceptibilities, using bad language, being 'rude', showing curiosity about sex, not saying 'please' and 'thank you', and so on.[29] Parent-child interaction was less intense, and of shorter duration than that in middle-class families where the period of exclusive dependence on parents and the nuclear home has always been longer. Children in working-class areas tended to grow up in larger families; consequently the wider kin as well as sibling and peer groups were important influences on behaviour at a much earlier age. In such conditions punishment-avoidance patterns are easily formed. In contrast, middle-class determination to exercise as much control over the child's activities as possible has been facilitated by spacious homes and private gardens. Autonomous living patterns and intimate parent-child relationships are more effective in emotional conditioning, and it has been suggested that this facilitates the development of an internalised conscience. It is likely that mother-child separation during early childhood will result in greater damage to the child's personality in such a setting than in the group setting of the traditional working class.

The middle-class professions and semi-professional occupations have grown rapidly in the course of this century, together with technological, scientific and administrative developments. At the same time growing affluence has had a considerable effect on the life styles of manual workers, many of whom have adopted, or are about to adopt, middle-class patterns of living. The literature describing 'spiralist' or 'aspirant' working-class families emphasises the connection between opportunities for job improvement and parental interest in education. Douglas, for instance, found a trend of upward mobility in families who were better educated than their reference group, and the wife's education was almost as important as that of the husband.[22] Upward mobility has been aided by large-scale geographical movements of populations from old-established working-class communities to new estates and new towns. The spread of mass media, especially television, has aided the adoption of new styles of life.

But there is a sector of the working class which does not share in heightened aspirations: it is largely composed of families of unskilled workers, who have more than the average number of children, low incomes, little interest in education, and few social skills. There is a high incidence of such families in sub-standard housing of the inner ring areas of large cities, but they are also found on housing estates, largely through city development schemes. Mitchell found two distinct status groups on a Liverpool estate;[30] Kuper speaks of the respectables, with the ultra-respectables at one end, and the ordinary families, with the really rough ones at the other end of the social spectrum.[31] Mogey found the same divisions on an Oxford estate.[32] Such divisions create estrangement and hostility in place of the tolerant attitude of 'live and let live' in traditional areas, and they add to the strains of living in families who have neither the material nor the personal resources to cope without the aid of wider kin and old-established friendships. R. Wilson discusses the effect that the challenge of a new neighbourhood has on those who have not got the psychological resilience and the robustness of family relationship to take it.[33] In some families such a change destroys personal inner strength; and in a small minority of families behaviour becomes overtly anti-social. This in turn increases the anxiety of aspirant and respectable families in the neighbourhood, so that considerable tensions build up.

The new child-centred attitudes go hand in hand with rising standards of living. A mother who does not get a good night's rest, who is physically run down, and who is overburdened with the difficulties of raising a large family on an inadequate income, will not find it easy to adapt to a situation in which each individual child in her family is a focus of attention in his own right. Moreover, space and privacy for play and the necessary equipment may not be available. In a comparative study of 'coping' and 'non-coping' large families, Pauline Shapiro found sharp differences in respect of the children's play.[34] 'In the non-copers' homes there was no provision for indoor play; usually there was pandemonium—coaxing and slapping, often ending in money for lollies or sweet biscuits from the corner shop. . . . ' The absence of provision for play did not refer to toys, for these seemed to exist at times, such as Christmas; but there was 'a complete lack of play material for constructive and imaginative use, and a lack of understanding or tolerance of children's play needs.'

The Newsons found in Nottingham that there are significant differences in the amount of daily contact of mothers and their young children in various socio-economic groups. The children of the lower socio-economic groups, who on average have larger families, tend to be out in yards and streets, and supervision tends to be negligible. The mothers let their children settle their own differences during play, and 'You can't fall out over your kids' is a standard answer of a mother who lives in close proximity to her neighbours. In very crowded districts mothers are sometimes forced to intervene to stop their children fighting, but they prefer 'not to have noticed it'. This pattern of behaviour is carried into the estates in spite of greater privacy and space for play; and here the fact that the children are out of earshot is considered an advantage. When they get really vicious, unwilling mothers are finally goaded into intervening, but little attempt is made to apportion blame correctly, and punishment falls equally on the just and the unjust. The Newsons found that two-thirds of the mothers in the families of semi-skilled and unskilled manual workers actively encourage their children to hit back to defend themselves in any fights that take place. Over-aggressiveness seems to worry them much less than under-aggressiveness.

There are other aspects of child-rearing found in some of the non-aspirant working-class homes which do not aid personality development of the child. Mention has already been made of the limited language facilities in such homes. The Newsons point out that perhaps the most salient way in which total patterns of upbringing differ in the different classes is seen in the kind of control mothers exert over their children. Whereas middle-class mothers tend consciously to reason with their children, whether to persuade or to prevent bad behaviour, the mothers of the lower socio-economic groups tend to issue bald commands. These are frequently reinforced by verbal threats which are not carried out. The child will be told that some person, the policeman, the teacher, or some other authority figure, will come and take him away if he does not obey; or that he will be sent away, or that mother will leave him. Furthermore, false information is frequently given about the consequences of undesirable behaviour, such as 'There's maggots under your nails' for nail biting, or 'You might have your fingers drop off' for masturbating. Three-quarters of mothers in unskilled manual workers' families resort to false stories concerning the birth of babies, such as 'Dug up in the back garden' or 'Bought at Woolworth's'. Such obviously untrue pieces of information tend to undermine the trust between parents and children. In the words of the authors: 'He learns at an early age that authority in the person of his mother (despite her pretensions to have his own welfare at heart) is yet not averse to using trickery whenever this suits her purpose of controlling him'. As the authors point out, words in these families do not carry the same symbolic meaning as agents of truth that they have in the homes of more educated parents. However, all parents tend to be 'very self-consciously aware of the responsibility to achieve some sort of long-term moral training which will have a lasting effect upon the character of the child. . . . [They] seem more concerned to point the generality of the principles which they try to instil.' Such training will later form the basis of some more or less consistent moral philosophy, which the middle-class mother continually makes explicit in verbal terms. This is not to assume that the Newsons found entire consistency in child-centred training methods of educated parents. There was much confusion, although the intention was frequently mentioned that rigid authoritarian methods were not acceptable. The major dilemma of these parents, especially those further up the social scale, was a rejection of plain coercion, but a simultaneous worry over habits of the children which cannot be suppressed by persuasion. Many parents did not succeed in being consistent, and many were self-critical about their results, finding they had to use disciplinary measures they did not really approve of. Three-quarters of all mothers were found to use smacking; the professional classes rather less frequently than the lower working classes.

The picture obtained by the investigation of J. and E. Newson is summed up in the statement that permissive mothers find again and again that they have to change their policy from the rational permissiveness to which they are ideologically committed towards authoritarian methods which they thought they had put behind them. The authors ask the final question: 'Working-class parents lag always a few years behind their middle-class counterparts as trends in child-rearing change; will they meet them one day on the way back?'

While this question is of no immediate concern in a discussion of socially deprived children, it focuses on the areas within which the problem of social deprivation must be set. The problem may be defined in the following way: Modern industrial society requires skills of a sophisticated type for a successful adult life. Success will come to those who from an early age have been trained to be resourceful and self-reliant; who have learned to subordinate immediate satisfactions in the interest of long-term objectives; who are able to exercise forethought and plan their time; who are responsible, well-mannered and courteous; and who have learned to cultivate technical and academic skills. The prerequisites for child training which lead to the acquisition of these skills are on the material level adequate diet and rest; space and privacy for play and work; and availability of toys, books and other equipment which stimulates development of mind and body. More important than material provisions, however, is the existence of a warm relationship with parents who can impart to the child a feeling of security, who can stimulate his curiosity, and who steer the satisfaction of the child's instinctual drives into socially acceptable channels. The main areas of socialisation cannot be put in order of priority. In terms of the child's development they may be listed as the areas of feeding and toilet training; the control of aggression; the protection of safety and health of the child; the protection of possessions; inculcation of a sense of responsibility towards others; and development of the child's creative potential and his independence. The methods by which these objectives can be achieved are much discussed, and changes from traditional authoritarian methods to permissive ones must be seen in the light of the aims which parents wish to achieve.

The general focus on child-centredness, however, must not be confused with the strictness-permissiveness variable. Responsiveness to the child's demands, participation in his activities, availability of the mother (or mother-substitute) when needed by the child, and an appreciation of the child as a person in his own right are all traditional middle-class attitudes which are essential for the development of the autonomous personality. What is new has sometimes been referred to as 'the Spock approach'[35] which followed the rather authoritarian methods advocated by Truby King in the pre-war era. While Truby King had advocated scheduled feeding, early potting, and a rigid programme of daily events for the child, Spock introduced more democratic methods of relaxed child handling, demand feeding, and general guidance of parents in terms of total enjoyment of their children and a more elastic attitude in matters concerned with the satisfaction of the children's needs. This new and more permissive regime in the nursery is now very widely followed.

The art of socialising children in this new fashion lies in finding a balance between the permissible and the proscribed. This is made more difficult in a period of history in which norms and values are very generally under scrutiny, and in a society the middle class of which no longer acknowledges one single set of such norms and values. The inculcation of this is the task of parents who help the child to achieve an internalisation of their value systems in the course of his childhood, and they do this as much by verbalisation of their own thoughts and feelings as by their example. Parents who are in the course of adopting new life styles and are just getting acquainted with new ideas and sets of values are somewhat handicapped in this process, and especially when in their previous setting they had heavily relied on the support of the wider family and the neighbourhood in general in the upbringing of their children. However, it is here that good schools can give much support, as has been documented by Douglas and also in the Newsom Report.[36, 37, 38]

The problem is a different one in families who have not reached the level of living at which child-centred child-rearing methods are practicable. The hypothesis of a threshold is helpful in this context in differentiating between homes which do supply the minimum stimulus for development of the child's potential, and homes which do not. Again, there is little documentation so far in Britain which would make a statement of the nature of the difference possible. The literature concerned with socially deprived families is descriptive rather than analytical. A good summary of child-rearing practices in such families appears in J. Klein, *Samples from English Cultures*.[39] The children in these families are usually not planned, and the first child may be born out of wedlock, or conceived before marriage. The mothers tend to be very young, inexperienced and not trained in mothercraft. In many of these families there is no systematic restriction of the children's impulses, and this must not be confused with permissiveness. It is an indulgence of an extremely inconsistent kind characteristic of helpless mothers, who cannot plan ahead or constrain their children except by the inappropriate use of physical force. The parents may themselves have little control over their impulses, and this may account for the 'battered baby syndrome' which has recently figured large in the press. Such events are not necessarily synonymous with rejection of the children, although they amount to physical neglect and what might be called maltreatment.

The present trend towards permissiveness in child-centred handling of children does not facilitate the task of parents who themselves have problems of self-discipline and problems in relationship with others. They are trebly handicapped: first through their own personality limitations; secondly through the absence of a supporting kinship system which would have carried them through the child-rearing period in a paternalistic community of former days; and thirdly through the demands of a permissive open society. The problem is aggravated by the fact that many of the vulnerable groups of families are handicapped, physically or mentally. A. F. Philp, in *Family Failure*, discusses the health aspects of 129 families with whom Family Service Units were in contact, and found that 37 per cent had either one or both parents of poor or very poor general health, and 87 per cent of the parents had mental health problems.[40] This assessment was made entirely on the basis of symptoms, and only broad distinctions could be maintained between psychotic reactions (10 per cent), personality disorders (63 per cent), epilepsy (4 per cent), neuroses (1·7 per cent), intermittent reactions to external stress, and other conditions. In a sample of fifty-two families known to a local authority for suspected child neglect, H. Wilson found fourteen disabled fathers, thirteen chronically physically sick, seven mentally ill, and one mentally subnormal father.[41] Twelve of the mothers suffered from chronic physical conditions which were disabling, three were mentally ill, and eight mentally subnormal. On correlating parental handicaps it was found that only five families had parents of average physical and mental health, and the main disabling factor in this group of families was the very large size of family. One of the families had ten children; the other four had eleven children each.

Such findings indicate the vulnerability of the population under discussion, but they cannot be taken to be necessarily causally connected with the circumstances in which the families find themselves. Poor physical health may lead to a bad work record with consequent reduction of the family income; but conversely a low family income affects general health. Similarly, mental instability is likely to bring about a general lowering of living standards as it affects capacity for work, but here again stress situations in low income groups may precipitate a mental breakdown. Continuous stress situations are likely to affect the personality in general, and to generate feelings of persecution and aggressiveness. The so-called 'immature personality' so frequently described in the literature concerned with socially handicapped families (as for instance Bodman[42]) may be a personality presenting symptoms of retarded development, or a personality which has regressed under stress, or a combination of both.[43] None of the above-mentioned physical or mental conditions suffice as an explanation of the low status of such families, as these conditions occur in all socio-economic groups. It is only when they occur in combination with the absence of material resources that they become significant.

One of the important features of the living patterns of socially handicapped families appears to be relative isolation. While some of the old-established poor communities, such as Spinley's deprived group in *The Deprived and the Privileged*,[44] or Kerr's *People of Ship Street*,[45] had the benefit of mutual support, the majority of families in the FSU sample described by Philp had difficulties in their relationships with neighbours, and although most of them came from large families they lived at a distance and were not in close touch with kin. The findings of H. Wilson were very similar. The great majority of the research families had severed their connections with kin, some because of rehousing, others in pursuit of work, others again due to family quarrels. A number of parents had grown up orphaned or in institutions. Social isolation has grave consequences in the field of child rearing, not only because of the parental inability to manage the children unaided, but also because of the absence of close relationships with adults other than the parents. The children are deprived of suitable adult models in personality formation. They also forego the experience of mutual give-and-take which is natural in human groups. In some exceptionally hostile environments, such as that described by H. Wilson as experienced in one area by a group of families, the children will actually develop pseudo-paranoid features of persecution and hostility.

MALFUNCTIONING OF DEPRIVED CHILDREN

Educational under-achievement and early leaving

Most of the above-mentioned surveys of the incidence of poverty and cultural deprivation give us evidence concerning the effects of such conditions on individual children. For a more detailed examination of such possible effects we must turn to the psychological and educational literature. The consistent tendency of children of semi-skilled and unskilled manual workers to perform less well in school than the rest, and for high-ability pupils of the working class to leave school earlier than their middle-class peers of the same ability, call for explanation.

The problem of the early school leaver was first documented by a report of the Central Advisory Council for Education (1954), *Early Leaving*, which showed that there are profound social class differences in the length of school life.[46] The Crowther Report (1959) gave a disturbing picture of wasted talent, especially among the sons of manual workers: in a survey of National Service recruits it was found that 63 per cent of young men of the highest level of ability had left school aged sixteen or younger; and 95 per cent of the second highest level of ability.[47] In 1963 the Robbins Report produced similar evidence.[48] Of the top ability group (IQ 130 plus), 18 per cent of manual workers' children reached university compared with 37 per cent of non-manual occupations. Of the second level ability group (IQ 115-129) only 8 per cent of manual workers' children, compared with 17 per cent of non-manual occupations, reached university. The latest piece of evidence concerning early leaving is found in J. W. B. Douglas, *All Our Future* (1968), which shows that social class differences, already obvious at the primary school level, had increased at the secondary level and extended to pupils of high ability. Nearly half the lower manual working-class pupils in Douglas's cohort sample in the top 16 per cent of the IQ range had left school before they were sixteen and a half. Dr Douglas states:

'Early leaving and low job aspirations make it probable that as many as 5 per cent of the next generation of manual workers will be recruited from pupils who, in other circumstances, might have qualified for administrative or professional occupations.'

The concept of under-achievement is a complex one, and very little experimental work has been undertaken on socially deprived children which would make a theoretical formulation possible. Children who have been removed from very poor homes in which the natural parents have sub-normal IQs, to foster homes with foster parents of average or superior intelligence, have eventually obtained IQs ten to thirty points higher than predicted if they had remained in their own homes, and their educational attainments were even higher than expected (Skeels).[49]

As A. R. Jensen has pointed out, in the United States where most of the research is at present carried out, the main aim of ameliorative programmes seems to be to explore the educational potential of children whose measured intelligence lies in the dull range, that is from IQ 75-95.[50] The relatively rarely identified slum child with a measured intelligence which is above average is not considered an educational problem, although it appears to be reasonable to postulate that he, too, has a depressed educational potential. Educational retardation must be clearly distinguished from biologically caused primary retardation. Intelligence is inherited as a result of a large number of genes, and because of the random assortment of these genes the total effect will be normally distributed in the population, in much the same way as height. The majority of dull children who do not show neurological signs of organic impairment are at the lower end of the normal curve of distribution. It is, however, difficult to discriminate between genetic and cultural retardation, but this is a problem which does not affect middle-class children. Jensen suggests that there are some indications that the environment acts as a threshold variable and not as a simple linear function of the degree of environmental impoverishment. There are degrees of cultural deprivation, but once the threshold is reached the individual's full potential will be more or less realised. He supports this hypothesis by the observation that there is a bulge in the lower half of the distribution of IQs when the Stanford-Binet Intelligence Test is administered to a large and representative sample of the population. An American study shows that the distribution closely approximates the normal if subjects of low socio-economic status are removed from the sample.

A further line of evidence which is quoted by Jensen in support of the threshold hypothesis is the work done by Honzik, who showed that the IQs of foster children are not correlated in the least with those of their foster parents, whose own IQs span a wide range.[51] Once the threshold of an adequate environment is reached, it appears that the IQ of foster children is primarily determined by genetic factors.

It was stated that the curve of distribution of intelligence becomes a normal one after removing subjects of low socio-economic status. There remains, however, a slight bulge at the very lowest end of the curve of distribution, below IQ 50, which is due to brain damage and major gene defects like mongolism, phenylketonuria, and amaurotic idiocy. These genetic defects result in severe degrees of mental retardation of a nature different from that which constitutes part of the normal variation, and they are not here under discussion. Standard intelligence tests, such as the Stanford-Binet and the Wechsler, are measures of specific knowledge and problem-solving skills. Ability for school learning is, however, a more complex concept than intelligence. Intelligence plays a part in determining it, but family and environment are of greater importance; and motivation, work habits, school attendance, parental interest and other cultural stimuli play a vital part in shaping the child's readiness for learning.

A number of studies have shown that children from low socio-economic backgrounds are not given the educational support which they need for the full development of their potential. J. W. B. Douglas, in a national cohort study of all children born in one week of 1946, had found that these children 'seemed to be saddled with a cumulative series of educational handicaps'.[36] They lacked stimulus at home, and many were also at a disadvantage at school because of early streaming into ability groups. Assessments of intelligence at the age of seven are not reliable, and especially in the case of culturally disadvantaged children. Douglas found that the children in each stream conformed to earlier assessments: those in the top streams improved in tests, and the children in lower streams fell behind. Such trends are reinforced by inadequate buildings, inferior equipment, shortage of staff, and rapid teacher turnover in many of the older schools containing large proportions of children from the lowest socio-economic groups.[52]

Douglas found later that social class differences in educational opportunities increased at the secondary stage, but pupils from the manual working class were less handicapped, compared with those from the middle class, when they were in well staffed and well equipped schools.[37] This was particularly the case when the studied cohort was aged fifteen, and the difference between scores made in attainment and in intelligence is a good indication of the extent of under-achievement of children from the manual working class. The total sample was divided into middle class and working class, and further subdivided into upper and lower sections according to the education and social origins of their parents. It had therefore a cultural element not normally contained in socio-economic classification. However, the entire group of semi-skilled and unskilled workers' families fell into the lower manual working class group. At each age social-class differences in test performances were greater in school attainment than in intelligence.

Taking non-verbal intelligence-test results, Douglas found that the differences between children from the upper and lower socio-economic groups showed at age eight, when they were first tested, and remained more or less constant from then on. He concluded from this that the major differences in the performance of the children have to be attributed to environmental influences acting in pre-school years. At the primary stage of schooling Douglas found one of the main factors in school success to be the support and encouragement that the parents give their children with their school work. This finding is supported by evidence given in the Plowden Report.[52] Parental attitudes, in fact, remain a decisive element when the decision has to be made whether or not to stay on at school beyond the official leaving age of fifteen, and again later when children choose whether or not to enter higher education.

The mothers who took little interest in their children's work included a high proportion of those who had been described earlier by health visitors as being 'poor managers'. It is important to look at this definition in some detail. Douglas classifies maternal standards of care by using the following five indices:

1. Mother's management of the child.
2. Adequacy of the child's shoes.
3. Adequacy of the child's clothes.
4. Cleanliness of the child.
5. Cleanliness of the home.

Since these indices are all closely linked with adequacy of financial resources, it is not surprising to find that nearly two-thirds of the mothers in the unskilled manual workers' group of families were classified as 'poor' managers. It must be recognised, however, that poor management, whatever it may mean, is highly correlated with lack of interest in the children's education. This is admitted by Douglas to be partly due to some of the schools who fail to involve the parents in the work they are doing. Apart from that factor, there is a close link of parental interest in the children's education of those working-class parents who themselves had any kind of education beyond the elementary level, such as night classes, or correspondence courses.

There are other environmental factors which exert an influence on measured ability. When either the father or the mother is in poor health, school attendance of working-class boys and girls (but not of middle-class children) falls off, especially that of the latter. As judged by the tests given at fifteen, this factor has some influence on the attainment and ability of the children. The group of parents in poor health included a whole variety of illness, ranging from the crippling ones to those that have little effect on ordinary activities. Taking those children whose fathers were unemployed owing to illness as a special group, the effects on school attainment were even more marked. While such misfortune occurs in each social class, there was an excess in the lower manual working class: 79 per cent of reported instances were in this class, which is nearly twice as many as would be expected. These families are also larger than the whole group: 58 per cent have four or more children compared with 33 per cent in the whole group. In view of the combination of these factors, one would expect the test performance and school progress of those with unemployed fathers to be relatively low, and this was actually the case. In the tests at each age (eight, eleven and fifteen) the children whose fathers were unemployed through illness made scores that were on the average six points below the average for the whole sample, and 1·7 points below the expected average when allowances are made for their social class, size of family, standards of care and housing conditions. In the same group children also tended to leave school at the earliest age, only 16 per cent in secondary modern schools staying on aged fifteen compared with an expected 35 per cent. Here then is a close association of poor progress of children at school and early leaving in a group of families who, through incapacitating illness of the father, experienced in many cases financial hardship. Another handicapping factor for children was the experience of long periods of illness of the father followed by death. The families in which the father died during the first six years of the survey were materially considerably worse off than the others, and a higher proportion belonged to the lower manual working class than expected. Standards of maternal care, as judged by the health visitors, were considered low, but this was not surprising since it included an assessment of the children's adequacy of clothing. Housing conditions tended to be poor, not only owing to the large size of the families, but also due to the fact that many shared their homes with relatives. The average aggregate scores of the children were considerably and significantly depressed at age fifteen to 5·5 points below those expected, after allowing for family size, standards of maternal care, housing and social class. On the other hand, the attainment of children who lose their fathers by sudden death, early or late, is no lower than would be expected.

Douglas concludes:

'Those that are handicapped are the children whose fathers have experienced long periods of illness before death, and the more recent this
experience the more affected they are. Prolonged strain, worry and adjustments in family routine to care for an ill parent, or the stresses thrown on
the family by a long period of unemployment of the father, take their toll
of a child's school attainment.'

It is commonly known that children from large families make, on the
average, lower test scores than those from families with one or two
children. Douglas obtained similar results. Large families are more frequent
in the lowest income groups, and therefore inadequate home conditions,
lack of parental interest in education, and poor school provisions have to
be taken into consideration, and they were found to explain about one-third
of the differences in test scores. Even in the most prosperous homes those
with many brothers and sisters made lower scores than expected in all the
tests. Douglas concluded that there are subtler influences at work. As there
were no divergences of test scores at the three ages measured, it seems that
the low measured ability of children from large families is determined by
factors that influence ability before they reach school. Family size differences are smallest in the non-verbal intelligence tests, and largest in
the attainment tests, especially in vocabulary tests. At ages eight and
eleven those with three or more siblings make vocabulary test scores that
are eight points below those made by only children, whereas in mechanical
reading they are only five points behind. In sentence completion tests aged
fifteen, the children from large families are seven points behind the only
children, but only five points lower in mathematics and three points in
non-verbal intelligence. It is therefore obvious that children from large
families are particularly handicapped in the use and understanding of
words. Douglas found, however, that the children of large middle-class
families whose births were widely spaced had higher vocabulary scores than
the children whose births were close together. This, he concludes, must be
connected with the verbal stimulation that young children get from close
contact with their parents while learning to speak.

Behavioural malfunction

Three behavioural problems of children appear to be associated with the
living patterns of socially deprived families. They are: (a) truancy; (b)
troublesomeness at school; and (c) early and persistent delinquency.

Truancy: The real prevalence rates of truancy, or staying away from school
without good reason, are not available for the population in general. Tyerman quotes teachers as believing that at least 4 per cent of the primary
school children who are absent at any time ought to be at school; few,

however, are brought to court for non-attendance.[53] The overall absence rate is around 10 per cent. During 1963-64 there were over 5,500 prosecutions, which is about 0·07 per cent of all children at school, according to an estimate by the Education Welfare Officers' Association quoted by Tyerman. These figures are not a good guide to the true extent of the problem, as usually only the most intractable families are taken to court. Figures for non-attendance or prosecutions are not published officially, neither by the Department of Education nor the Scottish Education Department. Tyerman points out the similarity of much of the research in the field concerning environmental factors. In research undertaken in a Welsh town as well as an urban and a rural area of Lincolnshire, he found distinct centres of truancy which generally coincide with slum areas. In a sample of 137 truants it was found that thirty-three came from poor homes, and seventy-four from extremely poor homes. Half of the sample came from broken homes, and a third from homes where the parents appeared to be unhappily married. Two out of three had a sibling who was also a truant, and one in three had a delinquent sibling. In more than three-quarters of the cases the parents 'set poor examples and had low standards. They neglected their children, were ineffective in their supervision, and took little interest in their welfare. . . . These children were deprived in nearly every way.'

Tyerman found that half his sample had started on their truant career at primary schools, and that the number of truancies increased with age, especially among the girls, reaching a maximum around age thirteen. Most truancies occurred in secondary modern schools.

A. F. Philp estimated the number of children in his sample of families with school children who did not attend school without good reason as being 35 per cent. He mentions 'Disorganisation and absence of routine which, particularly in the large families, often meant that the onus for getting to school was put on to the children themselves'. H. Wilson found, among 164 children of her research families for whom full attendance records were available over two terms, only 22 per cent could be classified as 'normal' attenders, i.e. whose percentage of absence from school did not exceed ten. A quarter of the children had absence rates over two terms of 40 per cent and over. These absence rates tended to increase for teenagers, and the juniors had on the whole better attendances. But bad attendance was much in evidence already at infant school, and increased to 45 per cent for the seven-year-old bad attenders. There was no clear pattern of bad attendance for the eldest child in each family; among the boys twelve had worse attendance records than their younger siblings, and seven had better records. Among the girls, thirteen eldest girls had worse records and nine girls better records than their siblings. In general, however, attendance records were bad right through the research sample, and the parents with fewest educational prosecutions were those with the younger children, whose combined number of school years were considerably less than those of the other families who had more prosecutions. One family with eleven children had paid seventeen fines for non-attendance.

Such school attendance records reflect clearly the reluctance of children from socially deprived families to attend school regularly, and the indifference of parents concerning their children's attendance. That education is not valued is frequently mentioned in attitude studies of the lower socio-economic groups in general. The children's passive resistance to compulsory schooling is partly connected with their parents' lack of understanding of the importance of education. It is also a reflection of their own difficulties in adjusting to demands made on them at school for which they had not been adequately prepared in early childhood. Communication is blocked through retarded speech development; punctuality and orderliness are unknown skills; to sit still and pay attention to the teacher is difficult for a child on whom such demands had not previously been made; manual dexterity is often much retarded, and this handicaps the child in handling small objects like pencils, or turning the pages of a book; motivation for learning and achievement in general is very low or may be absent altogether, as little stimulus for achievement is given to the child at home. Furthermore, there may be external factors, such as absence of toilet training, scruffy or inadequate clothing, habits like nose-picking, etc., which single out the child and possibly stigmatise him. In addition, physical conditions like impetigo, or head lice, under present regulations exclude a child from attendance at school, and such exclusions may well initiate bad attendance patterns. Child-rearing methods in very socially deprived families obviously do not prepare the child for school, and consequently the child's further socialisation in school and in interrelation with teacher and peers is detrimentally affected. No detailed studies exist of the relationship between different types of inadequate home, different types of children, and the effect schooling has on these variables, and it is therefore not possible to indicate which type of child tends to truant.

Troublesome behaviour at school: The same considerations apply to studies of troublesome behaviour. The national cohort study of J. W. B. Douglas contains teachers' ratings of children's behaviour. Teachers were asked to rate the children aged thirteen and again aged fifteen on a large number of items of behaviour and personal characteristics, and in addition to make an overall assessment of sensitiveness, shyness and aggressiveness for each pupil. The ratings for both age groups were finally combined to define five groups of pupils: three with high ratings for either nervousness, or aggressiveness, or both, and these three groups together formed 31 per cent of the sample; a fourth group contained medium ratings and formed 41 per cent of the sample; a fifth group had low ratings and formed 28 per cent of the sample. Douglas found on correlating work habits with nervous or aggressive pupils that those picked out as very nervous were on the average hard workers and well behaved in class, and seldom truanted. In contrast, those with high aggressive ratings or with mixed aggressive and nervous ratings were more often troublesome in the classroom and outside, neglected their studies, and were likely to be truant. It was not surprising, in view of these findings, that they also scored low in all the tests administered to the fifteen-year-olds. On the other hand, the nervous, hard-working pupils do hardly any better in their attainment tests. The symptoms of nervousness were those enumerated by the Underwood Committee (1955)[54] and included stammering, nail-biting, unexplained vomiting, abdominal pain, bed-wetting, thumb-sucking and similar habits. Apart from these very nervous pupils, who tend to be hard-working and well-behaved in class, the aggressive pupils or the pupils with mixed ratings of aggressiveness and anxiousness were more likely to be seen by their teachers as poor workers and troublesome, than the rest. In comparing intelligence and attainment tests of these pupils, it turns out that they are under-achievers and that their performance tends to deteriorate during their years at school. They are also the pupils who leave school earliest, and they 'present many educational and social problems, including a relatively high risk of delinquency'. More will be said about Douglas's findings in this area later on, and it may suffice to mention in this context that the highest risk group is that of the lower manual working class where neither parent had any education beyond the elementary level.

In an on-going, longitudinal study of an urban working-class neighbourhood, West and Gibson found that the boys who came from socially very adverse environments tended to be rated as badly behaved.[55] Conduct was assessed on the basis of combined teachers' ratings and social workers' ratings who had interviewed the parents. Whereas only 13·3 per cent of boys from a 'comfortable home' received a bad behaviour rating of five on a five-point scale, 46·7 per cent of boys from inadequate homes were so rated. In fact, conduct of the boys correlated so closely with the degree of environmental handicap that it was quite unusual to find a really well-behaved boy among this group. Social handicap was measured by a scale of seven items:

(1) The family income is inadequate.
(2) The main wage earner is an unskilled manual worker.
(3) Housing is very unsatisfactory.
(4) The family has six or more children.
(5) The children are physically neglected.
(6) The accommodation is very neglected.
(7) The family is supported by a social agency.

If a boy came from a home showing more than half these indices of handicap, he was classified as being exposed to a severe degree of social handicap; if less than half, the degree was moderate. A comfortable home showed none of the indices.

In relating parental management to the conduct of boys it was found that the following six ratings were positively correlated with poor conduct in boys: parents neglect the boy physically; they are uninterested in his education; there is inconsistency between the parents in handling the boy; there is lack of parental vigilance; there is laxity in rules; and a lack of parental praise. All these items of adverse parental behaviour were significantly more frequent among boys from poor homes. It is interesting, however, to examine the correlations of parental ratings and bad behaviour more closely in the light of the discussion on child-rearing methods which preceded this section.

Taking the group of parents whose vigilance was lacking, and also the group who showed inconsistencies between them in handling the boy, the relationship with bad behaviour held good at all income levels. Physical neglect did not appear at all in the group who showed no social handicap, but in the two groups of moderate and severe degree of social handicap this item was more frequently related to the worst behaved boys. It was found that parental lack of interest in education was largely a reflection of social class, and in itself of little importance as a determinant of the boy's bad behaviour; a positive interest in education was found to be quite unusual among the poorer families. Laxness of rules again was positively related with poor conduct of the boys at all income levels, but it was reported to be evident in only seven of the families classified as comfortably off. This latter group, it must be remembered, was a classification of income levels within the range of manual workers' wage levels, as the total population was a working-class one.

The most interesting single item was that of the obverse side of parental laxness: parental strictness in enforcing rules was associated with bad behaviour of boys from comfortable homes; but this was not the case with boys from poor homes, where it was significantly related with better behaviour. It seems apparent that strict rules reflect patterns of upbringing of the kind previously described as practised in traditional working-class communities. In homes where more permissive, rational, child-centred methods are not practised, the only way to keep a boy reasonably well behaved is to resort to authoritarian methods of socialisation. This finding points to the importance of relating single items of observation to the social context; only if this is done will such observations become meaningful.

Two further items will show the importance of this statement: Relating boys' conduct to parental disharmony, it was found that the percentage of boys from disharmonious marriages steadily increases as one goes through the categories from good to bad behaviour. This holds true for all boys except those from the poorest homes. Relatively few boys had good behaviour ratings in this group anyway, but there was no relationship between the degree of parental harmony and behaviour. Regardless of their conduct rating, half the boys belonged to disharmonious homes. The second aspect of parental behaviour which had a different connotation in the lowest income level was the rating 'Loving, normal mother'. In the better income groups this was correlated with good conduct in boys. In the socially handicapped group there was no such consistent relationship. The authors suggest that this might mean that a good maternal attitude is powerless to combat bad behaviour when social circumstances are very poor. But it was found that an 'anxious, over-protective mother' seemed to be related to better behaviour in the boys from poor homes, whereas in all less socially handicapped families this attitude was negatively related to good conduct.

It seems evident that deductions about the effect of parental attitudes upon the boys' behaviour can only properly be made by comparisons within groups of similar social level; and that such attitudes must be related to parental techniques of socialisation or the absence of such techniques.

Behaviour ratings of school children are subject to a good deal of subjective judgment, often made by a single person. The above study was based on combined ratings of teacher and social worker, and therefore had an element of concordance. In other investigations the instrument most frequently used in judging British school children's behaviour is the Bristol Social Adjustment Guide, which relies entirely on the observations of the teacher. This instrument was applied by Chazan to 169 educationally sub-normal children in South Wales and a matched group of children in ordinary schools.[56] While it is not possible to go into the detailed findings of this investigation in the context of this paper, there are some points relevant to a discussion of behaviour problems among socially deprived children. As is well known, the social composition of schools for the sub-normal contains a disproportionate percentage of children from the lower socio-economic groups, which may be connected with greater resistance on the side of middle-class parents to sending their children to these schools. In Chazan's sample only 7·2 per cent of the children from eight special schools came from white-collar occupations, and 45·6 per cent came from families whose fathers were unskilled or unemployed, or from fatherless families. Very few belonged to families with one child, and nearly half came from families with five or more children. On the basis of scores obtained for 'maladjusted' behaviour according to the Bristol Social Adjustment Guide, over one-third of the children were classified as maladjusted, which was nearly three times as many as among the controls. They showed considerably more symptoms of depression, hostility towards adults, inhibition and emotional tension. Chazan states that children in large families, which are more prevalent in lower socio-economic groups, are often at a disadvantage. There was a higher percentage of children who had had unsatisfactory attendances at school, had behaviour problems and were delinquent than in the control groups in ordinary schools. These behavioural problems may well be the main reason why children from poor homes and large families tend to be over-represented in special schools.

D. H. Stott, who devised and used the Bristol Social Adjustment Guide extensively in his own researches, has in recent years tended to interpret behavioural disturbance in terms of multiple congenital impairment.[57] On the basis of his published evidence it is unfortunately not possible to single out environmental factors, and although he recognises the close relationship between behaviour in terms of malfunction of children and the environmental factor of a critically stressful family situation, the latter is not analysed in terms of socio-economic or other relevant cultural indices. Furthermore, the syndrome of troublesomeness includes nervous behaviour as well as acting-out aggressiveness, so that it is not possible to relate his findings to those of the national cohort study by Douglas, or the on-going study by West and Gibson.

Delinquency: Finally, what is the relationship between a socially handicapping environment and delinquent behaviour? In criminological literature it is increasingly recognised that early and persistent delinquency is strongly class-linked. This must be differentiated from the bulk of adolescent delinquency which has a peak around age fourteen, does not usually persist, and has to be regarded as fairly trivial. Peter Willmott, for instance, in *Adolescent Boys of East London* sees two cycles in this type of adolescent law-breaking: an earlier one mainly concerned with petty theft, and a slightly later one with a peak age of about seventeen years, which involves motoring offences, hooliganism, and some violence.[58] He estimates that about a third of a local working-class population will be taken to court for one or other such offences during adolescence, that these episodes are transitory, and that the boys will settle down to a law-abiding life when they get married. But there was also a small group of boys who did not get on well at school, were not interested in education, and went in for manual unskilled or semi-skilled employment, often with no prospect of advancement. They tended to change their jobs frequently. They did not get on well with their parents, they disliked persons in authority. Willmott states that such boys are consistently rejected, and respond with frustration expressed in aggressive acts: they try to kick against society through delinquency and violence. Who are they?

J. W. B. Douglas gives details of the social characteristics of boys aged eight to seventeen who are delinquents.[59] This study is based on the national cohort study previously referred to. Using the social description referred to previously, which divided the total population into upper and lower manual working class, and upper and lower middle class, according to parental occupation plus education and social origin of both father and mother, he found the following percentage delinquency rates (related to boys at risk in each group referred to):

Upper middle class	2·7
Lower middle class	8·3
Upper manual working class	9·7
Lower manual working class	18·7

In *All Our Future* Douglas presents some of the more detailed findings on delinquent boys at school. The delinquents were those boys who were either cautioned by the police for delinquent behaviour, or sentenced by the courts. Those who were acquitted, or whose delinquent behaviour was not discovered or, if discovered, was not reported, were not included. Douglas states that it is recognised that many delinquents are poor scholars, and appear to their teachers as bored, badly behaved and inattentive in class; many also have a history of truancy. The highest risk group, as appears in the fore-mentioned statistics, is the lower manual working class, and within this that group of families in which the parents have a low interest in education and have had only elementary education themselves. The mothers were conspicuous for their failure to use maternity and child welfare services, and they were unfavourably assessed by health visitors for the standard of care they gave their children and their homes. The risk of delinquency is also greater in large families than in small ones, holding social class constant. There is much overcrowding in the delinquents' homes, and more than three-quarters of them never had a bed to themselves up to the time they were eleven years old. In the case of divorce and separation the risk of delinquency is twice as high as expected, but such information must be seen in its context. Taking the group of divorced and separated families by themselves, irrespective of class, three-quarters of their sons did not become delinquent. The chances of delinquency are not increased by death of father. Mothers who go out to work are no more likely to have delinquent sons than mothers who stay at home.

The most important finding is the fact that the boys who later become delinquent have already at primary school shown a record of poor work, laziness, lack of power of concentration, and they are found by their teachers to be difficult to discipline. In the secondary schools their teachers also find them badly behaved, but the trivial offenders are less so than the more serious ones. All delinquents have a bad attendance record: 38 per cent of boys who went to court for more than one serious offence were truants at some time during their secondary school years, compared with 10 per cent of non-offenders. The test performances in all tests were lower than expected after making allowance for size of family, social class, standards of maternal care and standards of housing. Douglas concludes that the reasons for their lack of involvement in school work lie in their pre-school years.

Gibson and West in *Some Concomitants of Early Delinquency* state that in a longitudinal study of a working-class population of schoolboys it was found that there was a close relationship between the incidence of early delinquency and unfavourable social features.[60] A definition of such features has previously been given on page 133. The majority of early delinquents belonged to the minority of severely handicapped families, and only one early delinquent came from the much larger segment of the sample described as having no social handicaps. The authors conclude that the risk of becoming delinquent at an early age is largely determined by comparatively crude external factors such as family income and housing, the main determinant being family income. Many of the parental characteristics were similar to those of the boys previously discussed under the heading of troublesomeness. The ratings of parental marriage as disharmonious, under-vigilance, laxity in rules, unstable personality of father, were all closely related to early delinquency. In a comparison with controls from the same social and intelligence level, the differences on certain items like lack of vigilance and laxity in rules, deviant paternal personality, and disharmonious marital relationships were not significant. The authors conclude that some of the most striking relationships between parental attributes and son's early delinquency may be nothing other than a consequence of a concentration of both parental pathology and delinquency at the lowest social level.

In an earlier study of delinquency in families of very low socio-economic status in a Welsh town, H. Wilson had found a very similar close relationship. The families were known to the medical officer of health for suspected child-neglect. It was found that the rate of delinquency per child at risk was eight times as high as the general rate for boys in the city as a whole, and it was also well over twice the rate prevailing in families other than the research families who lived in the closest proximity to them in two districts of the city which were well known to the police. Furthermore, the research families who lived in low-delinquency areas of the city had a rate of delinquency similar to that of those living in clusters in high-delinquency areas. The rate of recidivism was higher than that of the controls by about a third. The ratio of female to male juvenile delinquency in the research families was one to three, as against the national average of about one to ten. The figures related to detected indictable offences only, of which about 40 per cent are annually taken to court. The parental attributes in general were of a pathological kind, although there was a sizeable group of fathers who had regular work records. They were, however, considerably handicapped by low income, which in those cases where the family was unduly large was well beneath subsistence level.

In this study, as in the study by West and Gibson, it was found that differences in the personality of the mother, as well as marital relationships, had no effect on delinquent behaviour of the children. The main features which were shared by the children of all fifty-two families were extremely low material standards; absence of parental supervision; lax or erratic handling of the children; isolation of the families from their own kin; and in many cases hostility of the neighbourhood.

SUMMARY AND CONCLUSION

An examination of the literature concerned with socially deprived families in Britain makes a rough identification of vulnerable groups possible. Families whose incomes are at or beneath subsistence level consist of those with fathers in full-time work but earning low wages, families of chronically sick or disabled men, fatherless families, and families of unemployed men, many of whom are older workers or unskilled workers who became redundant. While these indices identify vulnerable groups they must not be taken to be sufficient as causes of social deprivation, for it is only in combination with lack of financial resources that they become handicapping. Low *per capita* income is correlated with dietary deficiencies, a low state of general health, a high incidence of prematurity, and perinatal and infant mortality.

Material aspects of deprivation are paralleled by cultural handicaps. Many workers have pointed out the importance of language in stimulating the development of cognitive skills. A child who grows up in the lowest socio-economic class is likely to use a restricted form of language which hinders the development of thought processes and the transmission of cultural values.

The transmission of such values and the training of children in the skills which will be required in adult life are primarily the task of parents in the formative period of childhood. This task has become more complex in the course of this century through industrial innovations, especially the trend towards automation, which makes the training of a highly skilled, literate, adaptable and mobile population increasingly necessary. National wealth has grown considerably in the course of this second industrial revolution, which has meant a constantly increasing general affluence and constantly rising standards of living. A rising standard of living is reflected in new styles of life. The process is aided by greater educational opportunities.

Equality of educational opportunity has not been achieved, but competition for higher education has shifted emphasis on achievement. Greater social mobility also implies greater geographical mobility, and this has important effects on patterns of community life. Close-knit family and neighbourhood networks give way to autonomous living patterns in nuclear family units. Marital relationships are affected by increasing opportunities for wives to work. The need for training the child to become an autonomous adult is increasingly recognised in those socio-economic groups who in previous generations relied heavily on traditional paternalistic patterns of child-rearing. Middle-class methods of child-centredness are gradually adopted and combined with a new tendency towards rational permissiveness. Such methods are not always found to be easy to adopt, and there appears to be much confusion.

One sector of the lower socio-economic group appears to be unable to share in the general rise of living standards. They are largely the families of unskilled manual workers, and may well contain the previously identified vulnerable groups containing specific handicaps, but no detailed work on this has been done. It is not possible, in conditions of material deprivation and in overcrowded living conditions, to practise the new forms of child-centred handling of children. Furthermore, it is difficult for parents whose personality resources are limited to adopt new techniques, especially when they are not supported by family or neighbourhood.

The incidence of malfunctioning of children from this sector of society indicates the considerable cultural handicap suffered by them. Educational under-achievement and early school leaving show that these children are not given the support at home which they need for the full development of their potential. A smaller but significant number of such children also exhibit behavioural problems, such as truanting from school, troublesomeness at school, and delinquent behaviour. While all these behaviour patterns occur in all social classes, the incidence is highest in the sector of socially deprived children. Early delinquency, as contrasted with later and more transient trivial delinquency, is almost entirely confined to this sector, judging by the rather scant information which is at hand.

No research has been done to relate poverty in general to the upbringing of children in particular. It is obvious from the available statistics on the incidence of poverty in Britain that not all the children who are materially deprived will show symptoms of malfunctioning. We do not know the dynamics of family life in such conditions, and we cannot say what personality resources are at work in those families that manage to bring up their children successfully in spite of considerable financial and psychological stress. It must not be forgotten that poverty in itself is considered a disqualifying factor in a society which is based on achievement and economic success. Fathers who do not remain solvent will sooner or later find themselves in trouble, be it as debtors in court, or as tenants in rent arrears. Children who are inadequately dressed may be in trouble over school attendance. Many school activities, like excursions, woodwork classes and domestic science classes, ask for extra money which they cannot supply. In a community with constantly rising standards of living it is not easy for a child whose parents are on a low level of income to keep his self-respect.

Nothing has been said about the effect that social deprivation has on the children themselves, on their feelings about life and their aspirations.

There is no information on those of the child population in poverty who do not get into trouble. Maladjusted or disturbed children are sometimes referred to child-guidance clinics, but children from homes of very low socio-economic status are not usually seen in the clinics, partly because of difficulties of communication with the mothers and in keeping of appointments. Some of these children will eventually find themselves in the care of a local authority children's department. This may be because the parents were evicted for rent arrears, or because of parental illness, desertion, or death. It is at that stage that one can get a glimpse of the tragic world which formed the environment of some of these children. Clare Winnicott discusses the problems that child care workers have to face : the children who are suspicious of anyone or anything outside themselves; the children who feel angry or hostile; the children who withdraw into themselves as a protective measure against frustrations and disappointments; the over-active children who prevent themselves from feeling, because it hurts; and the children who are in a state of depression.[61] It will not be inappropriate to conclude this summary on deprived children by quoting a passage from Mrs Winnicott's article; in discussing the aims of the child care worker she says :

'Our real aim is to keep children alive, and to help them to establish a sense of their own identity and worth in relation to other people. By keeping children alive I am of course referring to maintaining their capacity to feel. If there are no feelings, there is no life, there is mere existence. All children who come our way have been through painful experiences of one kind or another, and this has led many of them to feel angry and hostile, because this is more tolerable than to feel loss and isolation. Our work, therefore, is not easy, because it will lead us to seek contact with the suffering part of each child. . . . '

4. Combating Social Deprivation

Robert Holman

The three previous chapters have examined the extent and nature of social deprivation in income, housing and child socialisation. It would be false, however, to give the impression that some individuals experienced housing deprivation, others income deprivation, and so on. This concluding chapter will show that various forms of social deprivation are often experienced by the same persons. The chapter will then attempt to distinguish certain groups within the broad classification of the socially deprived. Finally, an examination will be made of the effectiveness of some of the social services in combating social deprivation, and some suggestions made for future development.

MULTIPLE DEPRIVATION

The three contributors have made it clear that social deprivation is still extensive. Professor Lafitte estimates that in 1966 in Britain (excluding Northern Ireland) 365,000 families, made up of 995,000 children and 615,000 parents, were in poverty by the old assistance standard, and 450,000 families made up of 1,215,000 children and 780,000 parents by the new standard. K. M. Spencer shows that in 1967 in England and Wales, 1,800,000 dwellings were considered 'unfit';* that 21·7 per cent lacked a hot and cold water supply at three points; 18·6 per cent had no internal water closet, and so on. Dr Wilson draws on educational research and reports which give estimates of those suffering in the field of child socialisation. For instance, it seems that well over half the sons of manual workers who are in the highest ability levels leave school at sixteen years of age or earlier. It would be tempting to add up all these figures and arrive at a total of the socially deprived. This is not possible, for it is clear that many individuals suffer more than one deprivation, and hence

---

* It must be remembered, however, that not all these dwellings would be occupied by families with children.

any totals would include double counting. Herein is contained an important factor, namely that social deprivation is frequently multiple in nature so that the same persons are likely to suffer more than one form. Admittedly, research has not yet concentrated on multiple deprivation, but there is evidence to show persons experiencing at least two deprivations.

Not surprisingly, poverty is associated with deprivation in housing and child socialisation. Spencer makes the general point that low income earners have a much greater chance of having unfit houses and those without basic amenities; a result associated with their greater chance of being in private rented property, which contains proportionately more of the worst housing. R. A. Parker similarly notes a correlation between private rented accommodation and 'poor' families with two or more children.[1] Further, in 1961-2 Greve found the homeless in London were not necessarily unemployed, but tended to have incomes around £10 to £14 which were simply too low to obtain accommodation for a family.[2]

The correlation between low income and deprivation in child socialisation is less well statistically established, except in the field of educational handicap. However, descriptive studies certainly suggest a relationship. For example, the government's wage stop enquiry showed many families unable to give their children pocket-money for school outings, cinema, swimming or holidays, and unable to buy them crayons or toys.[3] Clearly the lack of play and leisure experiences will handicap the social development of children. Further, it appears that the fathers of low income families are more likely to work overtime and hence have less time to spend with their families, less time to stimulate their children through conversation and play, and indeed through all the interaction which contributes to the socialisation process. Dr Wilson draws attention to the work of Douglas amongst others, to show the link between low income and educational deprivation. She concludes (p. 129):

'Here, then, is a close association of poor progress of children at school and early leaving in a group of families who, through incapacitating illness of the father, experienced in many cases financial hardship.'

The occurrence of families experiencing both housing and child socialisation disadvantages is clear. Tyerman's work, for instance, shows a correlation between truancy and slum conditions.[4] Spencer makes the point that poor housing areas also tend to have the worst schools, which further handicaps the children. Above all, the research carried out for the Plowden Report pinpoints the association between school under-achievement and overcrowding and lack of public amenities.[5]

These few examples serve to show that social deprivation—like wealth —is not equally distributed amongst the population. The deprived often suffer in more than one direction.* One reason is the causal relationship between forms of deprivation. For instance, bad housing is not only likely to create conditions which inhibit a child's educational progress, it may also adversely affect his health which, in turn, will lower his capacity as a wage earner, which will reduce his chance of ever obtaining adequate housing. Another, and related reason, is that whatever the type of social deprivation it is frequently — though not invariably — associated with income deprivation. Conversely, adequate income enables its owner to purchase not only comfortable housing but some of the factors which stimulate child socialisation, like play groups, nursery schools, schools with good teacher/pupil ratios, and so on. The point, so obvious that it can easily be overlooked, is that society works on an assumption: namely, that the avoidance of deprivation should largely depend on the possession and use of money. It follows that if social deprivation is to be reduced, combating factors must be made available outside of the power to purchase them (or their purchasing power must be provided). For example, that play groups, adequate housing, good schools should be available to the poor. Further, if social deprivation tends to be multiple in nature, then methods to attack it should be similarly on a multiple basis. This point will be taken up at a later stage.

WHO ARE THE SOCIALLY DEPRIVED?

So far points have been made about the extent and nature of social deprivation. There remains the question, who are the socially deprived? The contributors have mentioned various categories suffering from one particular deprivation. Spencer lists groupings of the housing deprived. An attempt will now be made to enumerate groupings which display deprivation in all three fields dealt with in this publication. The groups are: the low wage earners; large families; fatherless families; the unemployed; the disabled; immigrants; travellers and caravan-dwellers.

Low wage earners: One of the findings of the study by Townsend and Abel-Smith which caused most surprise was that the largest number of people in poverty were supported by a full-time wage.[6] The poverty level used by these two authors was not acceptable to all critics, but any remaining doubts about their essential point were dispelled by the later government enquiry showing, as Professor Lafitte says, that one-third of all the

---

* It must be noted that other forms of deprivation may also be associated with social deprivation. For instance, children suffering psychological deprivation through separation from their parents may also be in socially depriving circumstances. Moreover, the incidence of social deprivation can itself be a reason for children being separated from their homes. In 1967/8 in England and Wales, 1,983 children were received into public care because they were homeless. (Home Office, 'Summary of Local Authorities' Returns of Children in Care at 31st March, 1968'.)

families and children in new standard poverty 'depended on very low-earning fathers who were in full employment'. The families contained a greater than average number of children, but also a large number with two or three children. Some of the fathers were disabled, and hence overlap occurs with other groups in this section. None the less, there is no doubt that low earned income in itself is a major aspect of poverty.

The causation of low earning, and the reasons for its predominance in certain industries rather than others, is a complex subject.[7] However, there is little doubt that the individuals concerned are also likely to suffer in the fields of housing and child socialisation. The preceding section has shown the correlation between these deprivations and low income. Greve shows the low income level of the homeless, many of whom are in full-time work.[2] The 'Circumstances of Families' study reveals that, compared with the normal population of families with at least two children, the low earners had more chance of being housed in private rented unfurnished accommodation.[8] Further, whereas only two per cent of all families with full-time work were not in separate households, the percentage was 7 per cent amongst the poorest.[1] Similarly, the children in low income families will miss some of the socialisation advantages available to those with adequate income.

Large families: The sections on income, housing and child socialisation have all made copious references to large families, usually defined as those with five or more children. There can be little doubt of a relationship between deprivation and family size.

All recent studies of income poverty underline the vulnerable position of the large family. Townsend and Abel-Smith, Coates and Silburn, Hilary Land and the government survey are the foremost examples.[6, 9, 10, 8] Using the last study, Professor Lafitte draws out some most telling figures:

'The proportion in unrelieved poverty rose from 2 per cent of children in one- or two-child families to 11 per cent of those in five-child families, and to 20 per cent of those in larger families.'

Noticeably again, family allowances have not eradicated poverty for large families, even though they receive most from them.

Any family with five or more children will find accommodation difficulties in a country where the overwhelming number of dwellings have only two or three bedrooms. Naturally the problems are intensified when the family also has a low income, with the consequence of being driven into the cheapest part of the private market. Not surprisingly, K. M. Spencer shows that large families are more likely to be overcrowded than other family sizes. In areas of acute accommodation problems the plight of the large family is hard indeed. In the areas surveyed by the Notting Hill Housing Survey, over 80 per cent of all families with five or more children were in conditions of more than 1·5 persons per room.[11]

There is a danger of implying that income and housing deprivation are largely confined to large families. To rectify it, Professor Lafitte and K. M. Spencer add notes of caution. The former points out that nearly two-thirds of poor children were in families of under five children. The latter, that a higher proportion of large families than other families are in council houses, where general amenities are good. However, the picture is further complicated because they may well receive the worst council housing—often old property—because councils usually lack adequate houses of different sizes. Even where large council houses are available, their rent is sometimes such that large families cannot afford it.

If adequate child socialisation depends largely on a regular relationship with parents, it will not be surprising to find children from large families at a disadvantage. According to the Plowden Report their fathers spend less time at home—often because they work overtime and would hence participate less with their offspring; a finding confirmed by *Circumstances of Families*.[5, 8] Further, Dr Wilson calls on the work of J. B. Douglas to describe how children with three or more siblings fare worse than those from smaller families in intelligence, vocabulary rating and mathematical tests; a relationship also underlined by the Plowden Report. Chazan found that of children in schools for the educationally subnormal, over half came from families with five or more children.[12] Family size is not the only factor at work affecting intelligence and school attainment, but that it has a significant influence appears established.

Although outside the scope of this study, it must be interjected that size of family is also related to separation from the family. Packman's research into children in the care of children's departments revealed that 25 per cent of committals to care, 22 per cent of short-term admissions and 11 per cent of long-term cases were from families with five or more children at home.[13] It seems likely that a whole complex of factors is involved here. It is not just that the parents of large families necessarily care less for their children, but rather that they will lack the resources in terms of accommodation, money to buy day care, and so on, which is more available to the smaller family, and which helps prevent reception into care.

It would seem logical that the larger families with their problems of child socialisation should receive extra help in terms of income and housing. All too often, however, the reverse is true. Thus the mothers may be unable to afford the domestic appliances which could give them a little more free time with the children; the father has to work longer hours and thus not only spends less time at home but is probably more tired. Above all, low income and a large number of children may mean cramped accommodation, which can create extra family strains.

Fatherless families: In a study published in 1964, Margaret Wynn estimated a number of 540,000 fatherless families in Great Britain, including 785,000 dependent children.[14] She broke the number down to 175,000 widowed families, 55,000 divorced, 250,000 separated, and 60,000 unmarried. This, as Wynn says, was probably an underestimate, and the Seebohm Committee in 1968 estimated in England and Wales 1,390,000 children in families broken by death, divorce or separation, plus 672,000 illegitimate children under the age of sixteen.[15] However, it must be pointed out that the latter are not necessarily fatherless: for instance, many will live within a cohabitation. The Plowden Report estimates 5 to 6 per cent of the child population in England to be with only one parent.[5] This number would include children living with their father but not mother; in other words, 'motherless children' about whom very little is known.

Not all fatherless families suffer deprivation in the realms of income, housing and child socialisation. On the other hand there is a good deal of evidence to suggest that many do and, in fact, that fatherlessness is an 'at risk' factor associated with such deprivations. A number of studies establish the high incidence of poverty amongst fatherless families. The government report *Circumstances of Families* included relatively few unmarried mothers in its sample by virtue of excluding one-child families. None the less, Professor Lafitte shows that by the 'old standard' of poverty some 100,000 fatherless families with more than one child (amounting to 230,000 children) were 'initially poor'. Of these, some 77,000 were 'assisted' and so taken out of official poverty, but 23,000 families remained unassisted. Marsden and Holman also describe the financial plight of the unmarried or unsupported mothers,[16, 17] while the Plowden Report compares the income of fatherless and normal families as demonstrating the disadvantaged position of the former.[5]

It emerges that even amongst fatherless families there are degrees of income deprivation. For instance, widows receive pensions and hence more money (as well as more sympathy) than other fatherless families. But even amongst widows there are differences, and Marris points out that those with war pensions are better off than those with industrial pensions, while those with ordinary widows' pensions are the least well off.[18]

Divorced and separated wives can collect maintenance, and unmarried mothers can claim an affiliation order from the putative father. But these depend on the ability and willingness of the man to pay. Unmarried mothers appear in a particularly weak position, and Wimperis has shown that few are willing to go to the courts to obtain such an order.[19] Even if they do, the father may disappear or refuse to pay. It is true that attachment of earnings orders can be made by courts, but the difficulty in operating such a scheme is seen in the fact that in 1966 magistrates made such orders to the total of only 934 for the whole country. In addition most unmarried mothers have only one child and therefore cannot receive family allowance. Not surprisingly many have no recourse but to arrange care for their baby while they go out to work, or to draw supplementary allowance.

Even when the mother, especially the unmarried mother, of a fatherless family goes out to work she may still find herself in disadvantageous financial circumstances. A study of 'Mothers in Action', a society for unsupported mothers, found that 23 per cent of those who worked received as wages less than they would have got from supplementary allowance, and 41 per cent under £10.[17] There was evidence that promotion was often barred to them, while, needing employment near the place in which their baby was minded, they often could not seek better-paid posts. The additional expense of paying for baby care made even further inroads into the mother's income.

As with other groups, the lack of income precipitates housing and socialisation deprivation. *Circumstances of Families* showed 32 per cent of fatherless families having defective housing, 31 per cent in overcrowded conditions, and 22 per cent in non-separate households.[8] These proportions are much higher than the average for all families.

It therefore comes as no surprise that, as K. M. Spencer points out, the fatherless should comprise a significant proportion of the homeless. It is not income alone which prevents many fatherless families obtaining adequate housing. Holman found that the comparative youth and mobility of unmarried mothers could count against them qualifying for a council house, while a number of mothers complained that landlords were prejudiced against them.[17]

Poor housing in itself can constitute a handicapping factor in child socialisation. The cramped conditions, lack of play space, no garden, and washing ever-present indoors, not only fail to provide stimulating conditions for child development but can endanger the relationship between mother and child, already at risk because of the lack of a father figure. The effects of the absence of a father, leading to possible role confusion and adverse psychological growth, have been dealt with in other studies and are outside the scope of this volume. Two other factors, however, arise from the absence which may lead to further social deprivation, namely the possibility of the mother working and the placing of the child in day care.

The Plowden Report showed 57 per cent of mothers of fatherless families to be in full-time employment, compared with 38 per cent of those from complete families.[5] The effects on children of mothers working have raised much steam, but a comprehensive review of the available evidence by Yudkin and Holme failed to reveal any 'disastrous consequences'.[20] Indeed, for the unsupported mother the opportunity to live a more normal life by mixing with other people and of earning more money, can psychologically and materially benefit her child. On the other hand, the long hours worked by some mothers from fatherless families, as commented on by the Plowden Report, could lead to extra tiredness and less time spent with the child. What is most regrettable is that some mothers—for reasons of finance or even because assistance officers put pressure on them to work, as instanced by Pauline Morris's study—should have to work against their will.[21]

If a mother works, her child will require some form of care. Those over five years will of course attend school, although there may be difficulties between the time school closes and the time mothers return home. For the under-fives the alternatives appear to be a day nursery, nursery school, play group, care by relatives, daily minding* or private fostering.†

A recent study of these facilities agrees with the Yudkin Report that, generally speaking, the first three are not only preferred by the mothers, but actively benefit the child; while daily minding and private fostering can, by reasons of overcrowding or the inadequacy of the woman in charge, be damaging, although there are numerous exceptions.[17, 22] Placements with relatives have more disadvantages than might be thought, and have been discussed in a study of unsupported mothers.[17] Unfortunately the provision of day nurseries and nursery schools by the local authorities is extremely erratic, as is the provision of play groups by voluntary bodies. Therefore many mothers are forced to turn to the private market of daily minding and private fostering, and so use means of care which may be socially and emotionally damaging to their children.

Finally, research for the Plowden Committee indicated that children from 'atypical families' (mainly those with one natural parent) do not achieve educationally as well as those from normal families.[5] This, taken with the above evidence, constitutes a strong case for saying that fatherless families are an 'at risk' group, vulnerable in terms of the three forms of social deprivation.

The unemployed: The advent of comparatively full employment in postwar Britain reflects a major social advance. However, the 1960s have witnessed a slow increase in unemployment, so that in May 1969 the Department of Employment and Productivity enumerated 523,290 unemployed. There is a surprising lack of social research about unemployment in a full employment society, although *Circumstances of Families* provides some information and Adrian Sinfield of Essex University has undertaken a

* Daily minders are women who, as defined under the Health Services and Public Health Act (1968) look after a child for more than two hours a day for money.
† A private foster child is defined by the 1958 Children Act as one below the upper limit of compulsory school age whose care and maintenance are undertaken for reward for a period exceeding one month by a person who is not a relative or guardian. The 1969 Children and Young Persons Bill at present before Parliament proposes to delete the limitations of 'for reward' and 'one month'.

study of a random sample of unemployed workers in one area.[23]

Circumstances of Families enumerates the sick and unemployed families together, and working from this Professor Lafitte gives figures to show the 'initially poor' of this kind to number 310,000 families by the old standard (330,000 by the new standard), of whom 170,000 were publicly assisted, while 140,000 were not. Thus not only do many unemployed live on the minimum poverty income, others are below. Obviously some do not claim help, while some 15,000 were not brought up to the minimum level because of the operation of the wage stop.

Sinfield points out that the most serious problems of unemployment occurred among the unskilled, the disabled, and elderly workers. They tend to suffer recurrent unemployment, and hence have little chance of building up resources to tide them over rough patches.[7] Clearly they will have little opportunity to obtain adequate housing—apart from council accommodation—and the government survey established 40 per cent of families where the father was unemployed or disabled to be in defective housing, and 29 per cent to be in overcrowded conditions.

Although there are no recent British studies of the effects of unemployment on the socialisation of children, it is reasonably safe to speculate that the material disadvantages would promote handicaps in the ways mentioned in previous sections. Thus Dr Wilson draws attention to the description of the condition of families suffering from the wage stop. It might be thought that the more continued presence of the father at home might partially compensate for low material standards. However, there is no evidence that unemployed fathers do spend more time at home with their children; indeed, they might spend many hours looking for work. In addition the children have to cope with the social difficulty of unemployment, the feeling that their family is apart from most others.

The sick and disabled: There are few statistics relating to the sick and disabled. Townsend points out that about 3 per cent of the population is officially disabled or handicapped, but this is considered an under-estimate.[24]

The evidence already cited from *Circumstances of Families* indicates that housing and income deprivation is sorely felt by this group. The study by Harriett Wilson of fifty-two families suspected of child neglect found a similar correlation.[25] An earlier work by the Willmotts described the financial straits of many of the sick and how they were forced to cut down on such necessities as fuel and food.[26]

A recent survey of the disabled in Tower Hamlets has stressed their multiple deprivation: over one-third of the sample had a weekly income of under £6, and many had also a severe lack of housing amenities, with 45 per cent having no fixed bath and 38 per cent only an outside toilet.[27]

Immigrants: An objective assessment of deprivation amongst immigrants is made difficult by two factors: Firstly, definitions of 'immigrants' differ. References to immigrants usually mean coloured immigrants, although sometimes published figures include others. Moreover, sometimes the term only applies to persons resident in the country for a certain number of years; other times it counts coloured people who were born here. It follows that the few studies which do exist may not be strictly comparable. Secondly, the issue of immigrants has been taken out of perspective by racialist and political propagandists, who have used the question of colour for their own ends. The following sentences are made within these limitations.

There are few studies of income distribution amongst immigrants, although one study in a Yorkshire town showed the average income of Asian heads of households to be as low as £13 per week.[28] A number of cases reported in the press suggest that immigrants find difficulty in obtaining employment commensurate with their qualifications. Unjust though this may be, it does not necessarily mean that they live below the poverty line. Clearly the situation is confused by a lack of research, but three studies do offer pointers. A study in Birmingham of Handsworth (which contains well over one-third of the city's coloured school-leavers) in 1966 revealed 72 per cent of the coloured boys going into unskilled jobs, compared with 43 per cent of the white; 27 per cent into skilled crafts compared with 50 per cent; and none into skilled occupations compared with 7 per cent.[29] Therefore it may well be that proportionately more are to be found in the lowest paid jobs..The PEP survey *Racial Discrimination* also indicates that racial prejudice leads to immigrants having the jobs lowest in status and pay.[30] The recently published sample census (1966) Commonwealth Immigrant Tables showed coloured immigrants to be disproportionately found in manual jobs, and even amongst these few have the job of supervisor or foreman. It must be noted, however, that variants occur between immigrant groups, so that Indians have a higher percentage than West Indians in professional jobs.

There appears little doubt that coloured immigrants are deprived in the housing sense. In Birmingham, for instance, they are concentrated in areas of poorer housing like Soho, Handsworth and Sparkbrook.[32] The report of the Committee on Housing in Greater London described immigrants in general as being 'too heavily overcrowded' and particularly mentioned numbers living in single rooms for which they often paid over-high rents.[33] The housing survey in Notting Hill showed coloured immigrants more likely to be in furnished rented accommodation, that is the weakest form of accommodation, than white residents. They also received the worst value for their rents, and the West Indians had the highest rate of overcrowding in comparison with white groups.[11] The 1966 census confirms that immigrants from the West Indies and Asia are disproportionately found in overcrowded conditions, and in privately rented furnished accommodation, all over the country.[31] If, as believed, immigrants are amongst the lowest income earners, then clearly they will be driven into the worst housing conditions. Moreover, the PEP publication and the work of Burney suggest that sectors of the private and council housing market are prejudiced against coloured immigrants.[30, 34]

There is no national study of the socialisation of immigrant children in Britain. None the less, it is reasonable to assume that the location of many such children in low income families, overcrowded dwellings, and areas often characterised by overcrowded schools, would lead to social disadvantages. In addition there is the problem of immigrant mothers who wish to find substitute or foster homes for their children because they have to or want to work. The danger of inadequate substitutes, of the lack of local authority facilities, are as applicable here as for fatherless families. The present writer is undertaking research into private fostering, and has noticed situations where coloured children are placed with foster parents from a different culture. The young children will incorporate the attitudes, educational aspirations and behavioural patterns of the foster parents. When, as is usual, they return home, the different socialisation process incorporated by the children may well bring them into conflict with the natural parents. Most especially, there are cases of immigrants with high educational aspirations who receive back children from some lower working-class foster homes where educational values have not been instilled. The result can be disappointment and conflict. Lastly, there are cases of children left behind in their native land—particularly the West Indies—when young, while their parents emigrated to Britain. Brought up by relatives, often grandparents, it is frequent for the children to be sent to their parents in Britain when aged about ten or twelve years. Having been socialised in one culture, the children face the problems of adapting to a different culture and environment, to different parent figures, and often to new siblings and a different position in the family hierarchy. Child care officers report that sometimes such children find extreme difficulties in accepting their parents, who may use different forms of control and have different expectations from the grandparents; in fitting into a neighbourhood so different from their West Indian one; and in making the most of the British educational system.*

---

* Since this publication was written there has appeared an important work on immigration, namely *Colour and Citizenship* by the Institute of Race Relations.[35] Its findings confirm the trends specified above in relation to employment and housing. It calculates a total coloured population in Britain in 1966 of 924,200. It underlines the concentration of immigrants in poor housing conditions in twilight zones, making special mention of the containment policy of Birmingham.

Travellers and caravan dwellers: K. M. Spencer makes clear the distinction between the two groups who live in caravans. The first are mobile, are often descended from gypsies, and a conservative estimate of their number in England and Wales is 15,000 persons.[36] These are popularly known as tinkers or travellers. The second live on permanent residential caravan sites, and Spencer puts their number at more than 300,000.

Both groups suffer from housing deprivation in terms of overcrowding within the caravans and lack of amenities on their sites. Little is known of their income, although it is suggested that travellers earn less than a settled manual worker, while those on permanent sites appear to be there because they are not able to afford other types of accommodation.

Once again, income and housing restrictions are likely to affect adversely the upbringing of children. Moreover, traveller families tend to be much larger than average, the parents illiterate, and the children to attend school but spasmodically. A government survey estimated that less than 10 per cent of the school-age children attended school, while the teenagers appeared backward because of their restricted vocabulary and experience, although there was evidence to show they could make this up.[36] Their lack of education means that the opportunities of the children—if they so wished—to choose other forms of living are extremely limited. It is rare to find local authorities or voluntary bodies providing for travellers or those on residential sites the nursery schools, play groups, schools or youth clubs which play an important part in the socialisation of children in other parts of the community.

The above groupings are of necessity an over-simplification. They exclude certain groups such as alcoholics or the mentally ill, whose position relates to personality disorders yet who, as a result, may well suffer the social deprivations mentioned above. None the less it is useful to identify groups whose social circumstances mean not only deprivations for themselves, but involve a risk of their children being termed delinquent, of being separated from them, and in general of having little chance to break free from the material hardships experienced by their parents. Once the groupings are made clear, it is for government social policy to allocate resources where they are most needed.

WHERE ARE THE DEPRIVED?

Just as the identification by groupings of the socially deprived should enable social policy to focus its resources more effectively, so should their identification according to their geographical location.

Differences between regions in Britain are recognised in connection with certain measurables. It is known that housing conditions tend to be better in the south-east; that children tend to weigh more, and general practitioners be proportionately more in abundance in London and the south-east; that Ulster and the north-east have a higher rate of unemployment, and so on. The government has commissioned regional plans and inaugurated new regional machinery in the economic planning councils and planning boards in efforts to encourage economic growth in certain regions. But regional studies have failed to identify the comparatively small areas of intense deprivation. This requires highly specialised studies of communities, which have been notably lacking in post-war Britain. A partial rectification is now occurring and, apart from the completed studies mentioned below, there are on-going studies of parts of York, Liverpool and Newcastle.

The study of St Ann's by Coates and Silburn revealed a high incidence of the types of social deprivation with which this study is concerned—an incidence obviously much higher than in other parts of Nottingham.[9]

The study on parts of Notting Hill in the Borough of Kensington and Chelsea showed a similar concentration. The Borough as a whole has 26·9 per cent of its resident population born outside of the British Isles, compared with 3·6 per cent for England and Wales. In the wards actually surveyed the tenure patterns were owner-occupied 8 per cent, compared with 43·2 per cent for Greater London; local authority housing was 5·4 per cent compared with 21·6 per cent; privately rented unfurnished accommodation 42·8 per cent compared with 28 per cent; privately rented furnished accommodation 35·1 per cent compared with 4 per cent. Overcrowding was intense, with over 33 per cent of all households living at more than 1·5 persons per room. 13·1 per cent of households had no access to a fixed bath or shower, and a further 53·3 per cent shared a fixed bath or shower. Inhabitants were also characterised by low incomes, especially amongst large families.[11]

Rex and Moore's research on Sparkbrook in Birmingham has been severely condemned on methodological grounds.* None the less it shows how one part of Sparkbrook is characterised by a comparatively high incidence of immigrants and overcrowding.

It must be added that the areas surveyed so far are ones with a number of voluntary agencies, especially community work bodies, working in them. Indeed the surveys may have occurred there because these areas were 'fashionable' deprived areas. It is likely that studies of places less

---

* V. Karn in 'A note on *Race, Community and Conflict:* a study of Sparkbrook' in *Race*, 1967; and M. R. Atkinson, 'A critical interpretation of the sociology of John Rex', Discussion Papers Series 'C', 12; Birmingham University, 1969. Valerie Karn's criticism of the methodological errors and assessments made by Rex and Moore must be among the most devastating ever made on a piece of social research. She shows that they give a comparatively false picture of a piece of Sparkbrook; that they greatly exaggerated the degree of overcrowding; that the immigrants rather than becoming increasingly segregated in one lodgings house area of Sparkbrook may actually have become more dispersed in the period 1961-4; and that increase in their actual numbers was moderate rather than dramatic.

attractive to social workers may reveal even worse situations.

The Plowden Report undertook valuable research from an educational angle by correlating certain social symptoms with certain geographical areas.[5] It listed indicators of deprivation (which are given later in this chapter) as being clustered in certain deprived zones, especially inner ring areas. This research, described in Vol. II of the Report, included a study in the Midlands of the social services available to primary school children in different types of area. In the inner ring area they found that a much higher percentage of the children had to be visited at home by the social services for cases where the child's 'health, social adjustment or educational performance appeared to be suffering because of adverse home or other social factors', than in the small town and county area also studied. Significantly, children in the town's outer ring, mainly composed of council estates and often families rehoused from the inner ring, displayed far fewer problems, so indicating the probable positive 'influence of housing conditions and general environment'. In addition the city area suffered much more from shortage of social workers than the county or small town.

Putting together the above studies, and using material available from the census and from local authorities, there appears a strong case for saying that socially deprived families are frequently found in confined geographical areas identifiable by certain physical and social characteristics, some of which are as follows : *

(i) A geographical location between a city's business centre and the outer suburban areas. Frequently called 'twilight zones' they have been left behind as the business and outer rings have been developed.

(ii) A relatively high number of immigrants. A further example of their concentration is found in the Yorkshire town studied by Karn, where 54 per cent of its coloured immigrants were in two of the town's twenty-one enumeration districts.[28] Immigrants are not necessarily an indication of a deprived zone, and it would be a mistaken policy to give extra aid to areas simply because of their statistical preponderance. Indeed, many immigrants have given an area stability, and possess skills and leadership potential. On the other hand, their frequent lack of earning power, plus a lack of residential qualifications for council housing, does often drive them to the cheapest private rented housing commonly found in the twilight zones.

(iii) Housing conditions characterised by overcrowding and a lack of amenities. The housing stock is frequently of older, often Victorian houses. As Spencer points out, age of dwelling stock is highly

---

* Because so little work has been done on area deprivation, an attempt has been made to collect possible indicators of social deprivation according to geographical units so that they can be seen beside the national average. These are given in Appendices A and B.

correlated with levels of obsolescence and lack of amenities. This is likely to be privately rented property, which also displays the more adverse housing factors, although they do provide a greater variety of types and sizes than council or owner-occupied houses.

(iv)   Higher than average proportions of unskilled and semi-skilled workers.

(v)   Higher than average proportions of families receiving State supplements in the form of cash or kind.

(vi)   A higher than normal incidence of large families.

(vii) Comparatively large numbers of fatherless families.

(viii) A lack of play space and recreational facilities. Thus the Soho ward in Birmingham, an area with large numbers of children, immigrants and overcrowding, has no public play space. In 1963 in North Kensington, London, up to 80 per cent of children aged two to five had 'nowhere to play'.[11]

(ix)   Poorer health than is found in the population as a whole. Dr Wilson draws attention to Dr Asher's research in Birmingham, which found the number of untreated defects in primary school children greatest in the school serving an area of 'many decrepit houses, shifting populations, and many problem families', so that nearly one-third of the inner ring school had untreated conditions or defects. Noticeably, inner ring areas are also characterised by higher infant mortality rates.

(x)   A high incidence of child deprivation and delinquency. Dr Wilson establishes that delinquency and truancy correlate with 'slum' areas. Another indicator is the number of children who have to be taken into the care of or are supervised by children's departments. Thus statistics kept by the Birmingham City Corporation show wards with the other characteristics of this list to have many more children taken into care or supervised than council estates and suburban areas. Plowden suggests also that they are characterised by high rates of poor school attendance and truancy.

(xi)   There is also some evidence, as in the Plowden Report, that the areas have the worst social services. The schools tend to be older and classes larger, the staff turnover rate greater, the number of nursery places fewer. J. W. B. Douglas, in his study, says that children on council estates possess better education chances because they have both better schools and better housing.[37] It also appears that trained social workers are also at a minimum, perhaps being attracted to more pleasant surroundings, while day care in the form of day nurseries and play groups are conspicuous by their absence.

It is not claimed that socially deprived families are only in areas with the above characteristics. On the contrary, some are found on council estates and presumably in suburban areas.[38, 39] But generally there is a tendency for such families to be concentrated in particular and definable areas which come to be called deprived areas or communities. Although one result is that the families are embroiled in a circle of poverty, at least their location, if identified, should allow local and central government to allocate extra resources to them on an area basis.

COMBATING SOCIAL DEPRIVATION: SOME APPROACHES

It has been shown that social deprivation exists on a substantial scale and that it can be partially identified with certain groupings and localities. Nearly all people will agree with the desirability of eradicating deprivation, even though they may differ concerning the extent and type of help to be given, and even if they differ over the ultimate objectives of social policy.* Two questions then follow: Which services and approaches are employed to combat social deprivation? How effective are they?

Many readers will be familiar with the structure of the social services.† But a knowledge of their structure is not a sufficient account of the attack on social deprivation. For the social services—although they contribute to social policy—are the expression of and the means through which policy is executed. Hence they can represent the general approaches that the local or central government uses to tackle problems, while they themselves can also use these various approaches. This will become clearer if three available approaches are distinguished:

The general or universalist approach attempts to raise standards for all by providing services aimed at virtually all the population. The health and education services are open to all, and it is hoped that a general improvement — like raising the school-leaving age — will benefit the whole of society and not just the socially deprived. However, it would be naïve to believe that general approaches necessarily do benefit all to an equal degree. It may be that the more educated sections avail themselves more of these services, or, as Professor Kahn says, 'the sophisticated and the mobile cream the top'.[40] The result, therefore, could be a widening in educational attainment between sections of society.

The socially deprived can be classified into groups, and hence policy can use a specialised approach whereby benefits are available only to those

---

* 'Social policy' has various definitions. Slack thinks the most useful is that by Lafitte: 'In the main social policy is an attempt to steer the life of society along channels it would not follow if left to itself'. Quoted in K. Slack, *Social Administration and the Citizen*, Michael Joseph, London, 1966. Professor Marsh discusses the objectives of social policy in regard to the welfare state in *The Future of the Welfare State*, Penguin, London, 1964.

† The substance of this publication was presented to the United Nations as a report on Socially Deprived Families. It also contained, for the benefit of foreign readers, an outline of the British social services.

within the defined categories, with—hopefully—the benefit approximating to their particular needs. Obvious examples are pensions for the disabled, unemployment pay for those out of work, shelter for the homeless.

Deprivation can also be identified—as was shown in the previous section—according to geographical area. Therefore central or local government can use a priority approach by which resources are directed to areas considered most in need. Growing use has been made of this approach since the Plowden Report recommended 'positive discrimination' to divert extra educational resources to areas where children are at a disadvantage.[5] The recommendations have been partially implemented and 'educational priority areas' chosen. The government has also instituted an urban aid programme for the period 1969-1973 to tackle 'social problems of certain communities in areas of special need'. This programme will be discussed later, but it is as well to point out that Plowden did not invent the priority idea. The Newsom Report in 1963 recommended special educational help for slum areas.[41] Moreover, for many years the central government, in giving grants to local authorities for educational and other purposes, has taken into account the size of population and child population. Supplementary grants are geared to the number of children under five, people over sixty-five, school children in excess of prescribed population, density and sparsity of population, declining population, and metropolitan areas. Grants are also proportionate to the rateable value of areas. However, once receiving the money, the local authority determines how to spend it, it does not necessarily go to its most deprived parts. In housing, also, Spencer mentions the designation of 135 local authorities as 'priority areas' where more housing is allowed to be built. More positive priority housing help was called for by the Milner Holland Report with regard to areas of bad housing concentration, while the National Committee for Commonwealth Immigrants wanted areas with special difficulties accepted as a national responsibility.[33, 42]

The fact that at least three approaches can be distinguished does not mean the socially deprived can be helped by only one. A family with an unemployed father and school children living in a 'priority' area might benefit from the general, specialised and priority approach. Nor should the approach be equated with any particular type of social work skill. The use of casework, vocational training, material help, etc., might be appropriate to any or all of the approaches. The approach determines the persons or areas to receive the certain skills, materials or other resources.

COMBATING SOCIAL DEPRIVATION: EFFECTIVENESS

The second question posed was how effective is the attempt to combat social deprivation? A full answer would require a book to itself and involve a close examination of the intention, extent, practices and results of social policy, as well as of the social services. Such a book would be hampered by the lack of research studies which evaluate and measure the work of various types of approaches, services and skills. It might be thought that a decrease in deprivation would be a measure of a service's effectiveness, but the relationship between cause and effect is not a straightforward one. For instance, a betterment in children's health might be thought due to an improved school health service and the provision of school meals. In fact it may have stemmed from economic policy and full employment, giving most families a more secure income. More locally, children in a priority area may improve their educational attainment compared with similar children in a similar area not benefiting from educational priority resources. But the improvement may be due to other changes in the area, like better housing, or even because the children were stimulated by being researched.

The methodological problems posed by attempts to evaluate effectiveness are not insuperable. But as yet few reliable studies exist, and so a complete and comprehensive evaluation is beyond the scope of this chapter. Instead, the writer will pinpoint five subjects which appear particularly relevant to the services and approaches affecting the socially deprived. They spring from certain assumptions, namely, that help offered should be comprehensive in its coverage; that the quality and extent of services and resources should depend on need rather than other factors; that potential clients should have knowledge of their 'rights' to services and benefits; and that there should be some degree of consumer participation in the social services. These assumptions lead to a discussion of effectiveness under five heads: the coverage of the social security system; the distribution and quality of local authority and voluntary services; the non-take-up of services; the British 'poverty programme'; and client participation. Two points remain: No claims are made to comprehensiveness of evaluation. For instance, the National Health Service is given little attention because it embodies the general approach and covers the whole population and not just the socially deprived. None the less, it could be argued that its middle-class orientation discriminates against the socially deprived. Next, any criticisms of existing policies and services do not imply that they have not made great contributions. But the intent of the succeeding pages is to raise questions in order to discuss possible improvements.

THE COVERAGE OF THE SOCIAL SECURITY SYSTEM

The British social security system has much to commend it. Its centralised nature means that the level of income maintenance benefits does not greatly vary from area to area.* Moreover, the insurance payments are accepted as a right, not a charity, and the system does cover substantial numbers of the population. Few would deny that the post-war system is

---

* However, there will be variations in the discretionary payments which local officers make on the basis of their interpretation of central rules.

more comprehensive and humane than that of the days of widespread unemployment in the 1930s when, according to Lavers and Rowntree, 17·7 per cent of the population were in poverty.[43] None the less, the present system still leaves many in poverty. No social security system can be regarded as truly comprehensive when around 7 per cent of families and one in eleven of the child population is in poverty.

As Lafitte shows, families in poverty can be divided into those whose heads were in full-time work and those whose main income came through the social security system. Those actually receiving state assistance were, in the main, fatherless families, the unemployed and the disabled.* Generally speaking they had failed to qualify for insurance benefit; had exhausted their right to it; found it insufficient; were outside its scope; or suffered from the wage stop. They were thus helped through the Supplementary Benefits Commission, and hence had to experience the unpopular and, to many, humiliating means test. How can these groups be helped? The Child Poverty Action Group has long depicted the sufferings caused by the 'wage stop' and its modification—or even abolition—might well bring some relief.[44] Particular interest groups call for special allowances for their members at realistic levels; thus some want a fatherless families allowance, and the Disablement Income Group, an allowance based on the fact of rather than the cause of disability. Presumably the members would qualify regardless of insurance payments (as happens in regard to the health service). They are thus questioning the insurance principle, for so long dear to the heart of British social security. If this line is pursued the level of state payments would depend on need rather than on the type and cause of poverty and the person's insurance record. The implied distinction between the deserving (the insured) and the undeserving (the uninsured) would be abolished, but so also—presumably—would be the individual insurance payment contribution, which would be incorporated into the direct taxation system.

The second group are the low income earners. Professor Lafitte shows that a tenth of all manual workers earned two-thirds or less of the wage of the average manual worker, while half of these had earnings not exceeding

---

* Anomalies abound in the financial provision for the physically disabled. Those disabled at work are covered by the Industrial Injuries Scheme, which has a fairly comprehensive range of benefits. The victims of crimes of violence or someone else's negligence may be compensated through the Criminal Injuries Compensation Board or the courts. Those disabled through other causes, including those handicapped from birth, have had to receive Supplementary Benefit. However, in July 1969 the government announced new plans which included an 'invalidity pension', based on earnings, for people forced to retire early by illness, an 'attendance allowance' for the very severely disabled, and a relaxation of the earnings rule for wives who have to work because their husbands are disabled. *Social Insurance: proposals for earnings-related, short-term and invalidity benefits*, HMSO, Cmnd. 4124 (1969).

60 per cent of it. This supports the findings of the 1966 government survey, that low earning is a prime cause of poverty. What can be done to relieve this form of poverty? Professor Lafitte names three ways— reducing direct taxation on low incomes, raising the level of the lowest earnings by minimum wage legislation, and enlarged family allowances. He outlines the pros and cons of each, and it suffices to say that the United Nations study should provide valuable evidence of how these methods have worked in Europe. A fourth suggestion is to allow low earners to draw supplementary social security benefits in order to bring them up to the minimum level. (Noteworthily, the government has already conceded this principle by allowing low earners to claim exemption from health prescription charges). Conceivably, some employers might deliberately keep wages down, knowing that employees could reach the minimum level through the government services. However, it is equally conceivable that the government could recoup the extra outlay by taxation on employers —a moot point, for many low earners are actually in the employ of government industries and organisations.

All the foregoing assumes that the supplementary benefit level is a just measure of the poverty line. Using the May 1969 levels, an adult not of pensionable age, who is a householder, would receive or have his income brought up to £4 11s. per week, plus an allowance for rent. A married couple would get £7 9s. Additionally, allowances are paid for children, varying from £1 7s. for a child under five to £2 1s. for a child aged thirteen to fifteen years.* There appears to be a strong case for saying that although such levels can tide people over a temporary crisis, they are quite inadequate for long-term dependence as occurs with unmarried mothers and the long-term unemployed.† Research studies of unsupported mothers have shown the unrealistic nature of these levels, a point further illus- trated by a series of case studies of the disabled, unmarried mothers and the unemployed in the *Guardian* newspaper in 1969.[46, 17, 45] For instance, the cost of children's items such as shoes, clothes and toys—which are expensive and repetitive for growing children—does not seem adequately catered for, and objects like expanding gates or bars across windows for families in top flats are not catered for at all. In addition there seems little money to meet the unexpected crisis which most families can take in their stride—for instance, having to keep heaters on while a child is ill. Families suffering from these pressures appear to cut down their expenses in three

---

* The rates were raised in November 1969, a householder receiving £4 16s., a couple £7 17s., a child under five £1 8s.

† A recipient may receive discretionary grants for items of an exceptional nature like blankets, but this depends on local rulings by officers. In addition, after two years the weekly income is increased by ten shillings, although this is expected to replace discretionary additions up to this amount.

regrettable directions : on food, where they will miss out fresh fruit, salads and regular meat; on outings, holidays and play groups, the kind of items which help in a child's socialisation process; and on clothes, where many families still rely on second-hand clothes, often bought from jumble sales, which make the children who wear them feel inferior to their friends.[45] As Professor Marsh puts it, our income maintenance policies seem directed 'at the right to exist, rather than to live the full life . . . '[46]*

Reasoning of this nature caused Professors Townsend and Abel-Smith to devise a different measure of poverty. They used as a minimum 40 per cent above the lowest national assistance standard (plus rent) and by this means calculated that between 1953 and 1960 the numbers in poverty increased from 7·8 per cent to 14·2 per cent of the total population.[6] Of course their level is as arbitrary as any other, but few will deny that present levels are insufficient. Both in its coverage and in the levels of some of its benefits, the British social security system leaves much room for improvement.

VARIABILITY IN VOLUNTARY AND LOCAL AUTHORITY PROVISION

Any variables of provision should spring from the different needs of areas. One of the advantages of a centralised government service like the Department of Health and Social Security is its ability to direct resources over the whole country and hence—in theory—to maintain services of similar standards. An examination of the distribution of voluntary bodies and of the quantity and quality of local authority services gives a different picture.

Distribution of voluntary bodies: Voluntary bodies constitute resources which can be used to combat social deprivation. Ideally they should be in the areas of greatest need, but their distribution is limited and at times irrational.

First, consideration must be given to the great voluntary societies which have branches in many places. The National Society for the Prevention of Cruelty to Children has most of its workers in the industrial areas of Lancashire, Yorkshire, the Tyne Valley, South Wales and London.[13] Family Service Units are found predominantly in large cities such as Sheffield, Leicester, Liverpool, Manchester, Birmingham, and various boroughs in London. Smaller county boroughs and counties tend to lack units, as do some large towns, e.g. Bristol. The valuable work of the citizens' advice bureaux is sometimes more available in smaller authorities than in those with much larger populations. For instance, Tower Hamlets

---

* Professor Marsh makes a number of other stringent criticisms of the social security system, including its many anomalies. See D. Marsh, *The Future of the Welfare State*, Penguin, 1964.

with a population under 200,000 has six offices while Birmingham's populace of over a million has but one. Similarly, the London region has more offices than the West Midlands, East Midlands and the North East put together.

Similar patterns appear amongst the location of locally based voluntary groups and community work projects. A study of existing organisations in towns as recorded in the local directories of councils of social service reveals, for instance, a vast number of organisations in east and south-east London, but fewer in areas of a greater absolute population like Glasgow. If the Church is regarded as a voluntary social work body, then there is a very active and socially aware body of clergy in the Diocese of Southwark, compared with more inward-looking clergy in some areas.

Other examples of erratic distribution could be multiplied. They include important services like housing associations and play groups. Such distribution is justified if the areas most needing these services actually get them, but there is no such evidence. Packman, studying voluntary bodies and deprived children, found no correlation between distribution and need. She points out that voluntary children's societies largely draw their children from 'London and its surrounding counties, from East Anglia and from counties and boroughs along the south coast. On the whole the Midlands, Wales and the North contributed proportionately fewer children to voluntary society care.'[13] However, the latter areas did not have lesser need. Similarly, the comparative lack of NSPCC inspectors in the Midlands by no means meant that there was not a high incidence of the type of families they might help. Nor, Packman discovered, did the provision of voluntary services compensate for low standards in local authority services. Paradoxically, it may even be that the best local authority and voluntary services go together.

The uneven distribution of voluntary services can even be seen within single local authority units. For example, Soho and Sparkbrook, two deprived wards of similar population, for alphabetical reasons appear next to each other in publications of the Birmingham Statistical Office. On all the following indicators Soho is numerically more deprived than Sparkbrook—number of children under fourteen years, coloured immigrants, persons per occupied dwelling, persons per household, persons in density of over one-and-a-half per room.[47] In addition the child care problems are greater.[48] Yet voluntary help has most rapidly developed in Sparkbrook, where there are comparatively large numbers of play groups and a community association heavily financed by the local authority and with a seconded local authority worker, while outside trusts have also poured in a good deal of money. Nor do these voluntary efforts indicate a lack of local authority interest for, apart from financing the association, it has done more for Sparkbrook than Soho in regard to council housing, playing fields, recreational facilities, and public open space. Similarly in Notting

Hill, one of London's worst areas, there are twenty social action groups, two neighbourhood centres, five street associations, a district play group, a community workshop, and the Notting Hill Housing Service. Yet there are other areas in London as bad—if not worse—but with few if any voluntary organisations. Of course the Sparkbrooks and Notting Hills require their organisations, and more. The point being made is the haphazard development of voluntary help; the chances of inhabitants being helped depends not on need itself but whether they live in a 'fashionable' deprived area.

To sum up: Although it is not possible to discuss the quality of voluntary services, it is clear that nationally and locally their numerical distribution is extremely uneven. Nationally, London and its surrounding areas appear to have a preponderance of the voluntary societies, even taking population into account. Some reasons for this are obvious. Historically, the national societies have made their headquarters in London and, as a perusal of their addresses shows, remain there.[49] The capital's wealth no doubt explains why so many trusts, which can back voluntary bodies, are also there. It is less easy to understand why in a single city one part can receive the attentions of voluntary help, and others not. No doubt once started a snowballing effect occurs and a good publicity machine may attract the backing of the local authority. Or in the case of Notting Hill, the vision, enterprise and radicalism of the voluntary organisations—although far from winning local authority support—succeeded in attracting even more voluntary help and resources.

Whatever the causes, the distribution of voluntary organisations is not related to the needs of individuals, groups or areas. Can it be rectified? Possibly large voluntary bodies could co-ordinate activities. Some attempt might be made by them to assess need and to distribute resources accordingly. Perhaps more gaps could be filled if the government accepted some responsibility for funding local voluntary bodies in neglected areas—especially those outside of the metropolis—a subject which will be raised again.

Local authority variability: In contrast to voluntary bodies, local authorities have legal obligations to provide certain services, so more uniformity is to be anticipated. However, their interpretations of both duties and permissive powers vary so widely that vast differences are found between the same services in different areas, as can be illustrated in the fields of income, housing and child socialisation.

Income maintenance is mainly a central government responsibility, but local authorities are able to supplement the income of the families' school children through educational maintenance and clothing grants. As the authorities use different types of means test to assess eligibility, give varying levels of help, and advertise the grants with marked differences of enthusiasm, it is no surprise that even the Department of Education and Science concedes the existence of wide ranges of provision between authorities.[50]

Dr Harriett Wilson and the present writer have stressed the valuable role of play groups, day nurseries and nursery schools in aiding the *socialisation* of children from socially deprived families. Few local authorities are known to run play groups, although some grant aid to voluntary ones. More detailed figures are available for day nurseries, the work of Packman, the National Society of Children's Nurseries and the Plowden Report agreeing on the erratic nature of provision.[13, 51, 52, 5] For example, in the 1960s Derbyshire had 18·6 day nursery places per 1,000 of the population under five. Staffordshire had three, while twenty-seven county boroughs and thirty-seven counties had none at all.[52] Plowden showed that in the London area as many as 34 per cent of the under-fives had attended nurseries compared with meagre proportions in other areas. Not surprisingly, many areas have long waiting lists even for priority places reserved for children in difficult circumstances. In 1967 Birmingham had 290 priority cases waiting. In other areas these would have received a place.

In 1967 only 6 per cent of under-fives in England and Wales attended nursery education.[50] Even this low average hides great area differences. To take one example, Bristol had 48·2 local authority nursery education places per 1,000 children under five; Leeds had 3·7, and others had none at all.

Children in large families and single children in fatherless families are particularly liable to miss constant stimulation from adults and other children outside the family circle. As a preventive measure local authorities have powers under the National Health Service (Family Planning) Act, 1967, not only to continue financing voluntary bodies but to provide advice and contraceptives themselves. Contraceptive services for the unmarried, and domiciliary help for women with young families, is now feasible if local authorities fully use their powers. By the autumn of 1968 only 17 per cent had fully implemented the act.[53]

If, as generally thought, pre-school experience stimulates children's social and educational development, then those by chance resident in negligent authorities are at a severe disadvantage. Similarly, the chances of receiving local authority help to avoid illegitimate children or over-large families depends on the luck of where women live.

Local authority total contributions to day nurseries and nursery schools are not impressive. The former have actually decreased in number since the 1940s; the latter remain in the same proportion to the population as in the 1930s. Turning to housing deprivation the position is somewhat different, for local authorities can point to numerical improvements. The amount of local authority housing has steadily increased, and in the years 1965-1969 rose by 40 per cent compared with the previous four years.[54] Penelope Hall points out that overcrowding, as measured in persons per room, has decreased since the 1920s.[55] Without denying the fact of progress, three qualifications are necessary. Firstly, reduction in overcrowding is attributable to a fall in family size as well as housing policy. Secondly, some local housing problems, like homelessness, are if anything increasing. Thirdly, any general improvements mask enormous variations between housing authorities. Spencer has already depicted great differences concerning the numbers of dwellings built, methods of council house allocation, rent levels, interpretation of statutory standards of dwellings, and the use of powers to designate improvement areas. Attention will now be drawn to differing housing provision for three vulnerable groups who include socially deprived families—the homeless, unsupported mothers, and travellers.

Jean Packman studied the provision for homeless families over a large number of authorities.[13] Known as Part III accommodation (from the section of the National Assistance Act, 1948), it is usually regarded as a temporary expedient, not a permanent home. She found that some authorities had no temporary accommodation at all. The standards of others were sometimes so low—families were put in former workhouse buildings alongside the old and infirm—that child care officers often preferred to receive children into care rather than allow them entry. Some authorities enforced a strict time limit on tenure in temporary accommodation, perhaps as short as three nights, while refusing to take fathers at all, even at the cost of splitting up the family.*

By contrast, other authorities provided not only temporary but permanent accommodation for the homeless, refused to split fathers from their children, and helped with supporting services in the form of social workers, resident staff and half-way homes as a means of rehabilitation. Liverpool, for instance, cares for whole families in modern buildings, has intermediate accommodation, and makes council houses available for the homeless.

Local authorities have no statutory obligations to accommodate unsupported mothers or travellers.† A minority do give some preference to the former. The counties of Hampshire and Hertfordshire have made provision for travellers, and the London Borough of Redbridge encouraged the development of a play group and education for their children.[56] These are exceptions; generally, unsupported mothers — especially the unmarried —find great difficulties in obtaining council housing, while travellers are

---

* In 1966 a joint circular from the Home Office, the Ministry of Housing and Local Government, and the Ministry of Health, deprecated rigid time rules and the exclusion of husbands.

† Part 2 of the Caravan Sites Act, 1968, gives the minister power to make site provision for travellers and caravan dwellers a duty. As yet the power has not been enforced.

treated as 'undesirable', and in places council employees have resorted to physical force in order to move them on.

Leaving the distribution of services, further light is shed on area variability by examining the numbers of *social workers* and other workers employed by local authority social services. In 1962 health and welfare departments published their numbers of health visitors, home helps and social workers. Professor Townsend commented that, even taking population proportions into account, some 'councils possess from four to ten times as many home helps as others . . . there are three and four times as many health visitors and social workers'.[57] The Seebohm Report, referring to 1965, found the differences still great. In England and Wales health visitors varied between authorities from 0·02 to 0·21 per thousand population, home helps from 0·189 to over 1·260 per thousand. The number of social workers in health and welfare departments averaged 0·05, but they included one county borough with none at all, another seventy-seven authorities below average and, at the other extreme, thirteen authorities with over 0·1 social workers per thousand, and another fifty-six also above average.[15]

Child care officers, entrusted with much of the preventive work of local authorities as well as receptions into care, meet many fatherless families, large families, the homeless, and many others in socially depriving circumstances. For the year 1960, Packman calculated an average of one child care officer for every ten-and-a-half thousand children under eighteen in England and Wales. The range was from an officer to every three-and-a-half thousand to one for twenty-eight thousand, meaning that 'A few authorities had between seven and eight times more field staff in relation to their child population, than others'.[13] The places proportionately deprived of staff were the Welsh counties, the extreme North and North East, and the West Midlands.

Seven years later the extreme variability still continued. White, drawing on Home Office figures, depicted a range between authorities of one child care officer to 101,210 population, to one for every 3,467.[58]*

Proportionate numbers of officers tell something of the service given by local authority social services. The extent of training or qualifications of the officers and the kind of policies undertaken by their departments also indicate the quality of service, and allow room for even more variations. In the early 1960s in England and Wales, 28 per cent of child care officers were fully qualified, 36 per cent partially, and 36 per cent unqualified.†

---

* White used total population as the measure, whereas Packman used child population.
† Generally speaking, a qualified officer has completed a professional training course and received the Home Office Letter of Recognition. The partially qualified usually have a degree or other qualification in social science.

Again, wild variations occurred between authorities, from those with no qualified staff to those with 100 per cent.[13] By 1967 the variations had not been diminished. White further points out that qualified staff were attracted to authorities in London and the South, so that the London boroughs and the South West had 37 per cent of qualified staff, while at the other end of the scale the Midlands had 25 per cent and the North East 21 per cent.[58] Figures for some other types of social workers are given in Appendix A, and tell the same story. Great variations occur between authorities with, in addition, a definite tendency for London and its surrounds to come off best. This applies not only to proportions of qualified workers, but also to absolute numbers. Thus White shows that the London boroughs and the South East had, in *absolute* terms, over half the child care officers in the country.[58]

Few comparative studies have been made of the policies and practices of local authority social services. However, the oft-quoted Jean Packman, in comparing children's departments, noted differences in willingness to use their resources on behalf of private foster children, delinquents, the children of mothers entering hospital for short periods, and children of unmarried mothers.[13] Since Packman's study the Children and Young Persons Act, 1963, in giving departments greater powers, has also led to great variation in the provision of family advice centres, play groups, mothers' groups, family caseworkers, community workers and material help for families.

The tremendous variation between local authority provision would be explicable, indeed justified, if it correlated with need, so that the areas of social deprivation had the most workers, the best services, etc. Unfortunately this does not appear to happen. Packman underlines the point throughout her study; for instance, pointing out that authorities with similar problems of homelessness did not have relevant services of comparable standard.[13] Professor Townsend, writing of variations between health and welfare departments in 1962, said, 'There was no evidence to show that people's needs varied as much as this over the country', a point he reiterated after the findings of the Seebohm Report.[57, 59] The report itself added that the differences between authorities could not be explained in terms of needs, but were due to other factors such as differing policies and capacities to recruit staff.[15]

Davies, in his careful study of the services for the elderly and deprived children in a number of boroughs, establishes no consistent relationship between need and provision. For instance, taking the degree of *anomie* in a community as an indication of need of children's services, he shows that at times there is a positive correlation with the standard of provision, such as the probability of a reception home. But, equally, at times there is a negative correlation, as with the proportion of children in family group homes, while there is no correlation at all with gross expenditure or numbers of child care officers. He concludes, 'Most standards indices are positively correlated with need to only a small degree'.[60]

Nor is there evidence to show that authorities deficient in one service compensate with another. For instance, that a low number of day nursery places would go with a high number of nursery school places. If anything, the opposite is true, as Townsend points out from his examination of workers provided by health and welfare departments.[57] Again, the authorities with the proportionately lowest number of child care officers do not compensate by higher proportions of qualified staff; rather the reverse.[58] In addition, they tend to have more posts unfilled and to spend less on the service. Authorities who spend most on boarding out children also spend most on children's homes. Those with newer and more trained officers tend to have most reception home and nursery places.[60]

Diversity and variety are often regarded as virtues. This may be true of the social services, but only if initially similar services are available to all who need them. The present local authority structure leads to a system of social service inequalities so that the quality and range of help depends not on need but where people live. The consequences can be severe. The unlucky ones may lack skilled help because their authority has no qualified workers, while a person with a similar problem will receive skilled treatment by virtue of living half-a-mile away in another authority. Or they may get inappropriate help, like children needlessly received into care because an authority has little temporary accommodation. Or they may receive no help at all, for example nursery education being unavailable for socially deprived children. An appendix to the Seebohm Report estimated that in 1966 in England and Wales, 1,012,000 children had physical handicap, 1,061,000 had mental handicap, and 700,000 some form of social handicap. Of these, 96,000, 183,000 and 349,000, respectively, were actually receiving help from the social services. Although considerable overlap occurs between the numbers, the appendix stated, 'There are at least as many children in need of help as there are those receiving help'.[15] One reason many children are left by the wayside is their misfortune of living in local authorities which — in comparison with others — provide inadequate services.

Reasons for variability amongst local authorities: The division of local government into hundreds of authorities promotes hundreds of interpretations of permissive and mandatory legislation.* More similarity might be evident if policy decisions were largely in the hands of professionals or experts sharing similar training, values and objectives. But the nature of local government is such that officials are responsible to elected committees, who often have no relevant expert knowledge. Not surprisingly, the

* In 1966 there were 204 welfare, 173 children's and over 1,400 housing authorities in England and Wales.

committees may not only have political views of many shades, but their values and thinking about the social services may be sharply opposed to those professionally employed, and possibly even opposed to the spirit of some legislation. For instance, some committees, being convinced of the value of adequate numbers of qualified social workers, are prepared to pay for them. Others are content to pay minimum—or below—salaries, resulting in undermanned, unqualified services. Differences of objectives also account for varying services. Some committees, even in comparatively wealthy boroughs, have done little to overcome their poor housing conditions, instead choosing to spend money on what many would call luxuries. Others have put housing reform as a top priority. Similarly, some authorities—on moral grounds—refuse to give contraceptive aid to the unmarried; others pursue a more liberal policy.

Differences in resources further account for variability of provision. Rateable values—rates being the main local source of income—vary from £87 7s. to £15.8 per head.[61] Central equalisation grants do not abolish the differences, and hence some authorities cannot provide certain services even if so inclined. Smaller authorities appear particularly disadvantaged. To take an example from child care, they cannot afford the full scatter of residential care — reception centres, long-stay, short-stay homes, etc. — necessary to meet the needs of any range of children in their care.* In turn, as White points out, the limitations of the child care service plus the lack of finance reduce the chance of recruiting qualified staff.[58] The lack of staff causes extra strains and creates situations, as at present, where one authority is desperately short of residential provision and field staff, while a neighbouring authority has forty residential vacancies and staff underemployed.

PROPOSALS FOR CHANGE

'One insistent question not yet answered,' says Townsend, 'is how the government can prevent certain services in areas from falling far behind the national average.'[59] Proposals for reform have concentrated on the relationship between central and local government, the pooling of resources, the size and functions of local authorities, plus a basic questioning of local government as a vehicle for the social services.

In 1969 the Association of Public Health Inspectors, noticing that local authorities were rarely using their powers to compel landlords to improve

---

* It is fair to add that some writers believe small authorities have certain advantages such as offices being more accessible to clients, officers knowing the area more closely. See E. James, 'Frontiers in the welfare state', *Public Administration*, Winter 1966, and a critique of it by B. Davies, 'Local authority size: Some associations with standards of performance of services for deprived children and old people'. *Public Administration*, Summer, 1969.

properties, asked the government to pass mandatory, not permissive legislation.[62] Similar proposals have been made concerning legislation for family planning services and sites for travellers. However, not even mandatory legislation is always executed as intended, partly because it too is open to interpretation, partly because the government bodies with an oversight of services are extremely reluctant to put pressure on authorities to comply. Professor Marsh describes the central powers as varying from 'The dropping of a hint to a complete and absolute power of enforcement', adding that in either case there is 'Terror in the hearts of those in Whitehall that they may give the impression of appearing to be dictating a course of action to local bodies'.[46] Professor Griffith, in a detailed study of the relationship, concludes that the method and extent of central control depends not on the efficiency of local departments—which would include their capacity to meet local needs—but rather on their political importance.[63] It follows that calls for more mandatory powers will avail little if the centre will not exercise its powers—yet the centre is reluctant to be involved in battles with local authorities. Of course, central government often holds the power of the purse and has a number of inspectorates to make reports.* But the power is less when trying to encourage an unwilling authority to expand, and even the threat of financial withholding can provoke conflict and cries of political victimisation.

However much pressure the centre applies to local authorities, great variations in resources remain. A partial remedy is for authorities to pool resources. Some have combined to purchase educational materials on a cheaper basis. The Children and Young Persons Bill, 1969, provides for sharing of residential facilities through a regional planning scheme. But joint action creates problems, not least that of financial responsibility, and, as Forder points out, 'Very few have developed shared services on any scale'.[64]

Local social services could make better use of existing resources and have greater flexibility of action if their departmental system was rationalised. Developing this theme, the Seebohm Report recommended that one social service department should take over the following functions: those at present under the children's department; services for the old and disabled from the welfare department; educational welfare and child guidance services from the education department; home helps, day nurseries, mental welfare, adult training centres and other social work services of the health and mental welfare departments; the social welfare component of housing departments.[15] Profitable as these proposals are, they would do nothing about geographical boundaries, so leaving the multiplicity of authorities. A year later, almost as a complement to

* Marsh also criticises the part inspectors play towards local departments. D. Marsh, *The Future of the Welfare State, op. cit.*

Seebohm, the Royal Commission on Local Government (the Maud Report)
recommended a reduction of the number of local authority units so that,
in addition to the Greater London boroughs, there would be in England
eighty-one authorities grouped into eight provinces (including Greater
London). The authorities would have a population of between 250,000 and
one million, these ranges being thought to cover the optimum population
for the personal social services. In addition to the advantage of size, they
should have new sources of revenue including a local income tax.[61]

The above arguments, for all their radical flavour, do not question the
continued existence of the social services under the aegis of local government. They accept the well-known British assumptions that most social
services should be local and controlled by elected councillors. Marsh questions both assumptions, asking, 'Are we fully entitled to assume that local
democratic control by elected representatives is so vital, valuable, and
more effective than any other form of control?' He doubts whether lay
committee members can sufficiently understand the increasing technicali-
ties of their organisations in order to make rational policy decisions. In
any case he also doubts whether councillors can be called 'representatives'
when the turnout at local elections is usually very low, and when the
'selection of candidates to stand for local authority elections is a mysterious,
secretive and weird process, and not always democratic'. Turning to the
other assumption, Marsh asks, 'Does the process of child-bearing differ
from one locality to another?'[46] His colleague Eyden also casts doubts on
the local unit belief, saying, 'There is little factual evidence that the personal social services necessarily require to be administered in small local
areas', and she continues that the social security system has a large
organisation combined with small local units.[65] But neither Marsh nor
Eyden specify alternative systems for the social services.

What alternatives are there to local government? A government
ministry, such as social security, would hardly be acceptable to personal
social services requiring trained social workers, not non-specialist civil servants perhaps transferred from 'cemeteries' or 'ancient monuments'. Nor
would social service departments benefit from what Professor Robson calls
the 'caution and circumspection which is considered typical of government
departments'.[66] The present writer has suggested that public corporations
be considered as a model for a regional social work service.[67]* Not having
to coincide with the multiplicity of local authority boundaries, the regional
services could—like regional hospital boards—approximate to an optimum

---

* In his *Nationalised Industry and Public Ownership* (1960), W. A. Robson calls the
  public corporation 'the most important constitutional innovation which has been
  evolved in Great Britain during the past fifty years'. He says it is an organ of
  public enterprise, created by the government, with the following characteristics:
  freedom from parliamentary enquiry into the management of the concern as

size for social work practice. The rationalisation into a number of larger but fewer units would correspondingly minimise differences in policies and practices, allow more planning and capital investment for the future, and provide a greater range of resources to be used. In short, there could be all the benefits of economy of scale, including those of advanced administrative systems and techniques, so often missing in social work departments.

Benefits springing from size could, it is true, happen under any system which rationalised local authority boundaries. In addition, there are advantages springing from the nature of public corporations. Firstly, reliance on central rather than local finance should entail a more equitable allocation of resources according to need. For instance, a regional service with high social need yet lacking qualified staff could be given extra funds to attract them. Secondly, public corporations are free from control by elected councillors who, with all the good will in the world, are part-time amateurs. By contrast, boards of regional services could consist of full-timers with managerial, social work and research skills, plus representatives of clients, of the social work associations and of the local electorate. As in other public corporations, full-time board members would be appointed by the appropriate minister, who would also have overall responsibility. If ministerial influence is feared, it is as well to note that freedom from parliament and civil servants in managing its own affairs is considered one of the greatest advantages of public corporations.[66]

The foregoing suggestions are all attempts to meet the problems of size, multiplicity of units, resources, government, etc., which lead to such diversity in the quantity and quality of local authority services. In fairness to individuals, especially the socially deprived in neglected areas, it is vital to reach some solution, yet none of the suggestions have won common consent. The terms of reference given to Seebohm indicate the government will not consider any other basis than local government for the personal social services. Many of the medical profession have attacked the Seebohm recommendations concerning departmental reorganisation, the Maud Report has aroused the ire of many local authorities, and the government has not yet tried to implement either. A final suggestion—which need not necessarily be separate from any of the above—refers back to the priority approach. It argues that in areas of high need where local authorities will not or cannot provide adequate services, the central government should put in extra resources. The manner in which the British government has tried this approach will be shortly discussed.

distinct from its policy; 'disinterestedness'—it does not have to make a profit; personnel do not come from the civil service (nor local government); self-contained finance; board members are normally appointed by the minister for a fixed number of years. In addition, Robson adds, public corporations reveal 'a tendency to enlarge the unit of administration to a national or regional scale'.

THE PRIORITY APPROACH

The priority approach to combat social deprivation is currently being developed by the government through its educational priority areas, the urban aid programme, and the community development project (which, although part of the urban programme can be considered separately). Following on the heels of the American poverty programme, the press inevitably applied the same title to the British scheme, and in the sense that both involve central government attempting to help local areas of intense social need its usage is justified.[68] The strategy and effectiveness of the American programme has been upheld and denigrated on both sides of the Atlantic but few deny that potentially the priority approach could be an important means of help.[69,70,71,72] The present section will therefore describe briefly the three main parts of the British programme and attempt to evaluate their plans and objectives to date.

Educational priority areas: The Plowden Report recommended extra educational resources for areas containing schools with the greatest number of deprived children.[5] Without specifying how they should be weighted or proportioned, it recommended the following criteria for area selection; unskilled and semi-skilled workers; size of families; families receiving state supplements; overcrowding and sharing of homes; poor school attendance and truancy; retarded, disturbed or handicapped pupils; incomplete families; children unable to speak English.

These criteria were somewhat modified by the government when, in 1967, it invited local authorities to apply for grants over a two-year period· stressing that importance would be on:

(i) Evidence that children in a district were suffering from multiple deprivation because of the combination of several disadvantages, such as overcrowding of houses, family sizes above the average, high incidence of state supplements, poor attendance or truancy, a rapid turnover of teachers or difficulty in attracting them.

(ii) The general quality of the physical environment such as crowded, old, sub-standard and badly maintained houses.[73]

In April, 1968, the government authorised school building projects in fifty-seven authorities in England and Wales at a cost of £16 million. The largest amounts went to the Inner London areas, followed by Birmingham.

Urban aid programme: The Local Government Grants (Social Need) Act, 1968, enabling the government to give a new specific grant to areas of social need, was the springboard for an urban programme of up to £25 million in the fields of welfare, education, health and housing. Under the direction of the Home Office, but involving also the Department of Education and Science and the Department of Health and Social Security, the first phase invited applications for a 75 per cent grant, the main criterion being either a serious degree of overcrowding or at least 6 per cent of immigrants on the school roll. In January, 1969, twenty-three authorities were awarded a total of £3 million, mainly for nursery education but also for day nurseries and children's homes, the main beneficiaries being, in order, the inner London boroughs, Birmingham, Manchester and Liverpool. The second phase, in July 1969, agreed to finance some 500 projects in eighty-nine authorities to a total of £4½ million. Again the emphasis stressed education with nursery schools, teachers' centres, language classes for immigrants, but aid was also given through the local authorities to voluntary societies to run play groups, play centres and adventure playgrounds.

The community development project: The Seebohm Report recommended the government to take responsibility for community development in areas of special need.[15] This was not fulfilled by the educational bias of the two aforementioned programmes and in 1969 the government announced, as part of its urban programme, its Community Development Project to establish, 'in a few carefully selected areas of high social need, an experiment in community development'.

Two Home Office documents explain its objectives and strategy.[74, 75] It will 'find ways of meeting more effectively the needs of individuals, families and communities, whether native or immigrant, suffering from many forms of social deprivation'. Within this, the project will help people 'assume an increasing measure of control over their own lives', 'use constructively the services which exist', and 'take some of the load off the statutory services'.

The project will use two to three community workers in a neighbourhood of 3-15,000. After assessing needs their main ploy will be 'to give co-operation between (existing) services'. They will also 'seek to involve the people living in the area in community schemes flowing from their own perceptions . . .'. Lastly they might make existing services more comprehensible, for instance by reinforcing 'any efforts already being made to increase the relevance of the school curriculum to actual social needs'. In the summer of 1969, the Home Office announced the first three projects would be in Coventry, Liverpool, and Southwark, while negotiating for a fourth in Wales. (It was later announced that this would be located in the County of Glamorgan.)

The British poverty programme is now under way. Involving the co-operation of the major central social service departments, it is specifically directed towards the socially deprived. It is true its practice is just beginning but its objectives, strategies, resources and areas have been laid down, the paths of development have been settled. These must therefore be discussed and evaluated. Special attention will be focused on the community development project which is concerned with a wide range of needs with less concentration on education, followed by some points about the poverty programme in general.

Critique of the community development project: The project rightly recognises that large numbers of families with multiple needs are concentrated in particular urban areas where frequently the statutory local services either lack sufficient resources or are so structured, conducted and located that their effectiveness is reduced. The government therefore accepts that a fresh initiative must come from outside. However, the form and strategies of that initiative are open to criticism.

The project insists that control of resources must rest solely in the hands of existing central and local government bodies. It thereby *excludes other forms of local initiative* which might be more effective. From the start, the project has been devised by the Home Office in conjunction with local authority officials—not with the deprived themselves. Once established the four project teams will be controlled by a central and a local steering group overwhelmingly consisting of government and local authority personnel, plus representatives of voluntary bodies, able to 'contribute major resources', and community representatives. The actual workers may be seconded from the local authority services and will propose a 'solution by the services concerned', that is through the local authority services.[74, 75]

Undeniably a poverty programme needs to channel some of its input—nursery education, day nurseries, etc.—through existing statutory services. But to use only these excludes the deprived themselves and local voluntary groups from the part only they can play. The project assumes that efforts outside the existing 'establishment' power structure are not to be considered yet possibly they have more chance of local success.

The community development project does pay lip service to local participation but there is no suggestion that—even in one of the areas—the workers should be responsible to the local community, not the social services. Moreover, as a *New Society* editorial points out, the steering committees have no built-in representation of the deprived. Admittedly, provision is made for local representatives to be added, but not until they are 'identified' by the team which may not be 'until some quite specific plans for social action are put forward by the team'.[74, 75] An outsider may be forgiven for reading into these words the exclusion of anyone with ideas different from the local authority, the exclusion of the deprived or any other local radical leadership, and the inclusion instead of known community representatives such as doctors or clergy. No doubt the question of representation of the deprived poses problems, but it has been resolved in parts of America.[76] By choosing to ignore this, the project reinforces the practice of the enlightened middle class community worker leading the poor, inhibits local participation, and belies its claim to help people 'assume an increasing measure of control over their own lives'.

The refusal to initiate any programme outside of tight statutory control and personnel is the more difficult to understand as evidence on both sides of the Atlantic increasingly stresses the part local inhabitants and voluntary groups can play. In the USA their involvement has led to costly failures but also successes where professionals have failed. The employment of Harlem negroes—with no agency experience—to run youth programmes and to work with drug addicts, the use of local non-professionals amongst street gangs, etc., has flourished because they know the language of the streets and could more readily identify local needs than workers from a totally different culture. In addition to local participation, many American projects regard freedom from local or central politicians as an essential. Indeed, much of the story of the American programme centres on their struggle to retain freedom.[77] The potential of locally controlled movements to tackle social deprivation appears considerable, yet the community development project has ruled them out from the start.

In Britain, too, there are examples in deprived areas of local movements meeting local needs. Examples include tenants' associations, especially the Greater London Tenants' Action Committee and the Saint Ann's Tenants' and Residents' Association in Nottingham, client organisations of which more will be said later, the various Notting Hill projects in London, *ad hoc* groups operating from adventure playgrounds, immigrant associations, and so on. Such organisations are rarely able to overcome income deprivation but they help members obtain their rights in regard to housing and state benefits, provide services of the kind of playgrounds and play groups, give group support in times of crisis, pressurise local authorities to improve local amenities, and involve a range of people so that they do indeed exercise more control over their lives. Part of the success they have had appears attributable to an insistence on local grass roots control and participation. Unlike other voluntary bodies they reject aid, in form of cash or workers, from the local authorities if acceptance implies any modification in objectives or strategies. Certainly, the statutory social services have no comparable record on reaching and involving inhabitants of deprived areas.*

Despite their promise, such movements are few and limited by lack of finance. Sinfield points out the sad contrast between statutory services becoming 'even more isolated' from local needs while 'grass roots organisations multiply to help small areas and groups but without the power or the permanence to achieve more than a holding operation'.[78] With a membership largely drawn from the deprived, local financial income is limited.

---

* Occasionally a local authority does employ a community worker able to participate with local residents. An example is the Family Advice Centre of Birmingham Children's Department located in Brookfields. It is true to add, however, that as yet the Centre has not involved inhabitants in actions which might threaten the norms or policies of the local authority.

The radical nature of the movements may mean, as even the Notting Hill project found, that it is 'difficult to get any kind of official help for projects which seemed controversial and equally difficult to get help from charitable foundations'.[11] Here it would seem, is an outlet for any poverty programme wishing, as the community development project claimed, to break away from existing patterns of social service, wishing to experiment, wishing for local participation. Instead, however, of giving financial backing, without any strings, to such promising organisations, it has decided to work only through the existing local authority services.

A related outcome of the method of working is to reduce — or even exclude — the use of a strategy which might be particularly apt for socially deprived areas, namely *conflict strategy*. Epstein distinguishes consensus and conflict as two major strategies which promote change. The former includes research, reports and co-ordination, the latter includes claiming rights, political campaigning, rent strikes.[79] In the USA and Britain conflict strategy has some record of success in providing the focus which stimulates inhabitants in deprived areas to assume more control by actively attacking some of the inadequacies of their environment. For example, they have acted to prevent rent increases, pressurised public and private landlords to improve housing conditions, compelled officials to pay state allowances to the full. American professional social workers, although mostly disliking conflict, generally agree that conflict is the most 'effective' strategy for low income groups.[79]

The potential role of conflict as a change-maker in Britain was recognised by the Seebohm Report saying that participation 'may sometimes mean direct protest' and by its quoting approvingly the view that social workers will be involved in situations 'which lead to criticism of their service'.[80]

Despite its statement, Seebohm declined to say how institutionalised bodies like local authorities with their formally organised, publicly sanctioned structure, could countenance their workers using conflict strategy. They are characterised by hierarchies transmitting values and sanctions which tend to emphasise restraint, economy and caution—for instance not communicating with the press, not offending other departments, not acting in ways of which councillors or the public might disapprove. Not surprisingly there is little evidence of local authorities promoting strategies which might lead to conflict situations. On the contrary, there are examples of them getting rid of employees who so operate and of withdrawing financial support to organisations mildly criticising council policy or undertaking unorthodox work.[68] As Anne Lapping astutely perceived even before the community development project was announced, 'It will be difficult to appoint a social worker from the local department to do the work because he might too often find his community pushing him to bite the hand that's paying him'.[81] Equally, local authorities are unlikely to second workers to detect needs and inform of rights resulting in more pressures for receptions into care, housing repairs, etc. Thus by determining to operate only through the statutory services, a strategy with particular relevance to the socially deprived has been ruled out.

The disinclination to adopt radical solutions does not only spring from the relationship with the local authority, it is explicitly forbidden by the project. Supposing workers assess that local deprivation can only be countered by conflict strategy or by wholesale provision in housing, income, training, etc. They can use neither. The project states it will not 'involve the provision of facilities which are, individually, large, expensive or wholly new in conception'. Instead the workers must 'make familiar services more accessible' and secure 'the co-operation of the providing services'.[74, 75] *

Nothing in these paragraphs implies that the attack on social deprivation should not continue through traditional modes. As mentioned, the present statutory services are the only channels for certain services. Again, traditional voluntary bodies, reliant on local authority finance and employing consensus strategies, can play a valuable role in deprived areas. A good example in Birmingham is the Sparkbrook Association which works on 'a non-political basis', has 'no views on some of the most important issues of race relations: such as immigration control', and does not intend 'to deal with racial injustice'.[35] Within these bounds the association strives to improve amenities and to channel grievances into practical work. Rightly central and local government and such voluntary bodies will co-operate on lines suggested by the community project. The objection, however, is that it misses the opportunity to promote local. participation, to fund radical voluntary groups, and to allow different strategies. The American poverty programme was prepared to back new methods. It caused conflict with established bodies but also, in many cases, succeeded in helping the deprived. The community development project is the part of the British poverty programme with room to promote different forms of community work to meet social deprivation. This it has failed to do.

A further major criticism of the community development project concerns the *manner in which its resources have been allocated*. As part of a priority approach it is expected to develop measures of need so as to put resources where most needed, partly because this is socially just, partly to demonstrate the programme's effectiveness in the worst areas. The three local authorities chosen as recipients of the priority community resources —Coventry, Liverpool and Southwark, plus the likely choice of Cardiff—

---

* Problems of co-operation between local authority social service departments will be modified if, as expected, the recommendations of the Seebohm Report are implemented.

are areas of need but doubts arise as to their selection in comparison with other areas.

It is salutary therefore to look at some indices of social need applicable to the chosen and other authorities. The comparison immediately poses two major problems. Firstly, which geographical or administrative areas should be compared, the whole of the local authority unit or just a part like a ward or enumeration district? The projects are discussed both with reference to areas of three to fifteen thousand people and to the whole local authority. Available indicators mostly refer to the latter and although masking the highest concentrations of deprivation, do show in general terms which authorities have the worst areas. Moreover, an authority's resources, which must be balanced against need, can be concentrated on its worst parts if it so decides. In Appendix A material is presented for eighteen British local authorities. In Appendix B there is some material about wards.

The second problem concerns the indicators of need or deprivation. The possible indicators are discussed in Appendix A but as so often limitations are imposed by available statistics. The material is grouped into tables and is now used to compare the chosen authorities with others and with national figures.

Tables One and Two deal mainly with population structure, depicting groupings more likely to be eligible for the social services. These are pre-school children, school children, immigrants, adult males in unskilled and semi-skilled manual work, and large households. Taken together the authorities with high needs in nearly all groupings are Liverpool, Glasgow, Bradford, Coventry, Birmingham, Manchester, Tower Hamlets and Islington. Southwark, one of the chosen areas, is strangely low in the table having below average numbers of school children and its proportion of immigrants is lower than nearly all the other London boroughs.

Table Three offers three measures of overcrowding, population density of over one and a half persons per room, five or more persons per room, and shared dwellings. Notably Cardiff, Coventry and Southwark were among the better placed areas. Authorities with most overcrowding problems by these measures were Islington, Hammersmith, Lambeth, Hackney, Camden, Brent, Tower Hamlets, Birmingham and Glasgow.

Housing deprivation, it is recalled, means difficulties in the child socialisation process and extra strain on personal relationships as well as physical discomfort. Thus Table Four gives households lacking basic housing amenities. The listed London boroughs generally fared worse than authorities outside, with Islington by far the worst placed followed by Hammersmith, Hackney, then Southwark. Outside London, Liverpool, Birmingham and Glasgow suffered the greatest deprivations with Coventry and Cardiff among those with a high provision of amenities.

Table Five indicates mortality rates for infants and the whole population. Table Six draws attention to special needs groups who either do need, or have a high probability of needing, the resources of the social services. They are the illegitimate, children in public care, and those supervised under the 1958 Children Act (private foster children). The same authorities, as indicated above, stand out but particular attention is drawn to the abnormally high levels of Glasgow infant mortality rate and Tower Hamlets children in care.

Overall, without attempting to weight them and acknowledging they constitute but a limited number of indicators, the tables suggest the community development project has by no means allocated its resources to four areas obviously more in need than others. Certainly, Liverpool is an authority with high social need but with it rank the London boroughs of Islington, Hackney and Tower Hamlets. The inclusion of Cardiff and Coventry on the basis of the above indicators is hard to understand.

It must be remembered that the chosen areas are being compared only with the small number of local authorities listed in the appendix. In his study of over eighty local authorities Davies devised a social conditions index incorporating housing conditions, poverty and morbidity. Southwark was not included but the results show Cardiff and Coventry amongst the towns with the best social conditions. Liverpool was included but was by no means the worst. The worst conditions prevailed in industrial boroughs in Lancashire and the Midlands conurbation, none of which are listed in Appendix A.[60]

Turning from local authority units, it must be asked whether the use of smaller administrative areas justifies the project's choices. Material is less readily available but plotting in Inner London enumeration districts with more than 50 per cent households living in private furnished rented accommodation and those with more than 17 per cent of population living at over one and a half persons per habitable room suggests they are not predominantly in Southwark, the chosen London borough.[11] In Appendix B some figures are given for a few wards. It would appear that small areas of high deprivation occur in nearly all urban, industrial towns, and hence the existence of one cannot of itself be a basis for resource allocation.

Measurements of social need alone are not sufficient as grounds for priority allocation. They have to be balanced against the resources already at the disposal of authorities. Thus, returning to the eighteen authorities, Tables Seven to Twelve give some resource indicators. Tables Seven to Nine reveal the erratic nature of some service provision. For instance, Tower Hamlets, Southwark, Glasgow and Islington all have housing problems. Yet in the first three over 40 per cent of dwellings are council owned, in Islington only 20·4 per cent. Turning to pre-school provision, Glasgow records no play groups at all! The most amazing figure, however, concerns settlements—an acknowledged part of community work—for Southwark and Tower Hamlets each have far more than any other authority in England

and Wales. Tables Ten and Eleven give some idea of the distribution of social workers and doctors, and Table Twelve the proportion of qualified child care officers showing clearly the advantageous position of London authorities.* The advantage, Davies points out, applies to all local government positions, not only social work, for the administrative size and resources of the London boroughs enable them to pay higher salaries and offer a better career structure.[60] Taken in connection with the attraction of the metropolis to those anxious to reach the top in their careers it is not surprising that, both in terms of numbers and qualifications, London should prevail.

By no means do Cardiff, Coventry, Liverpool and Southwark stand out as desperately short of resources and provisions in comparison with other authorities. Indeed, in many ways they are better off. Southwark, in fact, appears so well endowed with resources—in comparison with other areas— that its selection is particularly puzzling. Tables Seven to Eleven demonstrate its advantageous position regarding services and social workers while having one of the best council housing records in London.[82] Information from other sources shows its product from a penny rate, expenditure on social services, and grants to voluntary societies compare favourably with other deprived London boroughs.[83] Most significantly, it has attracted community work. The number of settlements—some of which employ community workers—exceed most other authorities in the country put together. In 1968 the National Institute for Social Work Training established the Southwark Community Project which, backed by a wealthy trust, employs a team of community workers. In addition a comparison of directories issued by local councils of social service suggests Southwark is advantageously supplied with voluntary organisations and clergymen. The local planning department is one of few in the country with an interest in community work. Interestingly, especially as one of the functions of the community development workers is to encourage use of services, there are indications that services are more used in Southwark than many other parts. Rent appeal machinery is comparatively well used.[83] The activity of the well-known school care committee workers probably means a higher take-up rate of free school meals and educational benefits. In short, even a crude comparison with other boroughs makes the choice of Southwark, for extra community resources, an extremely questionable one.

Even a rough examination of a limited amount of available data does not bear out the project's initial claim to allocate resources to 'carefully selected areas of high social need'. Nobody will quarrel with the choice of Liverpool but there appear areas with more severe needs and fewer

---

* It was not possible to obtain figures on qualifications for other types of social workers.

resources than the other favoured authorities. The failure to develop and use social need indicators at the initial project stage is a sad start to a priority poverty programme.

If social need is not the instrumental criterion in selection, what is? The Home Office states four main criteria, three of which are, 'the need to obtain a geographical spread; the need to ensure a high degree of understanding and support among the local social service departments; a prospect of positive backing from a reasonably accessible University'.* It follows that a grossly deprived area located near a chosen authority, with un-co-operative local social services and inaccessible to a university, is automatically ruled out.

The fourth criterion, 'the desirability of making a connection between the Community Development Project and the Educational Priority Area Project sponsored by the Social Science Research Council', implies a form of pre-selection according to criteria used for EPA's.† Five objections can be made. Firstly, the EPA's were chosen from authorities who applied for help and not, therefore, necessarily from the most needy ones. Secondly, the criteria used did little to balance needs against resources. Thirdly, the measurement of educational need does not necessarily warrant extra community workers. Fourthly, educationalists have expressed doubts whether the EPA criteria will 'successfully identify the schools most in need of improvement' and which include most deprived children.[84, 85] Fifthly, the chosen authorities used different combinations of recommended criteria, different weightings, and sometimes added other criteria.[86] Consequently the EPA's are not strictly comparable so to use them as an indicator for also receiving community help really involves the use of a different set of criteria in each case.

Of course, to concentrate educational and community resources together is sensible provided the need for both is established. Doubts about the EPA's criteria and the apparent neglect of the community development project to use any social measurement, means the condition is not fulfilled. The result may be to locate two forms of scarce resources in areas less in need than others.

One other factor has influenced area choice. Politically it is important to 'sell' the priority approach to parliament. It has been argued that future support depends on the initial projects appearing a success, an outcome more likely in needy areas already equipped with co-operative social services and community resources rather than ones equally needy but with poor services and resources. Southwark is an example of the former and

---

* The information was obtained through private correspondence and conversation with government departments, June-July, 1969.

† It must be added that problems of identifying causation are increased if two research projects are located together.

being on the doorstep of parliament can be used as a showpiece.[87] Undoubtedly support must be won for a poverty programme but its case would be demonstrably stronger if successful in areas with minimum resources and services. Not least, a poverty programme should observe the basic principle of priority allocation to areas where the balance of needs and resources means the socially deprived have the least chance of help.

Poverty programme: gaps, resources and areas: Turning from the community development project, which constitutes one part of the poverty programme, consideration will now be given to the programme as a whole.

Perhaps the most striking point about the programme is its limited range and consequent *gaps of provision*. Emphasis being mainly upon education and community workers, it does not tackle social deprivation in two fields where this report finds it most extensive—income and housing. Clearly measures to relieve income deprivation rest mainly in the hands of social security and economic policy. None the less, American experience suggests that the income level of residents of deprived areas—most of whom are in low paid semi- and non-skilled jobs—can be raised. Their schemes have been located in priority areas, have trained the unskilled, the drop-outs and unemployed, and found them employment.[70] By contrast British training schemes often serve those with previous industrial experience, who are motivated sufficiently to seek out training. Moreover, their location may not be in a deprived neighbourhood so that extensive travel is required. American success in training married men and fitting unmarried mothers for paraprofessional roles makes British observers wish the same for the unskilled father with a large family and the impoverished unmarried mother. They would benefit not only from a higher income but also from greater job satisfaction.

Although the government allows certain housing authorities to undertake more building, the poverty programme to date has done nothing directly to provide more dwellings. The plight of those condemned to areas of housing deprivation has been graphically described by the Notting Hill Housing Survey which concludes, 'here is a problem far greater than can be tackled by the resources even of a wealthy borough . . . We are of the opinion that Greater London and government intervention is clearly called for.'[11] Similarly the thousands in overcrowded conditions or on housing lists elsewhere have little hope of immediate change unless extra resources are allocated to them.

Even if the poverty programme is prepared to tackle problems of income and housing, many deprived areas can only benefit if their authority decides to make a bid for priority resources. Some authorities do not apply for financial reasons—under the urban programme they have to contribute 25 per cent of the costs: others lack the desire to help the deprived or do not wish to be termed a poverty area: others, as *New Society* points out, lack the expertise, the statistics, and the prepared plans needed to get in bids in the short time sometimes allowed.[88] The government, by adopting a policy of refusing to designate areas of need, and instead inviting authorities to make out their own case for priority resources, is discriminating against the socially deprived in unco-operative authorities. Indeed, in some cases, as with the community development project, the resources may actually go to authorities already doing most to help the deprived. The result will be to emphasise the variability between services of different local authorities, instead—as was hoped—of compensating for them.

The weaknesses of the poverty programme can only be made good by a programme able to assess need, designate priority areas, allocate a vast range of resources, and prepared to act outside of some local authorities by funding voluntary groups or setting up its own schemes. Its scope thus becomes so great that some writers point to the American tactic of creating a new agency, the Office of Economic Opportunity, free of both the central bureaucracy and local government, to carry out their poverty programme.[71] A case can be made for a similar body in this country, Whitaker concluding his discussion with, 'In many ways, in the present climate of alienation from government the time is ripe for such a major innovation in Britain.'[71]

A body of this nature, concerned only with the poverty programme, would remove or alleviate many of its present limitations. Two further advantages would occur. Firstly, a concerted attack could be made on multiple deprivation. The deprived tend to suffer in more than one direction, hence to remove only one deprivation may do little good. American experience suggests the value of pre-school provision is reduced unless accompanied by improvement in home and neighbourhood conditions.[70] The correlation between educational attainment and housing makes educational priority help of limited value, if given alone. The deprived are, as Harrington said, caught in a 'downward spiral', poor housing, ill-health, the worst schools, the least provisions for children and so on.[89] The sheer range of need demands a concerted and comprehensive attack, possible only through one body with sufficient powers. The implementation of the Seebohm Report will strengthen the casework and other social work functions of the personal social services, but will not provide the range of powers—or resources—to free a deprived zone.

The second advantage of a new agency, on American lines, would be its separation from the central bureaucracy, namely the civil service. A previous section stressed the lack of specialisation and reputation for caution amongst civil servants, criticisms also voiced by Professor Marsh in speaking of the 'very selective recruitment of staff, narrow in-service training, strict adherence to the rules and to precedents'.[46] An authoritative work on the administrative class says its 'tendencies to give a low valuation to management, specialised knowledge and investigation . . . as a preliminary to action, constitute attitudes more appropriate to the Service of a Regulatory State than that charged with administering the Welfare State.'[90] Meticulous administration is not enough. As was argued in America a poverty programme requires specialised knowledge to assess need, a flair for winning public support, initiative and courage in adopting new methods and the ability if necessary to incur and meet local hostility.

British civil servants have earned a reputation for integrity and neutrality. But their limitations are already showing in the poverty programme. The community development project, for instance, not entrusted to specialists in community work or even social work, has formed quite unrealistic expectations. Amongst its thirty-five possible evaluation indicators are, 'reductions in dissatisfactions with employment (improvements in job retention; improvements in appropriateness of employment and prospects of promotion)' and 'reduction in short or long term care away from parents'.[75] Laudable objectives, but any social worker knows the former to be quite beyond the scope of two or three workers with limited resources. They also know that community workers, by detecting need, can lead to extra demands on the children's departments and hence an increase in care away from parents. The project's unreadiness to back any methods or bodies outside the traditional has already been discussed.

It is hard to avoid the conclusion that an effective counter to multiple and localised deprivation requires a new agency, with extensive scope, directed by specialists, and willing to try new methods. To end on a note of caution, it is as well to note a few of the difficulties of the American programme. The OEO had only limited financial autonomy, resulting in a disruption of its planning when Congress specified grants for particular projects.[70] The resources allocated OEO were far below the requirements of its intended programme.[91] Already the very limited British poverty programme is being allocated only minimal funds. The expenditure on educational deprivation is nowhere near that recommended by the Plowden Report.[5] The urban programme has had to reject many bids to improve services in highly deprived areas. The community development project is commencing in four (to rise to twelve) areas of 3-15,000 population. Similar areas, of probably greater need, can be numbered in the hundreds, if not thousands. Lastly, some Americans appeared to regard the poverty programme as a substitute for existing services. This it can never be for many deprived families are outside of priority areas.

The British poverty programme has many limitations but is endowed with the potential for an effective means to counter localised social deprivation. The writer can but echo the hope of Whitaker that 'it will benefit not just the whole of this country but also other industrial urban societies whose problems are depressingly similar'.[92]

THE NON-TAKE-UP OF SERVICES

Whatever the framework of present or future social services, their effectiveness is impaired if those eligible do not use them. Although there is no national comprehensive survey, examples given by the contributors suggest that non-take-up is extensive. Amongst the available evidence is the following:

(i)   Social security benefits. Professor Lafitte pointed out that numbers of sick or unemployed fathers had not availed themselves of income benefits. The Child Poverty Action Group claimed that, according to the survey *Circumstances of Families*, 5 per cent of fatherless families, with incomes at least £2 a week below the National Assistance rates, were not claiming their financial rights. Further, as many as one in six of the mothers concerned who had limited earnings were likewise not receiving National Assistance payments to which they were entitled.[93]

(ii) Rate rebates. The Child Poverty Action Group, drawing on the same survey, show that of the 130,000 poorest families, only about 10 per cent had applied to their local authority for the rates rebate to which they were probably entitled.[93] It is fair to add that some may have applied after the survey occurred.

(iii) Welfare foods. Professor Lafitte says that many children eligible for free welfare foods do not appear to receive them. The Child Poverty Action Group adds, 'Very few families with fathers in full-time work were receiving free welfare milk', although they believe about 90,000 were eligible.[93]

(iv) Aid for school children. 'More important and better documented than the welfare foods situation', says Lafitte, 'is the partial failure of the school meals service to reach all poor families whom it could help'. Lafitte also castigates education authorities for being 'secretive, unencouraging, and often mean' regarding grants for clothes, uniforms, holidays and maintenance allowances.

(v)   Medical prescription reimbursement. Although adults of low income are eligible for reimbursement of charges now made for medical prescriptions, it is estimated that among families with working fathers only 20 per cent of those eligible do apply.[94]

(vi) Industrial injuries benefits. An authority on this subject believes that sufferers from occupational injuries and diseases forfeit much money by failing to apply or to appeal for the appropriate national insurance benefits.[95]

(vii) Legal aid. Michael Zander, a lawyer, states that low income earners eligible for help from the legal aid and advice services, rarely use them. After giving the low numbers applying for legal aid he says that only 60,000 people per year, an average of three per solicitor, avail themselves of the legal advice service. 'Quite clearly', he concludes, 'the vast majority of people with legal problems never get anywhere near a solicitor.'[96]

(viii) Rents. In his chapter on housing deprivation, Spencer drew attention to the host of legislation concerning private rented property. Amongst the most important is the right of tenants and landlords to appeal to rent officers or rent tribunals for a determination of a fair rent for unfurnished or furnished accommodation. A survey in North London found a third to a half of private tenants had no knowledge of their rights in this connection.[97] Of 80,000 tenants in the *Circumstances of Families* survey, who thought their rent not 'fair and reasonable', only one in twenty had applied to a rent officer or tribunal.[8] Indeed, there is evidence in North London and Brighton that appeals concerning unfurnished accommodation are made more by landlords than tenants, and tend to lead to rent increases rather than decreases, although the spirit of the relevant legislation had been to protect tenants.[96, 98] Further, tenants still frequently believe that notices to quit are valid, when in fact they are not.[96]

The eight examples mainly refer to services open only to persons with low incomes. At the same time it seems that the lower social classes—if they are equated with low income earners—do not avail themselves of universal services to the same extent as higher classes. Undoubtedly the latter make more use of the education services.[5, 41] The Newsons found they received best use of certain hospital services such as maternity beds.[99] Workers in deprived areas have noted the reluctance of some residents to approach doctors.[100]

Reasons for non-take-up: Why do the socially deprived, and other eligible persons, fail to take up services and benefits which have been designed to help them? Lafitte believes 'feelings of shame' deter applications for income benefits, where a means test is involved. In some cases the agency concerned appears to play on these feelings, and Lynes talks of schools which not only identify free dinner children during the collection of money, but resort to 'segregating them in different queues and seating them at different tables'.[101]

Ignorance about services and rights would also appear a cause. The blame must rest partly on the social services for, perhaps because the take-up of services increases expenditure and work, they sometimes appear less than keen to spread knowledge. For instance, there is little publicity to inform low earners of their right to reclaim prescription charges. Local authorities have not circulated widely information about rate rebates. Where they have tried, their leaflets sometimes contain misleading information such as telling recipients of supplementary benefits that they are ineligible.[94]

Professor Lafitte mentions the 'reluctance of some local education authorities to make free dinner facilities for poor families widely known . . . '; a reluctance also shown towards other benefits in their hands. Lynes even accuses local authorities of a 'deliberate policy of secrecy' regarding some benefits.[101]

If services do not publicise adequately, it can be no surprise that people possess little knowledge. In many cases they will be dependent on the possible encounter with social workers, health visitors, teachers, doctors or other 'experts' to inform them about their rights and opportunities. Unfortunately, even this may not suffice. Evidence suggests that doctors and teachers possess little knowledge about the structure and functions of the social services.[102, 103] Even social workers and health visitors are rarely well grounded in the Rent Acts, security of tenure, and knowledge about supplementary benefits.[104]

Even where knowledge of a right is possessed, the procedures to be followed and forms to be completed may be sufficiently complicated as to inhibit many applicants. Lafitte refers to the difficulties associated with application for rates rebate. The secretary of the Child Poverty Action Group, talking about means tests, stated, 'Complicated forms had to be completed; much of the information demanded was difficult to obtain . . . and in many cases reference to past and present employers was necessary'.[101] Moreover, often the persons eligible for and in most need of the benefits were those who find forms most difficult to grasp, are the least articulate, and have the least confidence to push themselves forward.

Application would be the easier if the attitudes of officials were always encouraging and accepting. The Supplementary Benefits Commission has endeavoured to improve the attitudes of its officers; none the less it is still claimed that some are overbearing or off-hand, so deterring the questioning of the amount of benefit awarded, or the appealing to a higher body.[105] Michael Zander believes the reluctance to use legal aid and advice 'has something to do with the image of the lawyer, as not being the kind of person to whom the poor feel confident in going'.[96] The attitudes of some doctors can be equally off-putting. Those who do not look up when patients enter, who imply their time is being wasted, who treat adults like children, inhibit them from coming again. As Eyden puts it, the aims of the National Health Service are 'nullified if people are deterred from seeking advice at an early stage . . . because . . . the patient feels that he may be labelled a malingerer or hypochondriac'.[65] The socially deprived probably suffer most. Jefferies says doctors are more aware of the social problems of the middle class rather than the working class.[106] Possibly the restricted middle-class background and education of many medical practitioners serves to heighten the communication barriers. The socially deprived are the least well equipped to overcome the barriers, being frequently inarticulate and not versed in coping with authority figures. For them the result may be the reduction in the quality and quantity of a universal service to which they and their children have as much right as anyone else.

Increasing take-up: The non-use of services by those in need reduces their effectiveness in combating social deprivation. How can improvement be achieved? Increased knowledge can be communicated through the mass media, by greater use of letters, leaflets and advertisements. A notable step has been taken by Manchester City Council in the distribution to every household of a leaflet containing information about local and national welfare rights. But the written word has limits. Some people do not read widely; some do not read English; some are unable to read at all. Therefore the information-giving role of social workers, doctors, health visitors, teachers and others in personal contact with the public becomes essential. Training courses for these occupations will need to place more emphasis on a knowledge of practical details. Notably, one statutory social work agency recently appointed a full-time worker to keep social workers abreast of the rights of clients.

The questioning of official decisions is a daunting prospect, often requiring expert support. Many of the deprived are unable to do this unaided, yet the Birmingham Claimants' Union and Child Poverty Action Group have demonstrated that, when helped, appellants often win their case before supplementary benefit appeal tribunals. Social workers and lawyers are also in a position to help. The role of advocate on behalf of a client before appeal boards, although increasing, is not widely practised by social workers. Lawyers are often not even acquainted with the subjects where they could most help the deprived, Brooke saying that 'Legal education . . . is wealth-orientated, so that legal education does not cover housing legislation . . . or social security law.' [104] A wider scope to legal education is called for, but even so Whitaker points out that lawyers rarely live in deprived areas; the 'middle-class orientation of most solicitors, and the location of their offices (West Ham and Thurrock, for example, have none) result in many underprivileged people remaining ignorant of those minimal rights which they do possess'.[71] He believes the only answer is state-financed neighbourhood legal services, staffed by full-time salaried lawyers offering their services to the deprived.

Lastly, take-up will only be maximised if applicants feel at ease in claiming their rights. For instance, when in 1966-67 the Ministry of Social Security allowed the elderly to receive supplementary pensions from the same book as retirement pensions, the rate of applications for supplementary pensions rose markedly. Obviously, many now felt free of feelings of embarrassment. Similarly, those in need will only make full use of services if the attitudes of officials, doctors and lawyers make them feel accepted and respected. How can attitudes be changed or formed? Much of the answer must rest in selection and training procedures. A difficult position exists concerning social security officials, for they are primarily selected for the civil service in general, and not for their attitudes and aptitudes to deal with claimants. Hopefully, increased emphasis on training will give a wider number greater understanding of the needs and behaviour of clients.

Medical and legal training is a much longer process. The observation of the Seebohm Report that 'Undergraduate education surely is the most fruitful period for forming different attitudes among doctors' applies equally to lawyers. A teaching system more geared to the needs of the deprived would foster attitude changes and so better equip many practitioners for helping some of the more vulnerable members of society. It appears that doctors and lawyers are disproportionately drawn from a small part of middle-class society.[107] Intake from a wider stratum would do something to reduce the communication barriers that exist between the professions and many of the working class. Thus doctors and lawyers can combine with social workers, social security officials, administrators and all others concerned with the social services, to ensure that they are more fully used by many in great need.

THE EXCLUSION OF CLIENTS

From students to members of the Automobile Association, modern society is marked by an increasing call for participation. It appears based on a belief in the right—of both the persons who run an organisation and those to whom its ends are directed, such as students, members, consumers—to contribute to its purposes and policies.

At present, recipients of the social services are unlikely to have an established participation position. For convenience, they can be given a threefold classification, roughly approximating to the three approaches distinguished earlier. These are:

recipients of the universal services, such as health and education. No stigma is attached to receipt, as they are experienced by the majority of the population;

recipients of services for special need groups. They are frequently referred to as clients;

residents of a socially deprived area which is benefiting from priority help.

Interestingly, only the recipients of universal services have a built-in participation role, and that is extremely slight. Thus statute requires regional hospital boards to include lay members, some of whom will doubtless use the hospital service. Further, parents of school children are eligible for appointment as school governors. However, there is current discussion about, and even a movement towards, recipients of services for special need groups and residents of deprived areas participating in the organisations concerned. The ensuing discussion is about these recipients and residents, each of whom, for convenience, will be referred to as clients.

Cons and pros: The statements of statutory departments and committees contain little to suggest clients could or should make significant contributions.* As pointed out earlier, even the community development project keeps the deprived from policy-making decisions. Of all the recent official reports about the social services, only Seebohm devotes much space to client participation, and what it says is extremely limited.[15] It wants members of old people's clubs to participate in their management, and foster-mothers to recruit others. It concedes the possibility of local councillors and direct consumers of the services 'engaging in experimental bodies with an *advisory* capacity to area offices of social service departments'. Such people might even 'be included in the main social service committee or its sub-committees . . . they could carry out useful functions in the reorganised structure, notably in maintaining contact with residential and day-care institutions, and in strengthening the lines of communication . . . ' In sum, the report encourages 'respectable' clients, foster-mothers and pensioners, while making little mention of the unemployed, the unmarried mother, etc. Characteristically, it talks of 'citizen participation', not 'client participation'. They are to advise and communicate; little more. Perhaps most significantly, during its two and a half years the committee did not collect clients' views, although it had time to sound out everybody else concerned with the social services.

Why is there reluctance to offer any significant influence to clients? One explanation rests on the belief that the deprived, amongst whom are many clients, are too apathetic and submissive to want to participate. This may reflect Lewis's concept of a culture of poverty characterised by such features as apathy.[108] Secondly, doubts are expressed whether clients, who may lack education and emotional stability, have the capacity to contribute to anything but decisions about themselves. A third point is that social workers, mostly trained to operate within a structured role situation in which they give and clients receive, may feel uneasy at the prospect of interaction with them as equal participants.

Whatever the reasons, clients have not been allotted places on decision-making bodies. Their total exclusion is regretted by some social workers and clients, partly on the grounds that they should be represented on bodies whose policies virtually control their lives. In addition, client participation would promote a greater understanding of their needs and

---

* It can be argued that clients influence agencies by communicating needs to social workers who, in turn, persuade committees to meet the needs. The above paragraphs are not concerned with this indirect influence, but with clients knowing they are directly contributing towards decisions.

desires. At present, committees and chief officers make decisions largely on information provided by senior and field workers; they rarely have direct contact with those for whom the services were established. Reports, however skilfully compiled, contain subjective selections of material. Significantly, the few research projects directly interviewing clients and presenting their expressed needs, often reveal perspectives underestimated by agencies. For instance, unsupported mothers complain of the crushing demands of finding enough money, accommodation and adequate day care for their children. They not only feel that social agencies underestimate these aspects, but they are also critical of the kind of help they do offer.[16, 17, 21] Direct representation might serve to convey such feeling to committees. Not least, as Seebohm declares, the development of participation 'should reduce the rigid distinction between the givers and takers of social services, and the stigma which being a client has often involved in the past'.

PARTICIPATION IN PRACTICE

Progress towards participation has mainly occurred outside the statutory social services. A number of *ad hoc* locally based groups running adventure playgrounds, housing services and play groups in socially deprived areas take the participation of the deprived as a basic principle. Perhaps the most interesting advance has been made by the Haringey Family Service Unit.[109] Believing the traditional method of long-term, intensive visiting of so-called 'problem families' 'has sometimes served to perpetuate a family's sense of failure, and its exclusion from the social scene', the Unit wanted to break away from a reliance on casework and traditional community work. The approach most capable of 'drawing out and demonstrating the capacities of the families' appeared to be client participation.* Accordingly, families have gathered with workers and, as a result of decisions, have used the agency's resources to establish a legal advice centre, a mothers' club, and a discotheque for adolescents. The decision-making body is now to be shaped into a 'development group' with representatives of the families as permanent members. As well as participating in decision-making, the families have started to help each other and the neighbourhood. The workers have gained, by learning more of how the families perceived their needs and how they thought social workers could help them. Most valuable, however, has been the demonstration that even 'problem families' can participate, for they are the very group said to be most characterised by 'passive acceptance . . . the collapse of morale and complete abandonment of any effort to recover'.[110] It is one thing for a small, voluntary

---

* According to the Unit, client participation is 'attained when workers and families act together in deciding how the Unit should be used; and co-operated in securing and maintaining Unit resources'.

family agency to involve clients; it would be much more difficult for a large statutory body. None the less, the Haringey project, even in its infancy, has shown that clients have the motivation and capacity to participate.

Client organisations: Perhaps because the social services have been so reluctant to involve clients, they themselves are now attempting to influence policies and practices by forming client organisations. Until very recently in Britain, official client activities concerned only 'respectable' groups such as the Patients' Association, the Association for the Advancement of State Education, and old persons' movements. The less respectable had middle-class pressure groups working on their behalf — the Child Poverty Action Group and the National Council for the Unmarried Mother and her Child being prime examples. Abroad, however, the American National Welfare Rights Organization was showing that the poor themselves, if organised and united, could wield some power and act as a voice for the deprived. The years 1967-68 in Britain then witnessed the growth of organisations composed of clients, the most outstanding being the Birmingham Claimants' Union for those in receipt of social security benefits, and Mothers in Action, a society for unsupported mothers (mainly unmarried). Thus in 1969, Professor Kahn could say, 'The deprived are being heard and understood as never before'.[40] Prospects for growth are promising. A number of social workers, supporting the idea of client organisations, are prepared to encourage clients to join. The location of numbers of the deprived in concentrated twilight areas will facilitate communication and solidarity. Between the summer of 1968 and the spring of 1969, Mothers in Action increased its membership by over 700 without even advertising its existence.

To date, the British organisations have employed three main strategies: they have sought improvement for members' conditions, as would any pressure group; members have been informed of their rights and given assistance in claiming them; group activities have provided support for members, and lent numerical weight to complaints. Possibly they will now adopt conflict strategy, in emulation of the American NWRO which has 'sat in' at public assistance offices until unmarried mothers received their full financial dues, and engaged in protest marches. Already the Birmingham Claimants' Union has embarrassed officials of the Department of Health and Social Security by publicising on television and in the press the 'slum' conditions of their waiting rooms, criticising the long queues, and threatening to expose unhelpful officers by sending in claimants with tape recorders hidden in their clothes.[105] At least the activities of these organisations shatter the myth that all clients are apathetic and incapable of seeking solutions.

Although some social workers support client organisations, many are unsure of their attitude and others hostile towards them. If they fail to identify with them there is a danger of the organisations developing the view of some American negro movements—that social workers are just the lackeys of the establishment—so splitting two forces who could help each other. On the other hand, active social work support could pose awkward questions. Should social workers pass to client organisations information which is useful but obtained by virtue of their position as agency employees? Should they openly support militant action which is aimed at their own employers? One thing is sure: if client organisations continue to grow at their present rate, then the social work associations must work out their policies towards them.

A small number of social workers appear quite sure of their attitude and must be mentioned in any discussion of client organisations. Often with strong political affiliations, they see themselves working in partnership with clients towards the radical changing of a society which has allowed extensive social deprivation and is held responsible for the plight of clients. To them, the social worker's role is to help clients take over the control of the social services as part of the larger struggle whereby they will assume more power in society. Client power thus replaces client participation. Such social workers have to resolve questions concerning their relationship with and loyalty to their agency. They may well argue that their primary loyalty is to a political ideal or party, but there still remains the further question of their treatment of clients not sharing their political views, who need—and ask for—other forms of social work help.

If it is accepted that clients can and should contribute to agency decisions, then their involvement could develop in two directions. Firstly, forthcoming legislation on the reorganisation of the social services provides the opportunity to build-in client representation on the boards or committees which will control them. No doubt the problems of which types of clients are to be represented and how they should be chosen, are knotty ones. But similar problems have been resolved in other forms of consumer representation. Secondly, as mentioned elsewhere, the development of the poverty programme should allow for representation from socially deprived areas. In these ways the involvement of clients within services could enable them to be more geared to their needs. Outside the services, client organisations can present the case for their members at national and local levels. Clearly, not all clients will be able to contribute, but, equally clearly, at present the capacities of many are being neglected. Happily, present trends indicate a move towards a fuller use of their abilities in order to combat social deprivation.

TOWARDS CHANGE

By identifying the groupings and locations of the socially deprived, this chapter has allowed some evaluation of the efforts made to meet their needs. Commendable though they are, an examination of them revealed that improvements are required in at least five aspects, namely, to improve the coverage and nature of the social security system, to reduce the vast quantitative and qualitative variability between services in different authorities, to install a far more reaching and soundly based poverty programme, to promote greater take-up of available services, and to allow greater client involvement in the social services. Such reforms would entail changes in the organisation and structure of the social services, changes of policy, extra resources, and new attitudes. An enormous task but essential if social deprivation is to be effectively combated.

How can these, or any other changes on behalf of the socially deprived, be wrought? It is a platitude—but none the less true—to say that they can only derive from a multitude of interlocking factors: the political parties and their 'social engineering'; the economic position; the standard of living; the level of unemployment; public opinion and so on; all interact to create or allow change at a particular time. Amongst the factors will be the influence of researchers, voluntary pressure groups, client organisations, social workers, and militants. Because they are particularly connected with social deprivation, this chapter will close with an examination of their possible influence on creating change on behalf of socially deprived families, both in regard to national and local social policy and within social agencies.

Researchers: In the immediate past, social research helped confirm the extensive existence of social deprivation. Probably its findings contributed to some of the actions taken by the government in the 1960s. Much remains to be done. The contributors to this publication have underlined the lack of knowledge about the extent, nature and location of social deprivations. Hopefully, research will accept the challenge; hopefully, their findings will lead to action at both local and national level.

Interestingly, the recent survey by the Notting Hill Housing Service demonstrated the influence research can have.[11] Its substantiation and propagation of the plight of private tenants in a small area of London was succeeded by the local authority announcing its housing intentions, voluntary bodies undertaking a social action programme including a rent registration drive and a co-operative repair shop, and members of Parliament requesting the government that the security of tenure and rent fixing machinery applicable to unfurnished tenancies be extended to furnished.[111]

There is a danger that isolated research projects, in drawing attention to a particular area or grouping, win extra resources at the expense of even greater, howbeit less publicised, sufferers. The consequences are even worse if the research later proves to be ill-founded. The Sparkbrook survey exaggerated the deprivation of that area, and may have contributed to the diversion there of resources which were much more needed in other parts of Birmingham.[32] It follows that research has a responsibility to develop means of measuring need, in order to allow local authorities and the central government to distribute resources accordingly. Appendix 'A' lists some possible indicators of need amongst existing data. The detection and measurement of others, plus a system of weighting in order to produce an overall social need measurement, has still to be solved by researchers. Work of this nature has been pioneered by Davies but, as he says, he has been limited to available data.[60] Future development must concentrate on the devising and collation of new indicators.

Once needs can be satisfactorily measured, the next step is to establish which type of help is appropriate. The Younghusband Report complained of ' . . . the lack of any systematic study of the part played by social workers in meeting needs within the framework of the social services'.[112] A decade later little more is known. Thus a small area may score high on certain need indicators like number of applications for reception into care, number of private foster homes and daily minders, reports of child neglect, etc. The local authority may respond by taking more children into care, increasing the number of social workers, emphasising preventive work, harshly refusing applications, supplying a day nursery, and so on. The problem is, which of these types of help are required? Again, which problems and needs best respond to the general, specialist or priority approaches? Central and local government must make such decisions all the time, but they are doing so very much in the dark, and as yet research has given little help.

Researchers then, have a role in identifying deprivation, developing measurement tools, and advising on forms of help. If this were not daunting enough, they also may accept responsibility for 'selling' their goods to the authorities and the public. For a local authority, even if equipped with tools, may decide not to allocate resources according to social need because vast spending on the deprived might alienate the population—and votes— of other areas. The Plowden Report points out that authorities qualifying for extra resources did not always use them on their most needy districts. Thus researchers may feel they should propagate their works, possibly— as Professor Jones suggests—sometimes write them in popular form in order to shape public opinion at large.[113] But whether they do this or leave it to the pressure groups, most social researchers will hope, as Slack puts it, 'To produce factual evidence on which social policy, action or reform may be based or evaluated'.[114]

Voluntary Pressure Groups: Groups like the Child Poverty Action Group, Shelter, and the Council for Children's Welfare, are not client organisations but comprise mainly middle-class members concerned to work on behalf of the deprived. Including social workers and academics, they overlap with other groups mentioned in this section. The standing and connections of members of such organisations frequently place them in strategic positions for influencing social policy. Their magazines and publications may reach a wide audience, while some of their officers—as with the Child Poverty Action Group—may have direct means of communication with ministers and Parliament.

The emergence of client organisations will in no way diminish the role to be played by voluntary pressure groups. The former, although growing, are yet in the rudimentary stages, and the expertise and professional skills of the latter are still required to present reasoned cases to the public and to the government for, say, an increase in social security rates. They will also be required to articulate for those unable as yet to speak for themselves, such as the homeless, those 'without a settled way of life', and children under five.

The latter, for example, include a large section of socially deprived living in poverty, in crippling housing conditions, and in areas of general deprivation. Some are not even in the continuous care of their parents. At least 11,000 children are placed by private arrangements with private foster parents,* and a minimum of 17,000 are known to be with registered daily minders, with certainly as many more with the unregistered. Amongst these are many in overcrowded conditions and so vulnerable to social as well as emotional deprivation.[22] They comprise the children most in need of the socialising experiences of play groups, nursery schools and adventure playgrounds, whose most acute shortages are probably in deprived areas. Paradoxically, the same facilities are usually to be purchased on the private market by those able to afford, and probably in less need of them —a strange commentary on the welfare state. It follows that voluntary pressure groups could do well to 'move' public opinion on the 'at risk' position of many under-fives. To date they have achieved the Yudkin Report, giving some case histories and basic statistics.[22] But more is required—possibly, as some suggest, they should urge the government to institute a royal commission to consider the whole position of the under-fives, both at home and outside, both in deprived and non-deprived areas. The initiative for such a campaign would appear to rest mainly with the voluntary groups.

Client organisations: More than any other, client organisations can claim to be the voice of the deprived, and as such could win an influential position regarding welfare provision. The work of—*inter alios*—the Birmingham Claimants' Union has already demonstrated the effectiveness of action by clients to improve conditions and attitudes at local agencies. The next step

---

* Early indications from the present writer's own research into private fostering are that a substantial proportion, if not the majority, of private foster children are under five years old.

would appear to be for client organisations to claim the right of representation on local and central services, as well as in the poverty programme.
In this way they could win public recognition so that their views as a body
are sought even by the government, as happens with the NWRO in the USA.
   In a previous section the point was made that the organisations might
move from traditional to more militant methods, as used—with varying
degrees of success—by their American counterparts. Conceivably, for
example, a nationwide poverty movement could so flood appeals tribunals
with legitimate claims as to bring the whole machinery almost to a halt.
Thus being in a position to negotiate with the government, it could bar-
gain for the removal of an abuse like the 'wage stop'. Possibly, however, its
views will be heeded without militant action. In either case, client
organisations represent a new factor for change in the British social scene.

Social workers: Social workers have long been criticised for concentrating
their efforts on individual relationships with clients and ignoring their
potential for bringing about social reforms on a wide scale. Baroness
Wootton's barbs in 1959 have been resurrected ten years later by Adrian
Sinfield.[78] He believes that social workers have not analysed their relevance
to the basic issues of inequality and privilege in a 'modern and still class-
bound society'. He criticises the Seebohm Committee for ignoring the
question of whether social services do redistribute resources and so reduce
inequality. He cites the estimate that poverty and bad housing cause 'something like 60 per cent of the work that is now carried out by social workers',
and compares this with 'the apparent lack of interest on the part of social
workers in the command of resources . . . They do not pay sufficient heed
to the possible connections between the simple lack of resources and personal and family disintegration.' There are more instances than Sinfield
believes of social workers attempting to influence social policy and the
distribution of resources. None the less, few would deny the substance of
his case.
   Sinfield clearly believes that social workers have the capacity and the
responsibility to create social change by influencing policy. If these beliefs
are accepted, three objectives appear particularly within the province of
social workers: to argue the case for more resources for the social services;
to convince public opinion of the value and function of social work; to
oppose any punitive aspects still persisting within the social services.
   It is comparatively easy for social workers to show why more resources
are required. Their conferences, publications, and evidence to commissions
continually call for extra functions and more workers. Any reorganisation
of the social services—which they desire—will require extra resources, as
will an extended poverty programme and any steps to equalise the level of
services of different authorities. But resources are limited, and to date social
workers have failed to show how more can be diverted to them. In other

words, they need to argue the relative merits of the social services and the socially deprived vis-à-vis other claims. For instance, in 1966-67 local authorities in England and Wales spent £3·7 million (current and capital expenditure) on nursery schools.[15] In the same period government departments spent £4·8 million on fees alone to pay for children at direct grant or independent boarding schools. These were not children in need of special education, but children (often of high-ranking government employees) whom the state decided to assist financially at the main public schools. If the expenditure of local authorities on recognised independent schools is added, then over 10 per cent of the £85 million income of these schools—which serve a small minority of the population—comes from public sources. In addition the tax exemptions given them are valued at over £3·5 million per year, while the tax relief given to private fee payers cannot be valued.[107] Of course, many would justify such state expenditure, but equally social workers should make clear how public money is spent, and ask if it could better be used on the socially deprived rather than the socially privileged.

The subject of relative merits takes social workers into arguments of social justice. Similarly, they might campaign for large wage increases for low income workers on the grounds that income poverty is a prime factor in social deprivation. They might therefore argue against recent government decisions tending to allow the lower paid only small increases, while other occupations, such as doctors, judges and higher civil servants—already well paid and with the advantages of security, status and career prospects—have received very large increases.

Other examples are easy to find. Those who accept the claims of Titmuss and Whitaker that the income and wealth gaps between rich and poor are not decreasing — and are possibly increasing — might campaign for taxation reforms to reverse the trend in order to benefit the deprived.[115, 71] Or they might concentrate on social and educational advantages. The Public Schools Commission, in condemning the 'social divisiveness' of independent schools, says that their pupils gain unfair career prospects in comparison with pupils of similar abilities from other schools.[107] Social workers might wish to back the commission's proposals that the schools should also be used to help the socially deprived, or even argue that they so limit the educational and career opportunities of the rest of society, including the deprived, that only abolition is warranted.

If social workers actively campaign on such issues, they are seeking to create radical social change. Probably most readers will comment, 'All power to their arms', but two points must be made. Firstly, arguments about the distribution of limited resources are not as straightforward as they appear. It might seem simple social justice that low wage earners be brought above the poverty line before judges, for instance, received lucrative increments; but the counter-argument is the need to maintain the high standards of the legal profession. Social workers must be informed of the other side's position and be able to meet it, or the force of their campaigns will be lost. Secondly, questions of this nature take social workers into the political arena, for they frequently comprise matters on which the political parties have definite and opposing views. By backing one aspect, social workers, both individually and corporately, may lean to one party, with the possibility of a backlash if the opponents take office. Such a danger is not an argument against action. Indeed, the writer's personal view is that the plight of the deprived is so linked to politics that it is hard to see how workers committed to reform can stay apart from it. But the possible repercussions must be considered.

One way of influencing government decisions is to mobilise public opinion in favour of the desired objectives. On the other hand, government decisions may be largely nullified unless the public—or sections of it—are prepared to accept the spirit of the legislation. For instance, statute places a duty on local authorities to develop community care for the mentally ill, and boarding-out (fostering) when needed for children in care. Both would be impossible unless sections of the public had positive and accepting attitudes towards them. In two special respects social workers must do a public relations job.

Firstly, some of the socially deprived suffer unduly when public opinion blames and condemns. Although the elderly poor, young deprived children, the handicapped—especially the blind—receive public sympathy and support, the unemployed, the traveller, the parents of a large family, the delinquent, do not. Rejection and judgment probably further undermine confidence, making them feel increasingly isolated and different from the rest of society. Social workers, as the professionals actually in continual contact with such clients, are in the best position to explain to the public that their condition is no more deserving of blame—and no more helped by it—than that of the blind. They would do well, also, to make plain the inconsistency of a society which condemns the low income father who goes on 'the dole' if he thinks it means more money with which to keep his children, yet condones the Old Etonian who lives wholly on unearned income. To change public attitudes is a tall order, yet social workers can be encouraged by the greater acceptance of mental illness and, to a lesser extent, of illegitimacy, that has occurred in recent decades.

Secondly, if the public is to accept greater expenditure on the social services, social workers must play some part in convincing them of its necessity. The American poverty programme involved an increase in direct taxation, and hence had to be 'sold' to the public. The line taken was that a programme leading to more employment and better conditions would reduce numbers on the 'welfare rolls', so eventually cutting expenditure. A large-scale British poverty programme would only be contemplated by the government if it thought the consequent taxation increases acceptable to the populace. It too would have to be sold, although it is of doubtful honesty to argue reduced expenditure as a foreseeable result. Social workers, more honestly, could depict the misery caused to the socially deprived, reasoning that its alleviation is enough justification for more money. Alongside this it should be shown that welfare money is not just spent, but is an investment in the health and happiness of individuals which, economically and socially, benefits the whole of society.

Public opinion can be changed to accept expenditure. The publicity surrounding the death of a foster child did something to prepare the way for large public spending on behalf of deprived children in 1948 with very few voices raised against.[116] The effect of the film, *Cathy Come Home*, concerning the problems of finding accommodation, and the successful publicity campaign run by Shelter, further illustrate that the public can be moved by matters of social concern. The problem for social workers is to learn how to manipulate the means of mass media communication.

Apart from influencing social policy and public opinion, social workers cannot be content until their own house is in order. Unfortunately some social services still retain the residues of punitive attitudes, can still treat clients or applicants with a lack of dignity and respect, still appear to distinguish between the 'deserving' and the 'undeserving'. In short, clients can still be treated in ways which are diametrically opposed to the stated social work principles of acceptance and non-condemnation. Some examples follow:

Unmarried mothers complain that often social work agencies treat them as though they have committed a crime.[16, 17] Certainly, the tendency for housing departments to make housing especially available for the elderly but not for unmarried mothers, the fact that widows receive different forms of state incomes than the unmarried, imply that the former situations are considered more deserving of help than the latter.

The homeless are another category who may receive little sympathy. This chapter has already outlined the harsh policies some local authorities use, which actually lead to the break-up of families. Audrey Harvey, a person with much experience of housing conditions and policies, has written scathingly about local authorities who refuse to help the homeless, even unmarried mothers with no home of their own. In Outer London, 80 per cent of applicants to temporary accommodation were turned away.[117] Perhaps such punitive attitudes are not wholly unexpected if it is recalled that the relevant piece of legislation, the National Assistance Act, 1948, says temporary accommodation should be provided 'for persons who are in urgent need thereof, being in circumstances which could not reasonably have been foreseen, or in such other circumstances as the authority may in any particular case determine'. In other words, if the authority agrees, only those who could not foresee their homelessness deserve to be helped. Therefore need of help is not the sole criterion.

The last example concerns children's departments. A large proportion of children in care are short-term cases, particularly for the period of their mothers' confinement. Some departments, believing that applicants do not try hard enough to make their own arrangements, have adopted a harder, 'turning away' attitude. Research by the Schaffers, however, confirms such applications to be usually indicative of a family in need with limited social and economic resources, not of one trying to take unfair advantage of the social services.[118] To endorse a general policy of refusing help as the first reaction to short-term confinement cases is unjustifiably to treat them differently from other (non-confinement) cases.

Distinctions—other than on the basis of need—can also be discerned in the treatment of immigrants by a minority of children's departments. Their policy and attitudes are partly due to an influential publication by Katrin Fitzherbert, *West Indian Children in London*.[119] Stating that West Indians often needlessly apply for reception into care, she advises child care officers to adopt a tougher line, to put pressure on relatives or friends to take the children, indeed to 'resist the reception of West Indian children into care more strongly . . . even if this means refusing applications which, if they came from an English family, would be accepted'. This policy has been criticised as poor child care practice, but none the less some departments have taken Fitzherbert's advice.[120] The result is that immigrants are treated differently from other applicants, although there is no evidence that *en bloc* they apply for help more needlessly, or that their resources are different from other applicants. A member of the Birmingham Children's Committee even said that immigrants should be refused entry to the city because they placed strain on the child care services. To treat people—on the basis of colour—with a lack of dignity, and to refuse them a service available to white people, is firmly opposed to social work principles.

Children's departments adopting discriminatory practices may do so by decisions of their committees or chief officers, who may not be trained social workers. None the less, the latter are called upon to implement them, and are thus in a strong position to expose and oppose. Of course, punitive and discriminatory practices do not necessarily spring from the whims of sadistic or harsh policy-makers. They may be a means by which a department rations its over-strained resources. None the less, the upshot is suffering for those so rationed, a consequence which social workers must make clear to their departments and to the public.

To argue for resources for the socially deprived, to influence public attitudes, and to tackle punitive practices within the social services, must seem imposing objectives for social workers. Encouragingly, there are indications that, both within their agencies and outside, they have the potential to create change.

Donnison and Chapman's examination of the workings of social agencies suggests that the 'providers' (mainly social workers) are in a key position. Being the only layer of the agency in direct contact with the 'determiners of demand' (clients), they are able to communicate and interpret expressed need to the 'controllers' (committees). As the studies also revealed their capacity to gain the support of influential persons outside their particular agency, they are equipped to create change over the whole of their local authority. The authors concluded, 'They are not simply the instruments of their governing body—an impersonal link between the committee and its clients. They create, and continually modify, the service.'[121] Social workers are well placed, according to Donnison and Chapman, to initiate new developments.

Despite their powerful position, at times social workers will be reluctant to expose specific abuses within their own agency or authority for fear of dismissal, or even reprisals against the clients in question. At this juncture the social workers' professional associations could act by making complaints on behalf of members but without revealing their identity. To date the associations have been vocal mainly in urging reform of the overall structure of the social services, and in raising the levels of their own professional practice. Strengthened by the coming unification of most of the associations into one body, they will be poised both to act locally in regard to the failings of individual agencies, and nationally in influencing government policy makers and public opinion on behalf of the socially deprived.

The preceding pages have indicated the directions in which social work would operate if it accepted the exhortations to change the social environment as well as individual behaviour. The possible implications are profound. Social workers would not solely regard themselves as a means of social control, nor as 'adjusters' between clients and society, nor as caseworkers, but also as advocates for the socially deprived. For the rapidly growing social work associations there would be a re-thinking of their concept of professionalism. Social work strives to be a profession, yet its model is, to use Eyden's words, the 'mutual benefit associations' of medicine and law, where emphasis is placed on the position and status of members. A body committed to the socially deprived would be a 'commonwealth' organisation with emphasis as much on beneficiaries outside the membership.[65] The establishment of a professional model suitable to social work will exercise the efforts of its practitioners in the next decade.

The militants: Militancy, a current feature of society, is considered by some groups as a valid means of change on behalf of the socially deprived. Its advocates do not constitute a single connected group; indeed they are classifiable by their method more than any other factor, but they may be associated with *ad hoc* community organisations or with political groups. Instead of seeking redress through normal channels, they adopt radical, sometimes illegal methods. Some tenants' associations have withheld rent from landlords in order to fight rent increases or force repairs. The squatters have occupied empty houses and offices in order to persuade councils to house homeless families in unused property. At times, council chambers have been occupied by citizens—usually in connection with housing policies. Client organisations, as previously cited, may follow the same path.

It is easy to condemn militants, and indeed they usually receive a bad press. But their actions usually come at the end of a line of frustration, when change or improvement seems impossible by any other method. In deprived areas people have little control over their own lives, can do almost nothing to break out of the circle of poverty of income, environment and culture. They have the vote but little else, and even the vote looks meaningless if all political parties appear the same, and the great inequalities and lack of opportunities persist whichever party governs. The result may be apathy, social pathology, violence or militancy. Those who have witnessed all may agree that the last is the healthiest sign. Moreover, acquaintance with the families moved into empty property by squatters shows them desperate from years of despair and deprivation, and usually determined to find accommodation by any means rather than having their families broken up. Undeniably, militancy at times has paid off : repairs have been executed, some housing authorities have made fuller use of their empty property. Thus militancy and conflict is emerging as a tool in social manipulation. But this should not hide the fact that a society which allows deprivation so intense that the sufferers resort to extreme measures, itself stands condemned.

This report demonstrates that in income, housing and child socialisation, social deprivation still exists as—to use Beveridge's words—a giant, causing suffering to individuals, families, groups, and whole areas. To alleviate deprivation society has developed policies, approaches, services and attitudes. In many cases they are humane and effective; in others, not. The five groupings discussed in this chapter can play some part in remedying the defects. Similarly, the contributors to this report hope its contents will in some way be used to combat social deprivation amongst families.

Appendix 'A'

Some indicators of social deprivation in local authorities*

The purpose of Appendix 'A' is two-fold: to demonstrate some of the indicators used to measure social deprivation (or social need) and to show its concentration in certain authorities. The latter aim is achieved by selecting some local authorities generally thought to be trying to cope with severe deprivation, so that their need indicators can be compared with each other and with those for Britain (or England and Wales).†

The measurement of social deprivation is in a rudimentary state. The approach adopted in compiling the appendix was as follows: Firstly, accepting the validity of the indicators mentioned by the contributors to this volume, an attempt was made to collate them for the authorities in question. For instance, Spencer uses measures of overcrowding which could be obtained from the census. Secondly, an examination was made of the census and material published by local authorities and used if appearing to indicate social need. Thirdly, consideration was given to indicators suggested by the Plowden Report, by Davies, and by the government in allocating equalisation grants.[1,2] The results are presented in Tables 1-6.

The tables and indicators have many limitations. The following four points should be borne in mind:
(i) The tables refer to local authorities. Within the authorities will be areas which are not deprived; therefore the figures given will mask pockets with much higher levels of deprivation.
(ii) It is assumed that the indicators do measure social need or deprivation. In some cases this is straightforward: a high proportion of school children will make proportionately greater demands on the educational services. Again, high numbers of overcrowding per room clearly show housing deprivation. In other cases it is not so straightforward.

---

* Thanks are due to Mrs Rosamund Thorpe who compiled Appendices 'A' and 'B' and to the local authorities and councils of social service for supplying some of the information.

† One authority, wishing to remain anonymous, is given a code letter in the tables.

A large number of immigrants may create language problems at school and outside—but not necessarily; it will depend on the particular racial groupings. Again, they may make disproportionate use of some services, such as children's and education, but almost certainly they make less demand on welfare departments and social security.[3]

(iii) Many indicators proved unavailable. Among these were the measurement of morale in institutions and the degree of kinship support (both discussed by Davies); the non-take-up of certain services, incidence of vandalism, the inaccessibility of essential shops, amount of play space, proportion of motherless and fatherless families, illiteracy amongst adults. Other indicators were available, but not approximating to local authority units. For instance, statistics compiled by the local offices of the Department of Health and Social Security applied to their own administrative units, which differed from local authority ones. It thus proved impossible to give figures relating to income deprivation, but Table 1 indicates numbers in the lower social groups on the assumption that they will include those with the lowest incomes.

(iv) Almost certainly, some indicators underestimate the need position. For instance, Table 6 gives numbers of children in private foster homes. In fact, it records numbers known to the local authority; of necessity, it omits those of whom there is no recorded knowledge.

As mentioned in the text, social need must be seen against an authority's resources and standards of services. Davies talks of 'territorial justice' which he defines as 'a high correlation between indices of resource-use, or standards of provision, and an index measuring the relative needs of an area's population for the service . . . '[2]

The measurement of resources or services is even less developed than that of social need. It is complicated by the possibility that some services may substitute for others. For instance, an authority with little institutional provision is not necessarily failing to give a reasonable level of service, for its excellent domiciliary services may reduce the need for institutions. Again in Tables 10 and 11, Glasgow is shown to have a very low number of child care officers, but against this is an unexpectedly high number of probation officers.

Tables 7 to 12 give some indicators of resources available in the selected local authorities. They include 'physical' indicators such as the number of social workers per population, or numbers of voluntary agencies. But the numbering of agencies or workers tells nothing of their efficiency or quality. Therefore a 'qualitative' indicator is given in the number of qualified child care officers, assuming that trained officers operate more efficiently than non-trained.*

---

* It was not possible to obtain information concerning the qualifications of other types of social workers for all the authorities.

Two possible measurements, hopefully, to be used in the future, would
be the authorities' financial expenditure on certain services or groups in
need, and 'performance' measures such as the number of visits made to
clients, or even the degree of social work skills employed. It was not possible
to obtain material of this nature for the authorities in this appendix, but
it is hoped the Tables give some indication of the kind of measurements
that are available, and so show something of the provision made within
local authorities.

TABLE 1. POPULATION STRUCTURE (A)

	Total population	Population aged 0-4 years as % of total population %	Population aged 5-14 years as % of total population %	Economically active and retired males aged 15+ in unskilled and semi-skilled manual work* %
Great Britain	52,303,720	8·6	14·7	N.A.
England and Wales	47,135,510	8·5	14·5	N.A.
Greater London	7,671,220	7·7	12·4	22·4
Brent	282,490	8·3	11·8	22·6
Camden	217,090	6·2	9·1	23·1
Hackney	244,210	8·9	13·2	29·0
Hammersmith	203,240	7·4	10·6	26·1
Islington	235,340	8·9	12·3	32·1
Lambeth	320,780	8·4	12·7	26·3
Lewisham	278,450	8·3	13·0	25·3
Southwark	295,900	8·8	13·8	32·6
Tower Hamlets	196,830	8·7	14·8	37·3
Wandsworth	318,970	7·5	11·7	23·2
Birmingham	1,064,220	8·9	14·8	29·3
Bradford	290,310	8·8	15·1	32·5
Cardiff	253,920	8·8	15·3	23·6
Coventry	328,980	9·8	15·7	27·7
Glasgow	976,540	9·5	16·8	30·3
Liverpool	691,380	9·5	16·4	34·8
Manchester	598,640	8·9	15·0	28·9
City 'A'	249,240	8·1	14·9	26·8

* The figures refer to male workers in the socio-economic groups, 7, 10, 15 and 11,
  as used in the Census reports and as defined by the Registrar General's 'Classification of Occupations, 1966'.

N.A. = not available.
Source : 1966 Sample Census, County Reports. HMSO, 1967.

TABLE 2. POPULATION STRUCTURE (B)

	Total households	Large households with 6 or more persons % of total households %	Resident population born in New Commonwealth countries	Resident population born in New Commonwealth countries as % of total population %
Great Britain	16,960,560	6·7	852,750	1·6
England and Wales	15,359,680	6·5	829,750	1·8
Greater London	2,624,250	5·5	367,700	4·8
Brent	96,470	6·4	25,680	9·1
Camden	82,750	4·1	15,780	7·3
Hackney	85,500	5·7	23,630	9·7
Hammersmith	74,960	5·0	15,150	7·5
Islington	84,540	5·7	28,530	12·1
Lambeth	112,880	5·8	27,230	8·5
Lewisham	94,070	6·4	14,260	5·1
Southwark	100,860	6·0	14,480	4·9
Tower Hamlets	64,230	7·4	11,040	5·6
Wandsworth	110,420	6·0	20,690	6·5
Birmingham	332,810	9·1	49,870	4·7
Bradford	97,820	7·5	13,170	4·5
Cardiff	78,030	9·1	2,920	1·1
Coventry	103,070	7·9	10,770	3·3
Glasgow	304,970	9·7	6,260	0·6
Liverpool	205,500	11·4	5,130	0·7
Manchester	194,790	8·4	13,960	2·3
City 'A'	82,610	7·5	2,200	0·9

N.A. = not available.

Sources: 1966 Sample Census, County Reports. HMSO, 1967.
1966 Sample Census, Great Britain, Commonwealth Immigrant Tables.
HMSO, 1969.

TABLE 3. OVERCROWDING

	% of total households with density of population over 1½ per room %	Households with 5 or more persons in one room % of total households %	Households in shared dwellings % of total households %
Great Britain	1·6	0·02	6·7
England and Wales	1·2	0·02	7·3
Greater London	2·4	0·04	24·2
Brent	3·7	0·06	35·8
Camden	4·7	0·04	46·0
Hackney	5·4	0·06	43·1
Hammersmith	5·1	0·07	50·2
Islington	7·1	0·13	57·4
Lambeth	3·9	0·08	38·0
Lewisham	2·1	0·03	27·5
Southwark	3·0	0·04	32·7
Tower Hamlets	4·3	0·06	20·6
Wandsworth	2·4	0·04	35·0
Birmingham	3·0	0·09	8·6
Bradford	1·7	0·0	2·4
Cardiff	1·0	0·01	13·0
Coventry	1·5	0·01	2·7
Glasgow	11·8	0·17	1·2
Liverpool	2·6	0·08	8·4
Manchester	2·1	0·02	7·6
City 'A'	2·6	0·07	4·4

Source: 1966 Sample Census.

TABLE 4. HOUSING AMENITIES

	Households with shared use of hot water tap % of total households %	Households with no use of hot water tap % of total households %	Households with shared use of fixed bath % of total households %	Households with no use of fixed bath % of total households %	Households with shared use of inside W.C. % of total households %	Households with outside W.C. only % of total households %
Great Britain	2·0	12·5	4·1	15·4	4·4	16·7
England and Wales	2·1	12·5	4·3	15·0	4·1	18·0
Greater London	5·6	15·0	13·3	14·8	13·3	12·6
Brent	10·2	13·6	22·3	10·2	18·4	5·9
Camden	9·4	21·1	25·8	19·1	32·3	6·9
Hackney	6·7	29·2	18·8	30·5	24·2	16·7
Hammersmith	10·4	27·2	25·1	24·9	25·4	16·7
Islington	9·8	36·6	27·1	34·4	38·1	14·1
Lambeth	8·2	21·3	21·6	17·4	21·9	11·0
Lewisham	6·7	16·3	15·4	15·3	12·6	16·0
Southwark	5·1	28·9	10·7	34·2	13·1	21·9
Tower Hamlets	1·5	34·9	2·9	40·8	7·4	26·2
Wandsworth	7·8	20·3	18·9	20·3	15·7	18·1
Birmingham	4·1	17·5	6·3	18·6	6·0	27·8
Bradford	1·4	12·6	2·1	19·6	2·2	27·0
Cardiff	4·9	9·9	8·4	13·9	5·6	26·5
Coventry	1·4	15·2	2·2	10·4	2·0	17·6
Glasgow	1·5	23·8	1·8	32·7	16·1	1·8
Liverpool	4·0	20·2	6·0	25·6	6·4	31·6
Manchester	3·2	13·0	6·5	19·5	6·3	31·9
City 'A'	2·0	13·9	2·9	17·9	3·3	28·3

Source: 1966 Sample Census.

TABLE 5. MORTALITY RATES

	Infant deaths, under 1 year, per 1,000 live births	Crude death rate per 1,000 population
England and Wales	18	11·2
Greater London	18	10·8
Brent	20	9·8
Camden	20	10·0
Hackney	20	10·9
Hammersmith	16	11·2
Islington	18	10·3
Lambeth	22	10·7
Lewisham	16	11·5
Southwark	20	11·6
Tower Hamlets	17	10·7
Wandsworth	22	12·7
Birmingham	20	10·7
Bradford	28	12·8
Cardiff	21	10·9
Coventry	22	9·1
Glasgow	31*	12·7*
Liverpool	22	11·6
Manchester	23	12·6
City 'A'	24	12·0

* The year accounted is 1961; the figures were obtained from the Corporation of Glasgow.

Source: General Register Office, *The Registrar General's Statistical Review of England and Wales for the Year 1967*, Part 1. HMSO, 1969.

TABLE 6.   SPECIAL NEED GROUPS

	No. of live illegitimate births as % of all births %	No. of children in care per 1,000 population under 18 years %	No. of children supervised under 1958 Children Act per 1,000 population under 18 years %
Great Britain	7·7	N.A.	N.A.
England and Wales	7·9	5·2	0·08
Greater London	11·4	7·9	0·12
Brent	14·6	8·2	1·3
Camden	17·1	14·0	1·0
Hackney	15·6	11·8	1·1
Hammersmith	16·7	15·8	2·1
Islington	14·2	15·0	1·0
Lambeth	17·0	12·2	1·5
Lewisham	13·2	9·8	1·6
Southwark	13·1	11·2	0·6
Tower Hamlets	13·5	26·1	0·5
Wandsworth	14·3	12·4	2·0
Birmingham	11·3	7·4	0·9
Bradford	8·3	9·1	0·4
Cardiff	10·8	5·1	0·5
Coventry	9·0	5·1	0·6
Glasgow	5·4	9·1*	0·49*
Liverpool	10·3	5·4	0·4
Manchester	16·5	9·6	0·4
City 'A'	11·0	9·2	0·4

* The figures apply to the 30th November 1968, and were obtained from the Social Work Services section of the Scottish Education Department.

Sources : Illegitimate births data for England and Wales from General Register Office, *The Registrar General's Statistical Review of England and Wales for the Year 1967.* HMSO, 1969.
The Glasgow figure from the Corporation of Glasgow.
Children in care and supervised under the 1958 Act data from Home Office 'Summary of Local Authorities' Returns of Children in Care at 31st March 1968'.

TABLE 7. SOCIAL SERVICE PROVISION (A)

	Council housing as % of all dwellings* %	No. of play groups	Play groups per 1,000 of 0-4 population	No. of local authority day nurseries	Day nurseries per 1,000 of 0-4 population
Brent	8·7	39	1·7	11	0·5
Camden	20·4	36	2·7	10	0·7
Hackney	36·0	8	0·4	7	0·3
Hammersmith	17·3	10	0·6	7	0·5
Islington	20·4	17	0·8	5	0·2
Lambeth	27·9	32	1·2	10	0·4
Lewisham	28·5	40	1·7	3	0·1
Southwark	40·1	23	0·8	6	0·2
Tower Hamlets	51·7	15	0·9	4	0·2
Wandsworth	23·6	N.A.	N.A.	8	0·3
Birmingham	38·5	82	0·9	20	0·2
Bradford	23·5	25	0·9	6	0·2
Cardiff	26·6	N.A.	N.A.	2	0·0
Coventry	22·5	N.A.	N.A.	9	0·3
Glasgow	43·4	0	0	18	0·2
Liverpool	30·2	65	1·1	12	0·2
Manchester	28·6	26	0·5	22	0·4
City 'A'	34·1	4	0·2	5	0·3

Sources: In Tables 7 to 11 the material was obtained direct from the local authorities or from the local councils of social service in 1969.†

* The year accounted is 1966.

† The local authorities and councils of social service tried to relate information to 1968, but this was not always possible. Thus the 0-4 years population for Islington and Lewisham in 1968 was not available, so the 1966 population had to be used. Lambeth, Camden, Tower Hamlets, Wandsworth, Cardiff and Coventry also used 1966 as the base. Glasgow gave figures for the year 1961, the last full census year. For these reasons, and because Authorities may have different means of recording information, Tables 7 to 11 should not be regarded as authoritative but just as giving some impression of resource distribution.

TABLE 8. SOCIAL SERVICE PROVISION (B)

	No. of local authority nursery schools	Nursery schools per 1,000 of 0-4 population	No. of tenants' associations	Tenants' associations per 1,000 population	No. of Settlements	Settlements per 1,000 population
Brent	1	0·04	16	0·06	0	0
Camden	3	0·2	23	0·1	0	0
Hackney	0	0	N.A.	N.A.	0	0
Hammersmith	3	0·18	6	0·03	1	0·005
Islington	2	0·09	10	0·04	0	0
Lambeth	N.A.	N.A.	12	0·04	N.A.	N.A.
Lewisham	N.A.	N.A.	17	0·06	0	0
Southwark	3	0·1	12	0·04	10	0·03
Tower Hamlets	N.A.	N.A.	25	0·12	11	0.05
Wandsworth	N.A.	N.A.	N.A.	N.A.	N.A.	N.A.
Birmingham	23	0·2	33	0·03	2	0·001
Bradford	3	0·1	6	0·02	0	0
Cardiff	9	0·04	7	0·03	0	0
Coventry	1	0·03	12	0·04	0	0
Glasgow	41	0·4	N.A.	N.A.	2	0·002
Liverpool	30	0·5	14	0·02	2	0·002
Manchester	5	0·09	5	0·008	1	0·002
City 'A'	1	0·05	13	0·05	0	0

TABLE 9. SOCIAL SERVICE PROVISION (C)

	No. of community associations	Community associations per 1,000 population	No. of voluntary family casework agencies
Brent	9	0·04	2
Camden	0	0	4
Hackney	20	0·08	1
Hammersmith	N.A.	N.A.	N.A.
Islington	5	0·02·	3
Lambeth	N.A.	N.A.	2
Lewisham	6	0·02	2
Southwark	5	0·02	3
Tower Hamlets	3	0·02	5
Wandsworth	N.A.	N.A.	N.A.
Birmingham	31	0·03	5
Bradford	N.A.	N.A.	2
Cardiff	7	0·03	1
Coventry	14	0·04	2
Glasgow	N.A.	N.A.	2
Liverpool	9	0·01	30
Manchester	2	0·003	6
City 'A'	5	0·02	3

Sources: local authorities, 1969; local councils of social service, 1969.

Table 10.   SOCIAL WORKERS AND GENERAL PRACTITIONERS* (A)

TOTAL NUMBERS

	General Practitioners	Child care officers	Mental welfare officers	Welfare officers	Probation officers
Brent	301	18	9	14	22
Camden	164	35	15	22	12
Hackney	123	35	13	26	22
Hammersmith	114	26	12	28	17
Islington	117	43·5	15	29	17
Lambeth	N.A.	N.A.	15·5	N.A.	26
Lewisham	133	36	14	33	19·5
Southwark	180	36	23	83	22
Tower Hamlets	N.A.	54	9	34	17
Wandsworth	N.A.	38	N.A.	N.A.	26
Birmingham	438	89	30	19	72
Bradford	120	20	13	32	27
Cardiff	150	13	8	18	22
Coventry	132	20	16	13	18
Glasgow	535	26	14	27	98
Liverpool	431	41	27	22	75
Manchester	250	53	14	31	59
City 'A'	201	18	24†		21

* 'Social workers' refers only to field staff, and excludes senior staff with predominantly administrative duties.

The figures relating to general practitioners are particularly unsatisfactory, for some may practice partly outside their Local Authority or draw upon patients from outside. Figures given by the 'Annual Report of the Department of Health and Social Security for the year 1968' (HMSO, 1969) are useful, but fail to break down the London figures into its various boroughs. Taking National Health Service principal medical practitioners only, the average list of patients according to region and Executive Council was as follows:

England and Wales	2,477
London, Inner	2,304
Birmingham	2,674
Bradford	2,742
Cardiff	2,307
Coventry	2,731
Liverpool	2,452
Manchester	2,515
City 'A'	2,419

† In City 'A', welfare and mental welfare officers are combined.

Source: local authorities, 1969.

TABLE 11. SOCIAL WORKERS AND GENERAL PRACTITIONERS* (B)
NUMBERS PER 1,000 POPULATION

	General practitioners	Child care officers	Mental welfare officers	Welfare officers	Probation officers
Brent	1·2	0.07	0·04	0·06	0·07
Camden	0·8	0·16	0·07	0·1	0·055
Hackney	0·5	0·14	0·05	0·1	0·090
Hammersmith	0·6	0·13	0·06	0·14	0·09
Islington	0·5	0·18	0·06	0·12	0·07
Lambeth	N.A.	N.A.	0·05	N.A.	0·081
Lewisham	0·5	0·13	0·05	0·12	0·070
Southwark	0·6	0·12	0·08	0·28	0·074
Tower Hamlets	N.A.	0·27	0·05	0·17	0·086
Wandsworth	N.A.	0·12	0·05	N.A.	0·081
Birmingham	0·4	0·08	0·03	0·02	0·07
Bradford	0·4	0·07	0·04	0·11	0·09
Cardiff	0·5	0·05	0·03	0·07	N.A.
Coventry	0·4	0·06	0·05	0·04	0·05
Glasgow	0·5	0·02	0·01	0·03	0·09
Liverpool	0·6	0·05	0·03	0·03	0·1
Manchester	0·4	0·09	0·02	0·05	0·1
City 'A'	0·8	0·07	0·1†		0·09

* † See Notes to Table 10.

TABLE 12. QUALIFIED CHILD CARE OFFICERS

	% of cco's professionally qualified %	% of cco's semi-qualified %	% of cco's non-qualified %
England and Wales	38·2	20·8	39·9
Brent	31·6	36·8	31·6
Camden	37·1	20·0	42·9
Hackney	11·1	37·0	51·9
Hammersmith	35·5	35·5	29·0
Islington	27·6	36·2	36·2
Lambeth	57·2	6·1	36·7
Lewisham	27·3	13·6	59·1
Southwark	27·9	23·3	48·8
Tower Hamlets	66·1	13·6	20·3
Wandsworth	68·7	0	31·3
Birmingham	32·5	27·9	39·4
Bradford	21·1	26·3	52·6
Cardiff	7·7	53·8	38·5
Coventry	38·5	38·5	23·0
Glasgow	N.A.	N.A.	N.A.
Liverpool	27·3	6·1	66·6
Manchester	27·5	34·8	37·7
City 'A'	15·4	38·5	46·1

Source: Association of Child Care Officers. Figures refer to 31st March 1967.

Appendix 'B'

Some indicators of social deprivation in wards

In order to give an impression of deprivation in smaller units than the whole of a local authority, Tables 13 to 16 present data on a ward basis. The local authorities themselves suggested wards which they expected to score high on deprivation indicators. The data comes from the 1966 Sample Census and was made available by the General Register Office. It was also able to provide figures on migration within and to the areas and, as they probably also relate to social need, are given in Table 16.

TABLE 13. POPULATION STRUCTURE

Wards	Total population	Population aged 0-4 years as % of total population %	Population aged 5-14 years as % of total population %	Economically active and retired males aged 15+ in unskilled and semi-skilled manual work %
Kilburn (Brent)	10,530	8·8	7·8	32·6
St. Johns (Camden)	8,850	9·2	9·9	26·8
Clissold (Hackney)	12,740	7·5	12·4	30·2
Sherbrooke (Hammersmith)	7,000	9·4	11·4	31·3
Barnsbury (Islington)	11,570	9·2	15·0	35·6
Tulse Hill (Lambeth)	17,130	11·0	14·8	27·9
Drake (Lewisham)	14,950	10·0	11·5	29·7
Faraday (Southwark)	15,070	6·8	14·9	29·3
Bethnal Green North (Tower Hamlets)	7,950	8·4	14·0	30·3
Shaftsbury (Wandsworth)	15,130	9·3	11·4	31·4
Soho (Birmingham)	27,690	13·9	14·2	36·0
Manningham (Bradford)	11,680	9·1	11·2	45·3
Canton (Cardiff)	11,820	8·8	11·8	22·2
St. Michaels (Coventry)	19,600	9·1	15·2	40·8
Woodside (Glasgow)	13,630	13·4	13·1	38·0
Granby (Liverpool)	17,040	15·6	18·3	42·4
Beswick (Manchester)	16,170	12·5	17·4	36·1
Ward 'B' (City 'A')	10,830	10·2	13·3	24·3

TABLE 14. POPULATION STRUCTURE AND OVERCROWDING

Wards	Total households	Large households with 6 or more persons % of total households %	% of total households with density of population over 1½ per room %	Resident population born in new Commonwealth countries	Resident population born in New Commonwealth countries as % of total population %
Kilburn	4,260	3·5	8·5	1,220	11·6
St. Johns	3,450	6·1	5·8	1,320	14·9
Clissold	4,610	5·2	5·0	2,100	16·5
Sherbrooke	2,740	5·1	5·5	310	4·4
Barnsbury	3,970	7·6	10·3	1,570	13·6
Tulse Hill	5,870	8·0	8·2	2,980	17·4
Drake	5,290	6·6	6·4	2,620	17·5
Faraday	5,000	4·4	1·8	240	1·6
Bethnal Green North	2,890	4·8	1·7	90	1·1
Shaftesbury	5,320	6·6	4·5	1,990	13·2
Soho	8,620	12·9	11·5	5,900	21·3
Manningham	4,180	5·5	3·8	1,680	14·4
Canton	3,830	7·6	0·5	40	0·3
St. Michael's	6,200	10·8	3·1	1,830	9·3
Woodside	5,030	8·0	21·5	270	2·0
Granby	5,230	12·8	10·1	1,130	6·6
Beswick	5,340	8·6	2·8	70	0·4
Ward 'B'	3,830	6·5	1·8	240	2·2

TABLE 15.　HOUSING AMENITIES

Wards	Households with shared use of hot water tap % of total households %	Households with no use of hot water tap % of total households %	Households with shared use of fixed bath % of total households %	Households with no use of fixed bath % of total households %	Households with shared use of inside wc % of total households %	Households with outside wc only % of total households %
Kilburn	22·5	30·3	49·5	17·4	47·4	8·0
St. Johns	9·0	39·4	37·4	31·3	51·6	7·8
Clissold	11·3	33·8	24·7	36·0	31·2	19·1
Sherbrooke	12·0	37·6	23·0	44·9	20·1	28·8
Barnsbury	6·8	44·6	20·9	51·9	39·3	18·1
Tulse Hill	15·0	28·8	37·5	17·2	36·3	10·4
Drake	15·7	21·0	35·7	15·7	34·0	9·3
Faraday	2·2	30·4	3·6	41·6	9·2	27·6
Bethnal Green North	—	27·0	8·0	31·8	10·4	27·0
Shaftesbury	9·4	36·8	23·3	36·5	17·7	32·5
Soho	15·2	31·0	18·8	32·6	19·7	37·4
Manningham	4·1	21·8	6·7	32·5	6·2	51·7
Canton	7·0	17·0	14·1	23·5	10·2	45·4
St. Michaels	3·7	51·0	6·3	49·7	6·5	53·5
Woodside	5·0	54·9	5·8	76·9	40·2	4·2
Granby	15·3	41·1	23·9	42·8	28·7	40·5
Beswick	0·2	60·5	0·2	81·6	—	90·1
Ward 'B'	0·3	17·5	0·3	25·6	0·3	50·9

TABLE 16. MIGRATION

Ward	Persons moving within the LA area during the past year as % of total population %	Persons moving within the LA area during the past 5 years as % of total population %	Persons moving into the LA area during the past year as % of total population %	Persons moving into the LA area during the past 5 years as % of total population %
Kilburn	4·7	8·5	9·7	26·7
St. Johns	8·1	10·5	6·0	20·5
Clissold	5·0	14·8	7·9	20·3
Sherbrooke	5·0	10·1	6·3	15·9
Barnsbury	4·7	14·3	5·0	19·2
Tulse Hill	8·2	19·1	4·0	16·7
Drake	5·4	15·1	7·8	19·1
Faraday	3·5	22·9	3·2	10·1
Bethnal Green North	3·9	14·2	1·6	8·6
Wandsworth	5·6	13·4	6·3	17·1
Soho	8·6	19·6	4·3	13·2
Manningham	9·8	21·7	4·3	17·6
Canton	6·5	16·8	2·3	8·8
St. Michaels	9·2	18·5	3·9	15·6
Woodside	10·0	25·1	1·5	7·6
Granby	8·7	27·2	3·3	6·7
Beswick	7·4	18·7	1·7	5·9
Ward 'B'	9·0	20·0	2·5	10·0

ACKNOWLEDGEMENTS

We are grateful for the co-operation of various government departments, and especially to the Controller of Her Majesty's Stationery Office, for permission to reproduce tables from the report *The Housing Survey in England and Wales*, 1964 published on behalf of the government's social survey; to use material from Housing Statistics No. 10, 1968, the Report of the Committee on Housing in Greater London of 1965, and Economic Trends No. 175; for material from the Family Expenditure Surveys, 1966 and 1967, the Employment and Productivity Gazette and the report *Circumstances of Families*, 1967; and for reproducing statistics from the report of the Home Office Statistical Branch, 'A Summary of Local Authorities' Returns of Children in Care at 31st March 1968'.

Similarly, we are grateful to the General Register Office for permission to reproduce tables and use material from their publications.

Notes and References

INTRODUCTION

1. Quoted in P. Hall, *The Social Services of Modern England*. Sixth ed., Routledge and Kegan Paul, 1963.
2. Ministry of Social Security, *Circumstances of Families*. HMSO, 1967.
3. B. Abel-Smith and P. Townsend, *The Poor and the Poorest*. Bell, 1965.
4. K. Coates and R. Silburn, *St Ann's: Poverty, Deprivation and Morale in a Nottingham Community*. Dept. of Adult Education, Nottingham University, 1967.
5. J. Floud, A. Halsey, and F. Martin, *Social Class and Educational Opportunity*. Heinemann, 1957.
6. J. W. B. Douglas, *The Home and the School*. MacGibbon and Kee, 1964.
7. J. W. B. Douglas, *All Our Future*, Peter Davies, 1968.
8. Central Advisory Council for Education, *15 to 18* (Crowther Report). HMSO, 1959.
9. Central Advisory Council for Education, *Half Our Future* (Newsom Report). HMSO, 1963.
10. Central Advisory Council for Education, *Children and Their Primary Schools* (Plowden Report), Vols 1 & 2. HMSO, 1967.
11. B. Rodgers, *The Battle Against Poverty*, Vol 2. Routledge and Kegan Paul, 1969.
12. D. V. Donnison, 'The contribution of research to housing policy', in *Essays on Housing*, Occasional Papers on Social Administration No 9, Codicote Press, Welwyn, 1964.
13. R. M. Titmuss, *The Irresponsible Society*, Fabian Tract 323. Fabian Society, London, 1960.
14. O. R. McGregor, 'Social Facts and Social Conscience', *Twentieth Century*, May, 1960.
15. M. Wynn, *Fatherless Families*. Michael Joseph, 1964.
16. Ministry of Pensions and National Insurance, *Financial and Other Circumstances of Retirement Pensioners*. HMSO, 1966.
17. A. Sinfield, *Poverty Research in Britain and Europe* (draft). Essex University, 1968.
18. R. M. Titmuss, 'The social divisions of welfare', reprinted in R. M. Titmuss, *Essays on the Welfare State*. Allen and Unwin, 1958.
19. R. M. Titmuss, *Income Distribution and Social Change*. Allen and Unwin, 1962.
20. S. Yudkin, *0-5*. National Society of Children's Nurseries, London, 1967.

1. INCOME DEPRIVATION

1. Social Science Research Council, *Research on Poverty*, 1968.
2. Ministry of Social Security, *Circumstances of Families*. HMSO, 1967.
3. Department of Health and Social Security, Supplementary Benefits Commission, *The Right to Help*. HMSO, 1969.
4. Ministry of Labour, *Sick Pay Schemes*. HMSO, 1964.
5. R. M. Titmuss, *Commitment to Welfare*. Allen and Unwin, 1968. Chap. 16.
6. Ministry of Labour, *Family Expenditure Survey, 1966*. HMSO, 1967; and Department of Employment and Productivity: *Family Expenditure Survey, 1967*. HMSO, 1968.
7. Ministry of Social Security, *Administration of the Wage Stop* (Report by Supplementary Benefits Commission). HMSO, 1967.

8. For information about low earners see:
   Judith Marquandt, 'Which are the Lower-Paid Workers?' in *British Journal of Industrial Relations*, 5, 3, Nov. 1967.
   Employment and Productivity Gazette, May 1969.
   Ref. 6 above.
   A. R. Thatcher, 'Distribution of Earnings of Employees in Great Britain' in *Journal of Royal Statistical Society*, 131, 2, 1968, Series A.
   I. Gough and T. Stark, 'Low Incomes in the United Kingdom, 1954, 1959 and 1963' in *Manchester School*, 1968, 2.
9. Department of Employment and Productivity, *Family Expenditure Survey*, 1967. HMSO, 1968.
10. 'The Incidence of Taxes and Social Service Benefits Particularly Among Households with Low Incomes' in *Economic Trends*, No. 177, July 1968.
11. *Local Government Finance*, Nov. 1968.
12. Hansard, 3rd July 1967.
13. Department of Education and Science, *Education and Science in 1968*. HMSO, Cmnd. 3950, 1969.
14. Hilary Land, 'Provision for Large Families' in *New Society*, 24 Nov. 1966.
15. Mike Reddin in *Social Services for All? Part One*. Fabian Tract 382, London, 1968.
16. Child Poverty Action Group, *Poverty*, 6, Spring 1968.
17. Government Actuary, *Occupational Pension Schemes* (Third survey). HMSO, 1968.
18. Department of Health and Social Security, *National Superannuation and Social Insurance—Proposals for Earnings-Related Social Security*. HMSO, Cmnd. 3883, Jan. 1969; and *Social Insurance—Proposals for Earnings-Related Short-Term and Invalidity Benefits*. HMSO, Cmnd. 4124, July 1969.
19. Richard Crossman, *Address to annual meeting of National Council of Social Service*, London, Nov. 1968.

2. HOUSING AND SOCIALLY DEPRIVED FAMILIES

1. D. V. Donnison, *The Government of Housing*. Pelican, 1967.
2. *Report of the Committee on Housing in Greater London*. HMSO, Cmnd. 2605, 1965.
3. Scottish Development Department, *The Older Houses in Scotland, a Plan for Action*. HMSO, Cmnd. 3598, 1968.
4. *Appraisal of the hygienic quality of housing and its environment*, World Health Organisation Technical Report Series No. 353, 1967.
5. B. N. Downie, *The Social Areas of Birmingham*. Occasional Paper Series of the Centre for Urban and Regional Studies, Birmingham University (to be published 1970).
6. J. B. Cullingworth, A *Profile of Glasgow Housing, 1965*, Glasgow University Social and Economic Studies, Occasional Paper No. 8, 1968.
7. Ministry of Housing and Local Government, *Old Houses into New Homes*. HMSO, Cmnd. 3602, 1968.
8. *House Condition Survey, England and Wales, 1967*, Economic Trends, No. 175, HMSO, 1968.
9. J. B. Cullingworth, *Housing in Transition*. Heinemann, 1963.
10. F. T. Burnett and S. Scott, A *survey of housing conditions in the urban areas of England and Wales*, Sociological Review, 10, 1962.
11. M. Woolf, *The Housing Survey in England and Wales*. Government Social Survey, HMSO, 1967.
12. J. B. Cullingworth, *Scottish Housing in 1965*. Scottish Development Dept., 1967; and A *Profile of Glasgow Housing, 1965, op. cit.*
13. Ministry of Housing and Local Government, *Housing Statistics, no. 10*, 1968.

14. R. A. Parker, *The Rents of Council Houses*. Occasional Papers in Social Administration, No. 22, Bell, 1968.
15. W. B. Harbert, 'Who owes rent?', *Sociological Review*, vol. 13, No. 2, 1965.
16. H. Land, 'Provision for large families', *New Society*, 24 Nov. 1966.
17. Housing Act, 1957, Section 4(1).
18. Ministry of Housing and Local Government, Central Housing Advisory Committee, *Our Older Homes, a Call for Action*. HMSO, 1966.
19. Scottish Development Department, Scottish Housing Advisory Committee, *Scotland's Older Houses*. HMSO, 1967.
20. Housing (Scotland) Act, 1962, Section 24(1).
21. Ministry of Housing and Local Government, *Housing Statistics No. 12*.
22. Ministry of Housing and Local Government, *Current trends in housing progress*. Economic Trends No. 175, 1968.
23. J. Greve, *Private Landlords in England*. Occasional Papers on Social Administration, No. 16, Bell, 1965.
24. Housing Act, 1964, Part III Section 13(1).
25. Ministry of Social Security, *Circumstances of Families*. HMSO, 1967.
26. S. Alderson, *Britain in the Sixties: Housing*. Penguin, 1962.
27. Ministry of Health Circular 20/66, Home Office Circular 178/66, and Ministry of Housing and Local Government Circular 58/66.
28. A. Harvey, 'Homeless? You can't come here', *New Society*, 323-324, 27 Feb. 1969.
29. J. Greve, *London's Homeless*. Occasional Papers on Social Administration, No. 1 Codicote Press, Welwyn, 1964.
30. *Report of the Committee on Local Authority and Allied Personal Social Services* (Seebohm Report). HMSO, Cmnd. 3703, 1968.
31. City of Birmingham, City Council Meeting Summons, 7 Feb. 1967, *Housing Management Committee Report*, item 19.
32. National Assistance Board, *Homeless Single Persons*. HMSO, 1966.
33. D. V. Donnison, *The Government of Housing, op. cit.* The nutrition study he refers to is R. Lambert's *Nutrition in Britain*, Occasional Papers on Social Administration, No. 6, Codicote Press, Welwyn, 1964.
34. L. Needleman, *The Economics of Housing*. Staples Press, 1965.
35. E. Burney, *Housing on Trial*. Oxford University Press for Institute of Race Relations, 1967.
36. Political and Economic Planning, *Report on Racial Discrimination*, sponsored by the Race Relations Board and the National Committee for Commonwealth Immigrants, 1967.
37. J. Rex and R. Moore, *Race, Community and Conflict*. Oxford University Press, 1967.
38. Ministry of Housing and Local Government, *Gypsies and Other Travellers*. HMSO, 1967.
39. P. Gray and E. Parr, *A Survey of Residential Caravan Life*. Government Social Survey, 1959.
40. The Consumer Council, *Living in a Caravan*. HMSO, 1967.
41. J. W. B. Douglas, *The Home and the School*. MacGibbon and Kee, 1964.
42. Central Advisory Council for Education, *Children and their Primary Schools*. HMSO, 1967.

3. THE SOCIALISATION OF CHILDREN

1. Ministry of Social Security, *Circumstances of Families*. HMSO, 1967.
2. Ministry of Social Security, *Administration of the Wage Stop*. HMSO, 1967.
3. P. Townsend, 'The meaning of poverty', *British Journal of Sociology*, Sept. 1962.
4. B. Abel-Smith and P. Townsend, *The Poor and the Poorest*. Bell, 1965.
5. P. Townsend, *The Disabled in Society*. Greater London Association for the Disabled, 1967.
6. J. Veit Wilson, 'The Resources of the Disabled' (draft). University of Essex, 1967.
7. H. Land, 'Provision for large families', *New Society*, 24 Nov. 1966.
8. II. Land, 'Large Families in London' (draft). London School of Economics, 1967.
9. D. Marsden, *Mothers Alone—Poverty and the Fatherless Family*. Allen Lane, Penguin Press, 1969.
10. A. Sinfield, 'Unemployed in Shields' (draft). University of Essex, 1967.
11. P. Marris, *Widows and Their Families*. Routledge and Kegan Paul, 1958.
12. V. Wimperis, *The Unmarried Mother and Her Child*. Allen and Unwin, 1960.
13. P. Morris, *Prisoners and Their Families*. Allen and Unwin, 1965.
14. M. Wynn, *Fatherless Families*. Michael Joseph, 1964.
15. K. Coates and R. Silburn, 'St. Ann's—Poverty, Deprivation and Morale'. Dept. of Adult Education, Nottingham University, 1967.
16. K. Coates and R. Silburn, 'The Morale of The Poor'. Dept. of Adult Education, Nottingham University, 1968.
17. R. Lambert, *Nutrition in Britain, 1950-1960*. Occasional Papers on Social Administration, No. 6. Codicote Press, Welwyn, 1964.
18. Office of Health Economics, *Malnutrition in the 1960's?* Publication No. 23, London, 1967.
19. W. Berry and D. Hollingsworth, 'The indices of nutritional change in Britain', *Proc. Nutr. Soc.* 22, 48-55.
20. Department of Education and Science, *The Health of the School Child, 1964-65*. HMSO, 1966.
21. J. W. B. Douglas, *Children Under Five*. Allen and Unwin, 1958.
22. P. Asher, 'One thousand school children', *The Medical Officer*, 16 June, 1967.
23. P. Asher, 'A Survey of the Health Services for Children in the City of Birmingham'. Institute of Child Health, University of Birmingham, 1966. (Restricted circulation.)
24. N. R. Butler and D. Bonham, *Perinatal Mortality*. Livingstone, 1963.
25. J. C. Kincaid, 'Social pathology of foetal and infant loss', *British Medical Journal*, 17 April, 1965.
26. B. Bernstein, 'A socio-linguistic approach to social learning', in *Penguin Survey of the Social Sciences*, ed. J. Gould. Penguin, 1965.
27. A. Luria and F. Yudkovitch, *Speech and the Development of Mental Processes*. Staples Press, 1959.
28. J. and E. Newson, *Four Years Old in an Urban Community*. Allen and Unwin, 1968.
29. L. W. Shaw, 'Impressions of Family Life in a London Suburb', *Sociol. Review*, 11, 2, 1954.
30. C. D. Mitchell, 'Neighbourhood and Community'. Dept. of Social Science Research Series, Liverpool University, 1954.
31. L. Kuper, *Living in Towns*. Cresset Press, 1953.
32. J. Mogey, *Family and Neighbourhood*. Oxford University Press, 1956.
33. R. Wilson, *Difficult Housing Estates*. Tavistock Pamphlet, London, 1963.

34. P. Shapiro, 'Children's play as a concern of family caseworkers', *Case Conference*, 9, No. 7, January, 1963.
35. B. Spock, *Baby and Child Care*. Bodley Head, 1955.
36. J. W. B. Douglas, *The Home and the School*. MacGibbon and Kee, 1964.
37. J. W. B. Douglas, *All Our Future*. Peter Davies, 1968.
38. Central Advisory Council for Education, *Half Our Future* (Newsom Report). HMSO, 1963.
39. J. Klein, *Samples from English Cultures*. Routledge and Kegan Paul, 1967.
40. A. F. Philp, *Family Failure*. Faber, 1963.
41. H. Wilson, *Delinquency and Child Neglect*. Allen and Unwin, 1962.
42. F. Bodman, 'Personal factors in the problem family', *Case Conference*, 5, No. 4, September 1958.
43. H. Wilson, 'Problem families and the concept of immaturity', *Case Conference*, 6, October 1959.
44. B. Spinley, *The Deprived and the Privileged*. Routledge and Kegan Paul, 1954.
45. M. Kerr, *The People of Ship Street*. Routledge and Kegan Paul, 1958.
46. Central Advisory Council for Education, *Early Leaving*. HMSO, 1954.
47. Central Advisory Council for Education, *15 to 18* (Crowther Report). HMSO, 1959.
48. Committee on Higher Education, *Higher Education* (Robbins Report). HMSO, 1963.
49. H. Skeels, 'Adult Status of Children with Contrasting Early Life Experiences: a Follow-up Study'. Child Development Monograph, published by the University of Chicago Press, Society for Research in Child Development. (Serial No. 105, Vol. 31, No. 3, 1966.)
50. A. R. Jensen, 'The culturally disadvantaged: psychological and educational aspects', *Educational Research*, Vol. 10, 1, 4-29 (USA, 1967).
51. M. P. Honzik, 'Developmental studies of parent-child resemblance in intelligence', *Child Development*, 28, 215-228.
52. Central Advisory Council for Education, *Children and their Primary Schools* (Plowden Report). HMSO, 1967.
53. N. Tyerman, *Truancy*. University of London Press, 1968.
54. Ministry of Education, *Report of the Committee on Maladjusted Children* (Underwood Report). HMSO, 1955.
55. D. J. West, *Present Conduct and Future Delinquency*. Heinemann, 1969.
56. N. Chazan, 'The incidence and nature of maladjustment among children in schools for the educationally sub-normal'. *British Journal of Educational Psychology*, 34, 292-304, 1964.
57. D. H. Stott, *Troublesome Children*. Tavistock, 1966.
58. P. Willmott, *Adolescent Boys of East London*. Routledge and Kegan Paul, 1966.
59. J. W. B. Douglas, *et al.*, 'Delinquency and social class', *British Journal of Criminology*, 6, 3, 1966.
60. H. B. Gibson and D. J. West, 'Some Concomitants of Early Delinquency' (draft). University of Cambridge, Institute of Criminology, 1968.
61. C. Winnicott, 'Communicating with children' in *Disturbed Children*, ed. R. J. N. Tod. Longmans, 1968.

4. COMBATING SOCIAL DEPRIVATION

1. R. A. Parker, 'Where the poorest live', in *Poverty*, 4, Autumn 1967. Child Poverty Action Group, London.
2. J. Greve, *London's Homeless*, Occasional Papers on Social Administration, No. 10. Codicote Press, Welwyn, 1964.
3. Ministry of Social Security, *Administration of the Wage Stop*. HMSO, London, 1967.
4. N. Tyerman, *Truancy*. University of London Press, 1968.
5. Central Advisory Council for Education, *Children and Their Primary Schools* (Plowden Report), Vols. 1 and 2. HMSO, 1967.
6. B. Abel-Smith and P. Townsend, *The Poor and the Poorest*, Occasional Papers on Social Administration, No. 17. Bell, London, 1965.
7. A. Sinfield, 'Poverty Research in Britain and Europe' (draft). University of Essex, 1968.
8. Ministry of Social Security, *Circumstances of Families*. HMSO, 1967.
9. K. Coates and R. Silburn, *St. Ann's—Poverty, Deprivation and Morale*. Dept. of Adult Education, Nottingham University, 1967.
10. H. Land, 'Provision for Large Families', *New Society*, 24 Nov. 1966.
11. Notting Hill Housing Service, *Notting Hill Housing Survey*, 1968.
12. N. Chazan, 'The incidence and nature of maladjustment among children in schools for the educationally subnormal', *British Journal of Educational Psychology*, 34, 292-304, 1964.
13. J. Packman, *Child Care: Needs and Numbers*. Allen and Unwin, London, 1968.
14. M. Wynn, *Fatherless Families*. Michael Joseph, London, 1964.
15. *Report of the Committee on Local Authority and Allied Personal Social Services* (Seebohm Report). HMSO, 1968.
16. D. Marsden, *Mothers Alone—Poverty and the Fatherless Family*. Allen Lane, Penguin Press, London, 1969.
17. R. Holman, 'Unsupported Mothers and the Care of their Children' (draft). Birmingham University, 1969.
18. P. Marris, *Widows and their Families*. Routledge and Kegan Paul, 1958.
19. V. Wimperis, *The Unmarried Mother and her Child*. Allen and Unwin, 1960.
20. S. Yudkin and A. Holme, *Working Mothers and their Children*. Michael Joseph, 1963.
21. P. Morris, *Prisoners and their Families*. Allen and Unwin, 1965.
22. S. Yudkin, *0 - 5, a report on the care of Pre-school Children*. National Society of Children's Nurseries, London, 1967.
23. A. Sinfield, 'Unemployed in Shields' (draft). University of Essex, 1967.
24. P. Townsend, *The Disabled in Society*. Greater London Association for the Disabled, London, 1967.
25. H. Wilson, *Delinquency and Child Neglect*. Allen and Unwin, 1962.
26. P. and P. Willmott, 'Off work through illness', *New Society*, 10 Jan. 1963.
27. Tower Hamlets Council of Social Service, *Physical Disability and Community Care*. Bedford Square Press of the NCSS, London, 1969.
28. V. Karn, 'Property values amongst Indians and Pakistanis in a Yorkshire Town', *Race*, July/August 1969.
29. D. Beetham, *Immigrant School Leavers and the Youth Employment Service in Birmingham*. Institute of Race Relations, London, 1968.
30. Political and Economic Planning, *Racial Discrimination*. PEP, London, 1967.
31. Sample Census, 1966, Great Britain, Commonwealth Immigrant Tables. HMSO, 1969.
32. J. Rex and R. Moore, *Race, Community and Conflict*. Oxford University Press for the Institute of Race Relations, London, 1967.

33. *Report of the Committee ʼon Housing in Greater London* (Milner Holland Report). HMSO, 1965.
34. E. Burney, *Housing on Trial*. Oxford University Press for the Institute of Race Relations, 1967.
35. Institute of Race Relations, *Colour and Citizenship*. Oxford University Press, 1969.
36. Ministry of Housing and Local Government, *Gypsies and Other Travellers*. HMSO, 1967.
37. J. W. B. Douglas, *The Home and the School*. MacGibbon and Kee, 1964.
38. R. Wilson, *Difficult Housing Estates*. Tavistock Publications, 1963.
39. K. Coates and R. Silburn, *The Morale of the Poor*. Dept. of Adult Education, Nottingham University, 1968.
40. A. J. Kahn, 'Perspectives on access to social services', *Social Work*, Vol. 26, No. 3, July 1969.
41. Central Advisory Council for Education, *Half our Future* (Newsom Report). HMSO, 1963.
42. National Committee for Commonwealth Immigrants, *Areas of Special Housing Need*, London, 1967.
43. B. Seebohm Rowntree and G. R. Lavers, *Poverty and the Welfare State*. Longmans Green, 1951.
44. Child Poverty Action Group, *Poverty*, 3, Summer 1967.
45. *The Guardian*, April 1969.
46. D. Marsh, *The Future of the Welfare State*. Penguin, 1964.
47. Ed. A. Neale and G. Haine, 'City of Birmingham Abstract of Statistics', No. 11, 4, City of Birmingham, 1966-67.
48. City of Birmingham Children's Department, 'Admissions to Care and Children under supervision—by Wards' (duplicated sheet), 1968.
49. See, Central Office of Information, *Social Services in Britain*. HMSO, 1964.
50. Quoted in Appendix F, Seebohm Report, *op. cit.*
51. National Society of Children's Nurseries, 'A statistical analysis of day and residential nurseries in England and Wales', London, 1962.
52. T. Ryan, 'Day Nursery provision under the Health Service, England and Wales, 1948-63'. National Society of Children's Nurseries, London, 1964.
53. D. Barnard, 'Sex on the Rates', *New Society*, 31 Oct. 1968.
54. Letter from the Ministry of Housing and Local Government to writer, dated 4th June 1969.
55. M. P. Hall, *The Social Services of Modern England*, 6th edition. Routledge and Kegan Paul, 1963.
56. N. Swingler, 'Move on, gypsy', *New Society*, 26 June 1969.
57. P. Townsend, 'The timid and the bold', *New Society*, 23 May 1963.
58. T. White, 'Social Services and Local Government Reform', *Case Conference*, Vol. 15, No. 5, Sept. 1968.
59. P. Townsend, 'Seebohm Assessed', in *The Seebohm Report*, a *New Society* pamphlet, 1968.
60. B. Davies, *Social Needs and Resources in Local Services*. Michael Joseph, 1968.
61. *Report of the Royal Commission on Local Government in England* (Maud Report). HMSO, Cmnd. 4040, 1969.
62. *The Guardian*, 16 May 1969.
63. J. A. G. Griffith, *Central Departments and Local Authorities*. Allen and Unwin, 1967.
64. A. Forder, *Penelope Hall's 'Social Services of England'*. Routledge and Kegan Paul, 1969.
65. J. Eyden, *Social Policy in Action*, Library of Social Policy and Administration. Routledge and Kegan Paul, 1969.

66. W. Robson, *Nationalised Industry and Public Ownership*. Allen and Unwin, 1960.
67. R. Holman, in *The Guardian*, 25 March 1968.
68. R. Holman, 'The wrong poverty programme', *New Society*, 20 March 1969.
69. P. Marris and M. Rein, *Dilemmas of Social Reform*. Routledge and Kegan Paul, 1967.
70. E. James, *America Against Poverty*, forthcoming publication by Routledge and Kegan Paul.
71. B. Whitaker, *Participation and Poverty*, Fabian Research Series, No. 272. Fabian Society, London, 1968.
72. D. Moynihan, *Maximum Feasible Misunderstanding: Community action in the war on poverty*. Free Press, Collier-Macmillan, USA, 1969.
73. Department of Education and Science, Circular 11/67.
74. Home Office, 'Community Development', mimeographed, 1969.
75. Home Office, 'Community Development Project, Objectives and Strategy', mimeographed, 1969.
76. 'Britain's poverty programme', *New Society*, 16 Jan. 1969.
77. Quoted in E. James, *America Against Poverty*, *op. cit.*, chapter 8.
78. A. Sinfield, *Which Way For Social Work?*, Fabian Society Tract No. 393, London, 1969.
79. I. Epstein, 'Social workers and social action', *Social Work* (USA), Vol. 30, No. 2, April 1968.
80. Quoted in Seebohm Report, *op. cit.*, para. 494.
81. A. Lapping, 'Social action', *New Society*, 2 Jan. 1969.
82. *The Guardian*, 10 Sept. 1968.
83. Director of Research and Intelligence, Greater London Council, '1967 Annual Abstract of Greater London Statistics'. Greater London Council, 1969.
84. T. Blackstone, 'The Plowden Report', *The British Journal of Sociology*, Vol. XVIII, No. 3, Sept. 1967.
85. 'Children and their Primary Schools', *Municipal Review* (Supplement), Vol. 38, No. 453, Sept. 1967.
86. For instance, compare the criteria and methods employed by Birmingham and the Inner London Education Authority:
Chief Education Officer, 'School Building in Educational Priority Areas', City of Birmingham Education Committee, 5 March 1968.
'ILEA Index of Educational Priority Areas' (duplicated), Inner London Education Authority, 1968.
87. The content of this paragraph arises from communication with a government official to whom thanks are due for reading this section and making constructive comments
88. *New Society*, 5 June 1969.
89. M. Harrington, *The Other America*, Macmillan, New York, 1962.
90. G. Fry, *Statesmen in Disguise: the changing role of the administrative class of the British Home Civil Service, 1853-1966*. Macmillan, London, 1969.
91. See the review article of Moynihan's work (72) by P. Marris, *New Society*, 3 July 1969.
92. B. Whitaker, 'Tentative steps towards an anti-poverty programme', *The Times*, 24 July 1969.
93. Child Poverty Action Group, *Poverty*, 4, Autumn 1967.
94. Child Poverty Action Group, *Poverty*, 6, Spring 1968.
95. J. Bell, *How to Get Industrial Injuries Benefits*. Sweet and Maxwell, 1966.
96. M. Zander, 'Poverty and the legal profession', in R. Titmuss and M. Zander, *Unequal Rights*. Child Poverty Action Group and London Co-operative Education Dept., London, 1968.

97. M. Zander, 'The Unused Rent Acts', *New Society*, 12 Sept. 1968.
98. K. Worpole and S. Yeo, 'Rent Act in Brighton', *New Society*, 31 Oct. 1968.
99. J. and E. Newson, *Infant Care in an Urban Community*. Allen and Unwin, 1963.
100. For instance, recorded in the conference, 'Poverty and Child Health' organised by Birmingham Branch of the Socialist Medical Association and Birmingham Branch of the Socialist Education Association, Birmingham, 16 March 1968.
101. T. Lynes, in the foreword to R. Titmuss and M. Zander, *Unequal Rights*. Child Poverty Action Group and London Co-operative Education Dept., 1968.
102. B. Rodgers and J. Dixon, *Portrait of Social Work*. Oxford University Press, 1960.
103. Central Advisory Council for Education (Wales), *Primary Education in Wales* (Gittins Report). HMSO, 1968.
104. R. Brooke, 'Social services and the law', *British Hospital Journal and Social Services Review*, 21 Feb. 1969.
105. *United Claimants' News*, Birmingham Claimants' Union, various issues, 1968-69.
106. M. Jefferies, *An Anatomy of Social Welfare*. Michael Joseph, 1966.
107. The Public Schools Commission, *First Report*, Vols. 1 and 2. HMSO, 1968.
108. O. Lewis, *The Children of Sanchez*, Secker and Warburg, 1963, and *La Vida*, Random House, New York, 1966.
109. Haringey Family Service Unit, various duplicated papers, privately circulated, 1968-69.
110. T. Stephens (ed.), *Problem Families*. Pacifist Service Units, Liverpool, 1945.
111. *The Guardian*, 23 June 1969.
112. Ministry of Health, *Report of the Working Party on Social Workers in the Local Authority Health and Welfare Services* (Younghusband Report). HMSO, 1959.
113. K. Jones, 'Human Relations in Social Research', unpublished paper, presented at Birmingham University (1969).
114. K. Slack, *Social Administration and the Citizen*. Michael Joseph, 1966.
115. R. M. Titmuss, *Income Distribution and Social Change*. Allen and Unwin, 1962.
116. J. Heywood, *Children in Care*, 2nd edition. Routledge and Kegan Paul, 1965.
117. A. Harvey, 'Homeless? You can't come here', *New Society*, 27 Feb. 1969.
118. H. and E. Schaffer, *Child Care and the Family*, Occasional Papers on Social Administration, No. 25. Bell, 1968.
119. K. Fitzherbert, *West Indian Children in London*, Occasional Papers on Social Administration, No. 19. Bell, 1967.
120. R. Holman, 'Immigrants and child care policy', *Case Conference*, Vol. 15, No. 7, November 1968.
121. D. V. Donnison, V. Chapman, *et al.*, *Social Policy and Administration*. Allen and Unwin, 1965.

APPENDIX 'A'

1. Central Advisory Council for Education, *Children and their Primary Schools* (Plowden Report), Vols. I and II. HMSO, 1967.
2. B. Davies, *Social Needs and Resources in Local Services*. Michael Joseph, 1968.
3. Institute of Race Relations, *Colour and Citizenship*. Oxford University Press, 1969.

Index

Socially Deprived Families in Britain

Supplement

EDITOR'S NOTE

Socially Deprived Families in Britain was first published in 1970. Three years later, two factors have led the authors (with the exception of Professor Lafitte who was unable to help) to issue this Supplement. First, demand for the book has been maintained. Second, a number of important developments have occurred in social policy and the social services. All that can be presented now is a brief outline of the major developments but consideration will be given in the future to providing a completely revised edition of the book.

September 1973   R.H.

Dr Robert Holman is now Senior Lecturer in Social Administration and Social Work in the University of Glasgow.

Distributed by Research Publications Services,
Victoria Hall, East Greenwich, London SE10 0RF

Design and typography by NCSS Publications Department
Printed in England by Lewis Reprints Limited, Tonbridge.

Housing deprivation

Kenneth Spencer

In relation to the physical condition of the housing stock, annual slum clearance rates in England and Wales have continued at just below the 1968 level, varying between 68,000 and 70,000.[1] In 1971 a second national house condition survey indicated that some 1,244,000 dwellings remained unfit (this figure represents 7.3 per cent of the housing stock, compared with 12 per cent in 1967).[2] There still exists the need for an urgent drive to clear the statutorily defined slums, and one of the new subsidies of the 1972 Housing Finance Act is aimed at this.

The emphasis upon the improvement of the older housing stock has been continued under the impetus of the 1969 Housing Act. In 1969, 108,938 improvement grants were approved (45 per cent were the discretionary type), and by 1971 the 1969 Act's effects were beginning to be felt as 198,792 grants were approved (70 per cent discretionary). Hence the emphasis of grants has switched to the higher amenity level of improvement.[3]

However, improvement policies were not felt to be having the desired effect in areas where improvement was badly needed. The 1971 Housing Act identified the development and intermediate areas as those in a special need category.* In such areas, grants for dwelling and environmental improvement now cover three-quarters of the cost (within approved limits), whereas in the rest of the country the grant levels remain at one-half. Development

---

* To combat this form of housing deprivation a twofold geographic differentiation has been adopted, but grants still remain related to the physical structure of the dwelling and not to the ability or otherwise of a house owner to afford his share of the improvement costs. One can still argue that grants are in many cases not reaching those for whom they were intended and recent abuses of the system strengthen this case. One could also look upon the application of these higher grant levels as a form of economic aid to the building industry, especially the smaller firms in these areas, particularly as unemployment levels have been high.

and intermediate areas have thus received a boost and in the third quarter of 1971 (the first period of operation of the 1971 Act), some 9,802 discretionary grants were approved, a figure which rose markedly to 25,309 in the first quarter of 1972.[4] The number of general improvement areas declared has been 108 in 1970 and 163 in 1971.[5] However, progress with general improvement areas ought to be more rapid, as any advantage of living in a dwelling with improved amenities may be eroded by the poor environment in which it is situated.

With the continuing decline of privately rented accommodation (14 per cent of dwellings by 1971), there is a need to develop new forms of housing tenure, and to encourage more effectively the growth of the voluntary housing movement – an opportunity missed by the 1972 Act.[6] Our tenure options are too inflexible to cope well with the range of housing needs.

Housing policy has often been criticised as being too fragmented, based upon ad hoc decisions, lacking integration across tenure categories, partly due to the numerous private and public institutions involved in the housing process. Some movement has occurred in attempting to establish a comprehensive housing service (evolving around local authority administration).[7] Many calls for housing departments to diversify from the strictures of estate management have been made, and some have met with a level of success, tenants' groups are becoming more involved in management, housing aid centres are being established, mortgage facilities are provided and so on. However, the issue is not just one of diversifying activities, but the need to create a corporate approach at both local and national levels if any major impact is to be made upon improving the housing position of deprived families.[8] A fuller consideration of the roles played by different institutions in the housing market could lead to a restructuring, so that the deprived are more likely to get a better deal.[9]

The Caravan Sites Act of 1968 provided for more and better site accommodation for gypsies and other travellers. Local authorities were required to make provision for such sites; however, progress has been slow and contentious despite legislation.[10] A survey of these people in Scotland showed that in August 1969 there were 342 such families (1,598 persons), which is undoubtedly an underestimate. Average household size was high at 4.7 and 47.9 per cent of the families wished to settle permanently, while 32.5

per cent lived in tents (the similar figure for March 1969 was 25.4 per cent).[11] The housing conditions (if they can be called that), in which many of these families were found can only be described as atrocious and intolerable.

The subject of homeless families has been one about which knowledge has vastly improved in recent years.[12] Despite this, such families continue to increase at an alarming rate. Official figures reveal only the tip of the iceberg, showing by 1971 5,630 homeless families (26,879 persons) in local authority temporary accommodation in England and Wales of which 58 per cent were in Greater London. Amongst other things the evidence of London, and South Wales and the West of England, shows: very young children and large families were found in high proportions amongst the homeless; local authorities operated differing definitions of homelessness; official statistics indicated trends in the provision of temporary accommodation rather than numbers of homeless families; fatherless families constituted about one-third of temporary accommodation occupants; growing proportions of New Commonwealth immigrant families were becoming homeless; domestic friction remained an important cause of homelessness; while in London the housing shortage was itself a major cause, but was less so elsewhere; in times of high demand for temporary accommodation local authorities had to refuse admission because of lack of accommodation; in London 20 per cent of homeless families had been in temporary accommodation for over eighteen months, with large families often amongst this group because of difficulties in finding suitably sized accommodation, but in South Wales and the West of England only 6 per cent stayed in this type of accommodation longer than six months. The facts are now known and homelessness needs to be tackled with new vigour, otherwise it will become a growing sore upon society. However, the signs are sometimes pessimistic rather than optimistic.[13] The number and plight of homeless single people is a growing problem, and here even the semblance of an integrated policy to deal with this is lacking. If one were to become homeless, the treatment one would receive, including the rapidity or otherwise of decent rehousing, depends more than anything else upon geographical accident i.e. in which local authority area one became homeless. The London housing market in particular is unable to meet the demands placed upon it.[14]

Local government reorganisation in 1974 will result in housing being the main local government function in the county districts.[15] Entry into the Common Market may lead to influxes of European workers.

The 1972 Housing Finance Act represents the most significant change of emphasis in British housing policy since 1919.[16] It introduces fair rents into the public sector; speeds up changeover to such rents in the private sector; provides for rent rebates for council tenants and new town corporation tenants; provides rent allowances for housing association tenants and private unfurnished tenancies (furnished tenants are brought into the scheme, after much pressure, under the Furnished Lettings (Rent Allowances) Act 1973); gives a new emphasis to slum clearance. Basically the Act moves from subsidising council dwellings, to subsidising tenants irrespective of tenure, and is based upon a means test which considers the fair rent level, the gross household income and a needs allowance. It replaces locally determined rent setting and rebate schemes with a national scheme for both. Rent assessment panels calculate fair rents,[17] which are defined vaguely as discounting the scarcity element in the housing market. Rents in the council sector were raised in 1972 and will be raised further, over the next few years, until they reach fair rent levels. Politically, locally and nationally, the measure is highly controversial.[18]

Rebates will be put into effect by charging reduced rents, but allowances will be paid in cash to tenants and in both cases rents must be registered as fair rents in order to qualify. Rebates and allowances are calculated alike, and the weekly needs allowances of the Act have been increased under the prices and incomes freeze policy of 1973.* The maximum allowance or rebate is £8.00 per week in London and £6.50 elsewhere.

Where assessed income equals the needs allowance the tenant pays 40 per cent, or £1, of the fair rent (whichever is greater), and for each £1 by which income exceeds the allowance, rent payable increases by seventeen pence up to the fair rent. Where income is below the needs allowance, rent payable is reduced by

---

* They are: £14.00 for a single person; £18.25 for a couple, or an individual with a dependent child or children; £2.75 for each child. Registered handicapped persons have slightly higher needs allowances. Certain income is disregarded in calculating gross weekly income, eg. the first £2.50 of a wife's earnings, while certain deductions are made from rebates or allowances where there are non-dependants in the household.

twenty-five pence for each £1 by which income falls short.* Local authorities can increase the level of rebates and allowances by up to 10 per cent of the total cost, providing the rates meet the bill, and the scheme applies equally to rebates and allowances.

Many aspects of the Act provide valuable assistance for the deprived in the housing market, but it also raises questions. Is a fair rents principle appropriate in the public sector? A government report thought not;[19] and in Scotland standard rents, not fair rents, have been introduced. The objectives of housing policy are stated as: a decent home for every family at a price within their means; a fairer choice between owning a house and renting one; fairness between one citizen and another in giving and receiving help towards housing costs.[20] However, the Act excludes owner-occupiers and tax relief on mortgage interest payments (£300 million for the UK in 1970/71) ensures that higher income families, borrowing more, receive more subsidy through tax relief; at the same time their dwelling appreciates in value and is exempt from capital gains tax. This anomaly needs rectifying.

Under fair rents average local authority rents rise by about 25 per cent to 60 per cent or more, but averages conceal extremes. Controlled tenancy rents will double, treble or go up even more, as they start from a low base level.

Local authorities are empowered to pay only a proportion of any rebate or allowance if the tenant has a dwelling much larger than required, or is in a high rental cost area out of choice rather than necessity. This may well give rise to argument if taken literally.

Council tenants are easily identified and rebate take-up rates may be high, though many tenants are attempting to hold out against payment of these rent increases (and would thus not get a rebate). With private tenants the onus is upon them to claim every six months and take-up rates may well be low. Birmingham operated a rent allowance scheme for private tenants before the 1972 Act (it was the only authority to do so), and their experience was that by late 1972 the take-up rate was officially estimated at 6 per cent.[21] Experience shows that many deprived families will not benefit from policies enacted to assist them. The legislation

---

* A couple or single parent each with two children, income £24, fair rent £3, would receive £1.76; where income was £30, fair rent £5, they would receive £1.94.

may well have repercussions upon the social structure, affecting mobility rates, social differentiation, overcrowding and so on. The Labour Party has committed itself to repeal the Act if returned to power.[22]

Housing policy has moved further towards the point where subsidies are directed towards those in need rather than to dwellings of particular tenure categories. Yet we still have a long way to go before an integrated housing policy is devised which will ensure that the plight of the losers in the housing market struggle is overcome.[23] Nationally the resources we devote to housing are low compared with other European nations and this raises issues about the ordering of political priorities.[24]

The socialisation of children

Harriett Wilson

Since this chapter was written the first findings of research projects in educational priority areas have become available. One of these, the Schools Council research and development project in compensatory education, directed by Maurice Chazan, has been engaged on a number of enquiries involving infant school children in several areas of England and Wales. The aims are to provide a screening technique to enable children in need of compensatory education to be identified on entry to school; to make longitudinal studies of children in deprived areas; and to produce language materials for use in compensatory work in the infant school.[25] In a paper presenting preliminary findings Chazan and Jackson (1971)[26] showed that more five-year old children from deprived areas had aggressive behaviour problems than children from settled working-class or middle-class areas, but the actual numbers with such problems were relatively small; 11 per cent of boys in deprived, and 5 per cent in control areas.

The Educational Priority Areas action research project, directed by A.H. Halsey, sprang directly from the Plowden Report's recommendation that 'positive discrimination' should be exercised on behalf of deprived children. The criteria for identification of priority areas are described in Robert Holman's chapter of this book. The selection of educational priority areas, however, was deeply influenced by an endeavour to identify 'schools of exceptional difficulty' for purposes of additional remuneration of teachers under an amending order to the *Remuneration of Teachers Act, 1968*. In effect, educational priority areas came to mean the catchment areas of certain schools that had been identified on low socio-economic status of parents, absence of amenities in the children's homes, free school meals, and children with serious linguistic difficulties. As none of these criteria had been weighted, and the available data from the 1966 census are often seriously out of date in redevelopment areas, it is not surprising that the resulting choices of schools present quite substantial differences in populations. Of all schools recommended by LEAs only a small percentage were ultimately designated by the DES as presenting exceptional difficulties. EPA projects were set up in Birmingham, Dundee, Liverpool, London and West Riding. Responding to local opportunities and needs each project has produced different solutions to different problems. The findings, collated by Dr Halsey, are in course of publication.* The Birmingham EPA project has concentrated on three aspects: pre-school education, literacy work with selected primary schools, and the 'community school'. Experimental work with pre-school children was aimed at determining whether traditional pre-school procedures were effective in combating language deficiencies, and whether a more structured programme would be more effective. Paul Widlake,[27] in an article on language and learning in the pre-school, reports that comparison with middle-class controls showed that EPA children were very retarded on language measured by the English picture vocabulary test; even after a year's language intervention programme in EPA pre-schools, this gap remained substantial. Widlake concludes that traditional nursery school procedures in EPAs would be more effective if there were more child-adult verbal interaction, and that a structured intervention programme could help informal play groups to bring their standards of language work nearer to those of the nursery schools. All children in EPA pre-schools did significantly better than a group of deprived children who had no pre-school experience.

An as yet unpublished study of socially deprived children and their families in a Midlands city has been carried out by Harriett Wilson and G.W. Herbert.[28] Preliminary findings show the close correlation of social deprivation and educational measurements. Criteria for the selection of the sample of 174 six-year old and ten-year old boys were developed in the form of an instrument ascertaining degrees of social handicap. The choice of items was made on the basis of sociological data used in other researches concerned with educational performance; it was intended that it

*The first volume has now been published, A.H.Halsey (ed), *Educational priority* Vol 1.

should be used by the investigator in co-operation with the teacher. The items which are weighted on an eleven-point scale are: father's occupation, size of family, school attendance, adequacy of child's clothing, and parental contact with school. In the study under discussion the sample was located in high-need inner ring areas of the city, and therefore an item relating to housing was superfluous.

A pilot survey of a random sample of 400 boys in the same areas presented an overall picture of the distribution of social handicap. Practically half the boys' fathers were in semi-skilled or unskilled occupations, and the percentage of non-manual occupations was negligible. There was a striking preponderance of large families: 47 per cent of the boys in the sample came from families with five or more children. Compared with a national 'lower working-class' sample, as defined by Douglas,[29] the difference is highly significant: families with five or more children form less than a quarter of the national sample. The general level of parental contact with schools was low; only about 10 per cent of parents were rated as 'taking the initiative in discussing progress or supporting the school's efforts in an active way'. The information from teachers upon which these data are based must not be seen as a valid measure of parental interest in their children's education, still less of their potential capacity for concern, because it is probable that difficulties in communication and social insecurity play a large part in determining the quality of the contact between home and school.

The weighting system of the social handicap instrument was designed in such a way that children scoring five or more points show effects of material and social deprivation. On the other hand if a child scores only one or two points, he is likely to come from a home with a low social handicap. Children scoring three or four have a moderate social handicap. The pilot survey of 400 boys indicated that the 0-2, 3-4, and 5-11 ranges would account for about 40 per cent, 30 per cent, and 30 per cent respectively of the indigenous boys in the catchment areas of the research. Two groups of six-year old and ten-year old boys, 174 in all, matched for age in trios of social handicap, were subjected to a battery of ability and attainment tests and a personality rating of behaviour. Preliminary findings show that there is a close correlation of ability test results and social handicap: whereas the boys with mild degree of social handicap are very near national norms, the highly socially handicapped boys are very dull on all types of test, although they do slightly better on non-verbal than on verbal tests. The moderately handicapped boys occupy an intermediate position. In reading the difference between the groups is less great; at age ten even the low socially handicapped group are considerably retarded.

One of the aims of the study was to clarify the concept of troublesome behaviour of socially handicapped boys in school. Teachers were asked to rate behaviour on a scale designed for the purpose by G.W. Herbert. It was found that there is not much difference between the three groups of boys in 'acting-out' behaviour. A major difference, however, was found to exist in the highly socially handicapped boys' poor showing on a competence scale, which comprises such items as independence, reliability, length of attention, perseverance in difficulties and so on. Such 'problem behaviour' must be distinguished from bad conduct: it indicates a gap in the children's preparation for school life. The same group, aged ten, also showed a higher mean level of anxiety than the less socially handicapped boys, which contrasts with a lack of difference on anxiety in the younger age group. It is possible that, as they grow older, the highly socially handicapped boys become increasingly aware of their social incompetence and their inability to cope with the demands of school. These results could be interpreted as showing that they are more 'troublesome' at school, but this would only be true in the sense that they lack classroom skills, and that they require more supervision to keep at tasks. The study also indicated that a high proportion of the highly socially handicapped boys become delinquent at an early age. The data on classroom behaviour cast some doubt on the equation of social handicap, bad behaviour and delinquency. Some of the quietest ten-year old boys in the study had already been through the juvenile court.

Home circumstances were found to be stressful; on average the sample suffered from a severe degree of overcrowding. Basic amenities, such as hot water, indoor sanitation, and a bath were available in very few homes. There is a high degree of involuntary mobility; large, low-income families tend to be offered houses in older areas where rents are low. Often the life-span of the property is short, and families who are to be rehoused are offered a 'choice' of two or three similar types of house. With high mobility goes the inevitable disruption of kinship and social ties, and the children are unsettled on changing schools. The study includes an analysis of child-rearing methods, which appear to be closely adapted to a stressful environment, but prove to be inadequate as a preparation for school and a full personality development. It is open to debate and discovery what forms so-called compensatory education should take and what its effectiveness is likely to be, if considerable numbers of families are continuously exposed to severe degrees of material and environmental stress which disrupt normal family life and which leave a permanent mark on the personality of the growing child.

Combating social deprivation

Robert Holman

The years from 1970 have given little indication of a lessening of social deprivation. On the contrary, estimates made from both inside and outside government confirmed it to be a characteristic of many inhabitants. For some time, growing unemployment compelled more people to depend upon social security benefits. Many workers did receive wage increases in an attempt to keep pace with rising prices but low wage earners did not seem amongst those who made any relative improvement. The effects on these earners of the government's recent freeze on wages, rents, dividends and certain prices[30] is not yet known but there is little doubt that they still make up a substantial part of the working population. Official figures issued in 1972 estimated that over four million of the country's seven million manual workers were earning less than £30 a week.[31] Low wage earners also made up many of the over 100,000 families which a government survey on two-parent families calculated to be living below the basic level of supplementary benefit.[32] Even these figures, according to some critics, were a gross underestimation.[33] Of course, the figures do not include one-parent families and those without children. Nicholas Bosanquet claimed that two million people were living below the basic level, four million were on it, and another four million just above it, making in all about a fifth of the population.[34]

Whatever the exact numbers, it was not disputed that many thousands of families continued to experience depriving social conditions. The disadvantageous effects on children were made abundantly clear by a further publication of the study being made of 16,000 children born in March 1965.[35] It demonstrated, for instance, that those children whose parents held unskilled manual jobs were proportionately more likely than others to be abnormally light in weight or short in height, to have squints or stammers, to do less well at school, to have poor oral ability, to live in homes which were overcrowded and lacked amenities. And they were more likely to die. The depriving housing conditions were also subjected to the focus of a number of other studies. Shelter documented the position of a number of deprived wards showing. for instance, that in Central Leith ward in Edinburgh over 48 per cent of families were overcrowded (having over 1½ persons per room), while over 70 per cent lacked the exclusive use of a fixed bath.[36] The reports of Glastonbury[37] and Greve[38] documented the plight of and even an alarming increase in the number of the homeless. The *Annual Report, 1971* of the Department of Health and Social Security gave the number of homeless as 25,969 on 31st December 1971, an increase of 2,520 over the previous year.

SOCIAL LEGISLATION
If social deprivation continued unabated, it can be at least recorded that the period witnessed much social welfare legislation. The Local Authority Social Services Act, passed in the spring of 1970, seemed a flimsy paper when compared with its weighty parent, the Seebohm Report. Many of the latter's recommendations were not incorporated into the Act. Indeed, it concentrated on reorganising the functions of the former welfare, children's and mental welfare departments, along with certain social work aspects of the health and education departments, into one new social services department, and gave little attention to extending the powers and resources of the local authorities. Noticeably, it differed markedly from the Local Authority Social Work (Scotland) Act of 1968 which, in addition to the other personal social services, also incorporated the probation department into the new organisation; instituted children's hearings instead of juvenile courts; and gave the local authorities an additional community responsibility 'to promote social welfare by making available advice, guidance and assistance on such a scale as may be appropriate for the area' (section 12).

The new social services departments had not even been formed before a further Act, the Chronically Sick and Disabled Persons Act 1970, increased the scope of their work with a group whose needs had been consistently articulated by the Disablement Income

Group. The influence of· DIG probably also helped to persuade the government to introduce attendance and invalidity allowances for certain of the long-term sick. Useful as these measures were, DIG was by no means satisfied with the level of provision made while, before long, the explorations of the new departments began to reveal that local authorities had been unaware of the numbers of chronically sick and disabled persons needing help within their localities.

Not all the government action of 1970 was designed to extend the social services. The Secretary for Health and Social Services provoked a storm of criticism when he announced increases in the charges for NHS health prescriptions, dental and optical services. The removal of the subsidy for welfare milk for pregnant mothers and children under five added fuel to the fires of controversy. Even more so, the withdrawal of free school milk for children over seven years of age (except for those medically certified as requiring it) stirred a bitter political argument which continued for many months as a handful of local authorities sought means of continuing to supply the milk.

Before the eventful 1970 ran its course, another controversial bill became law. The Family Incomes Supplement Act was designed to help financially families whose wage earner's income was below certain prescribed levels. FIS (as it became known) could make up half the difference between the families' income and that level up to a maximum of £3 (raised to £6 for families with at least three children from October 1973). The heated discussions surrounding FIS, however, were small compared with those which greeted the Immigration Act of 1971. It was commonly held that it made explicit the different valuation which some sections of society placed on white as against black persons and that it would serve to reinforce discrimination against black citizens who already frequently bore the brunt of socially depriving conditions.

Much other social legislation found its way to the statute book in 1970-72 and a comprehensive list cannot be given. Mention must be made of the raising of the basic rates of national insurance and supplementary benefits. The latest increase of the latter, to take effect from October 1973, gives a basic rate of £11.65 for married couples and £7.15 for a single person. Old age pensions are raised to £12.50 and £7.75 and unemployment and sickness benefit to £11.90 and £7.35. Further, pensions were introduced for those over-eighty year olds who were not eligible under the 1948 insurance scheme.

Some of the most important legislation was prospective, that is, its implementation was timed for the future. Thus the major reorganisations of local government and of the health services were both timed for 1974 (for Scotland, the local government reorganisation was a year later). A new pensions scheme, fully explained in the White Paper *Strategy for Pensions* (cmnd. 4755) was announced in 1971 for operation in 1975. The new scheme puts particular focus on private occupational pension arrangements coupled with a basic state pension for which earnings-related contributions will have been made. Those outside occupational schemes will receive a reserve second state pension. At the time of writing, the proposals are being debated by parliament as the Social Security Bill (1973).

Less certain of implementation but supported by obvious government approval, a Green Paper *Proposals for a Tax Credit System* (cmnd. 5116), issued in October 1972, put forward a new idea for public debate. In brief, the suggestion is for a single assessment of income in order not only to calculate the tax to be paid above a certain level but in order to give out a social benefit to incomes below it. Covering 90 per cent of the population it would replace present child tax allowances, family allowance and FIS but not supplementary benefits. Lastly, in December 1972 the White Paper *Education: a Framework for Expansion* (cmnd. 5174), announced that expansion would be encouraged in nursery education, a service which many commentators thought would be of special help to socially deprived children.

The implications of so much legislation are varied and extensive but here only two developments can be mentioned. First, it soon became apparent that the motive behind much of the new government's legislation was a commitment to a doctrine of selectivity. Selectivity implies the attempt to limit social benefits to those persons deemed to be in need of them, with the tool of selection being a means test. Thus the raising of charges for school meals, health prescriptions, dental and optical services meant that more persons came within the orbit of such tests. The introduction of FIS combined with the growth of rate rebate schemes and the continuing dependence of many thousands on supplementary benefit gave rise to the gibe that the country had become 'a nation of means tests'. The passing of the Housing Finance Act (1972), whereby all council tenants became subject to such tests, gave it even more strength. Consequently, the old arguments between selectivists and universalists broke out again with the former stressing the need to reduce expenditure and the latter arguing that means tests might actually inhibit the most needy from applying for help. The latter gained extra ammunition from the detection of the 'poverty trap' which, as the Child Poverty Action Group demonstrated, could mean that a wage increase for some low-paid workers could leave them worse off because they lost their entitlement to certain benefits.[39]

Second, the passing of the Local Authority Social Services Act (1970) did appear to open a new chapter in the development of the personal social services. Most of the professional social work associations had supported the proposals of the Seebohm Report, arguing that its implementation would lead to more effective services. Consequently, much was expected from the new social services departments. However, the departments had to commence operations with the government declining to give an assurance that they would receive any more resources than had been available to the previous separated services. Sir Frederic Seebohm, who had argued the case for extra resources, described this decision as 'a great shock'.[40] While in the midst of reorganising, the social service departments further faced the challenge of providing additional services for the physically and mentally handicapped not to mention the implementation of the Children and Young Persons Act (1969).

With the new departments so young and facing so many demands, any criticisms must be made with some reluctance. Yet it is fair to observe that both within and without the departments some disappointment has been expressed that the new legislation does not appear to have resulted in an obvious improvement in the condition of the socially deprived. In particular, few departments have taken the opportunity to provide services basically different from those previously available. The hope had been expressed that certain groups in need would receive more adequate attention from the social services. Thus the National Council for the Unmarried Mother and Her Child commented in 1972 that 'Great hopes were raised in many of us by the inauguration of the new social services departments. We welcomed with enthusiasm the Seebohm Committee's recommendations about unmarried mothers and their children and the proposal that there should be a clear assignment of responsibility to the social services departments to ensure adequate social care and advice. . . . (but) it will be many years before all social services departments can offer a comprehensive service to this group',[41] Similarly, proposals had been put forward, for example by Sinfield, that the roles of social workers should be subjected to close scrutiny and changed in order to be of more relevance to persons in poverty.[42] Since the Act, social workers have manfully accepted the expansion of their duties and many now cope with a range of cases previously divided between specialist workers. But Sinfield's plea for a change in the nature of the roles has not been heeded. Indeed, the British Association of Social Workers has expressed concern whether new roles can be undertaken and questions whether the same social worker can undertake the new generalist functions and also be expected 'to advise on welfare benefits . . . and to act as a sort of second class solicitor and accountant for the poor'.[43] Further, no departments have placed their area offices around activities with a community focus, such as day care centres or adventure playgrounds, which reach out into the community. None have made the provision of day care facilities or community workers the cornerstones of practice; instead they are regarded as supplements to more traditional activities. Some departments have developed work with volunteers but groups made up of clients or residents of deprived areas are still regarded with some suspicion. Any ideas of promoting credit unions or similar projects which financially help the poor as a group do not seem to have been considered. Instead of promoting innovation, the new Act and new demands have channelled the departments into building up administrations and services akin to but larger than those of old. Organisational integration has occurred without changing the objectives and methods of helping the deprived.

Disappointment with the outcome of both central government legislation and local government development may have contributed to the increased activities of voluntary pressure groups in 1970-3. The work of DIG has already been mentioned. The Child Poverty Action Group not only gained a continued voice in some newspapers but also provided practical services to the poor in the field of welfare rights. Similarly, the National Association for Mental Health and the Society for Mentally Handicapped Children have hammered loudly on the door of the government. These are but four examples but they typify the now strident voice of pressure groups who have refused to be satisfied with half measures and who possess a barely concealed anger that in an era of affluence their particular concerns should suffer so much social deprivation.

THE SAME FAILINGS

The original edition of this volume identified a number of weak points or failings within the services which aim to help socially deprived families. Nearly three years later the same failings remain. The government's emphasis on selectivist services requires that those eligible are informed of and are prepared to submit to a means test to obtain the benefits. Yet despite increased publicity the take-up of such benefits has remained disappointingly low. A report by Task Force argued that fewer than 8 per cent of old age pensioners in London who received supplementary benefit were aware of a provision for claiming a heating allowance.[44] The introduction of rent rebates for council tenants (from October 1972) and for private tenants of unfurnished accommodation (from April 1973) was designed to aid low-income families. Yet it must be considered in the light of a pilot scheme in Birmingham which advertised rent allowances for private tenants and in a two-year period received only 250 applications from an estimated eligible 6,000. The most widely publicised scheme of all has been the government's Family Income Supplement. In a parliamentary statement the Secretary of State for Social Services admitted that at the end of March 1972 only 52 per cent of those entitled to FIS were actually receiving it. The low take-up has been attributed not only to ignorance about the services (to be countered by publicity) but also to a reluctance to submit to the 'shame' of means tests and the entering into a relationship with officials which stresses the inferior status of the applicant. The Child Poverty Action Group has been quick to point out that, in contrast, new benefits not dependent upon a means test, such as pensions for the over-eighties and constant attendance allowances for the disabled, have actually received more applications than the number originally considered eligible.

The failure to reach those most in need has been highlighted in other forms of services. Grants made under the urban programme have been criticised on the grounds that they are more available to traditional voluntary bodies than organisations which are run by the deprived themselves.[45] A study of playgroups financed under the urban programme in order to reach socially deprived children in Southwark found that many groups were not located in the areas of highest need while some contained as few as 7 per cent of their children with personal or social handicaps.[46] Again, the proposed expansion in nursery education may not be a means of benefiting the early experiences of the most needy children. Low-income families where the mothers have to go out to work require adequate day care for their pre-school children. Such care will not be available in nursery schools with their short hours and closures for long school holidays. The development of day care centres which can provide stimulating care within hours suited to working mothers would have better suited the requirements of these families. As it is, their children, in most cases, will probably be placed with more unreliable sources of daily care, in particular daily minders, while the extra places in nursery schools will go to children who already possess other advantages. A major delivery problem for the social services remains how actually to reach the persons most in need while doing so in such a way as does not reinforce their status as deprived persons.

Even where benefits do reach people, their standards may be lacking. In particular, the levels or rates of social security benefits have continued to be criticised as inadequate. Case studies have shown only too well that anything approaching normal living is impossible on the rates set by supplementary benefit. The FIS, therefore — although praised for incorporating one-parent and one-child families — came under fierce fire for not necessarily bringing recipients above the supplementary benefit minimum. Indeed, as rents were excluded from the assessment of FIS, cases were reported of families who qualified for free school dinners but were not eligible for FIS as their high rents were not taken into consideration. The minimal levels being used, Michael Meacher MP claimed, were the direct result of the low priority accorded to social welfare by the government. His statement that in real terms the expenditure planned for the social services was infinitesimal compared with that for roads and law and order provoked a public reply from the Secretary of State for Social Services.[47]

In 1970, this publication focused attention on the great variability between the social needs and resources of different areas in the country. Studies in the succeeding years have underlined the point even more clearly. At a regional level, government figures have contrasted the advantageous position of London, the south and the south-east with the rest of the country. In infant mortality rates, housing conditions, degrees of income and possessions, health and educational levels as well as in the quantity of hospitals, doctors and social workers, people north of a line from the Severn to the Wash were more likely to suffer deprivation.[1] The variations were not restricted simply between north and south, for certain cities were in a particularly poor condition. The Corporation of Glasgow itself published a comparative study of deprivation indices showing 'that in virtually every factor Glasgow presents a less satisfactory example than the other centres'.[48] The extent of housing deprivation identified in Glasgow was particularly staggering with 11.8 per cent of the population in overcrowded conditions as against a national average of 1.6 per cent while 88.7 per cent lived in multi-dwelling buildings as against 14.4 per cent. To take another example, some mental illnesses were shown, by the Psychiatric Rehabilitation Association, to be more common in deprived neighbourhoods either because these areas contained the stresses which provoked such illnesses or because the mentally ill could only find accommodation there.[49]

Area variability covers not only measures of need but also the services which are intended to meet need. A survey by the National Association for Mental Health documented wide discrepancies in the provision of hostels, day centres, social clubs and social workers.[50] Strong criticism has been levelled at those local authorities which have failed to discharge their duties towards the disabled as stated in the Chronically Sick and Disabled Persons' Act.[51] Further, in 1972 the Department of the Environment stated that only one county borough in ten in England had carried out its legal requirements to supply camp sites for gypsies according to the Caravan Sites Act (1968).[52] Further statistics have been collated to document the range of differences between local authorities in terms of home helps, nursery places, cash grants to families and so on.[53] The reorganisation of the social services at local and governmental levels has not, as one prominent director admits, led to a greater uniformity of provision. He points out that the Department of Education and Science 'is generally extremely successful in ensuring minimum standards of provision in schools . . . the Department of Health and Social Security has taken a much more *laissez-faire* approach and the minimum standard of provision in the health and welfare fields shows considerable variation'.[54]

As the established deficiencies of the social service agencies have continued unabated, more attention has been focused on their institutional mechanisms which appear to perpetuate rather than abolish deprivation. In the field of education, selection tests have been shown to discriminate against immigrant children so that they are thereafter deprived of certain educational resources and have less opportunity to achieve the qualifications which lead to higher paid jobs.[55] The study *From Birth to Seven* concluded that 'the educational system itself contains a built-in bias in favour of middle-class children' and thus it cannot be expected that the present system will change the position of the socially deprived.[56] Outside the school, concern has been expressed at the mechanisms by which some housing departments select tenants. By grading on moralistic and adequacy grounds, some applicants are offered only sub-standard property which is incapable of being improved and which thereby denies them the chance of raising their grading and so obtaining better accommodation. Further, Professor Cullingworth has claimed that discrimination can occur within housing departments not at a policy level but through administrative, managerial and clerical practices.[57] Lastly, Kemeny and Popplestone have discussed the ways by which social services departments may ration their services to clients and even inhibit their use.[58]

THE ANALYSIS OF SOCIAL DEPRIVATION

In the wake of the criticisms made of prevailing practices, the question must be raised whether the intervening years have brought forth further ideas on the means of combating social deprivation. One school of thought has advocated that the present direction of government policy be more rapidly developed and extended so that welfare is firmly placed within the private market system. Against this, there have been counter arguments for universal services and greater social planning.[59] These are by no means new ideas but, at least, the government was breaking fresh ground with its proposals – already mentioned – for a tax credit system. The Child Poverty Action Group has doubts about the proposals and in its publication *Family Poverty* expressed a preference for increased family allowances or a child endowment scheme as the most promising way of helping the poor.[39] At the same time, rising unemployment was prompting a demand for job creation in depressed areas, supplemented by improved re-training schemes in order better to equip people for more skilled and more highly paid occupations.

Implicit in many of the suggestions was the view that the central government should accept greater responsibility for supporting local needs. Shelter gave expression to many voices in claiming that the local authorities' inability to tackle housing deprivation constituted a case for direct government intervention.[6] The idea was expanded by a report from Shelter's neighbourhood project which had worked in a deprived part of Liverpool where unwieldy bureaucratic local authority services had imposed almost insurmountable barriers between officials and deprived residents. The report concluded that the only hope of social intervention now lay with the local authority asking the central government to designate deprived neighbourhoods as 'priority areas' into which extra resources could be poured. The mechanism of intervention would be akin to a New Town Development Corporation in having extensive powers and being capable of attracting capital and social investment to inner ring areas.[60]

It is a reasonable hope that policies which are selected to combat social deprivation should be closely related to an analysis and explanation of it. The years 1970-3 did witness some discussion of the causes of poverty. First, the view that many of the poor are morally to blame for their condition found expression in the publications of a former social security official, Robin Page.[61] Academically unacceptable, the charge is important in that it is widely held and distributed by the mass media. Second, the Secretary of State for Social Services focused attention on a cycle of social deprivation. According to this concept, some parents are unable to pass on to their children the social skills and attitudes necessary to avail themselves of educational and work opportunities. Consequently, the inability to cope with modern life is transmitted from one generation to the next.[62] The deduction made is that the cycle must be broken into by services which alter the behaviour patterns of the parents or which compensate the children for what they have lacked. Noticeably, the government report on educational priority areas places special emphasis on providing extra pre-school experiences for the children in such areas and on improving the communication between schools and parents.[63]

The cycle of deprivation theory has some links with researchers who focus on the child socialisation methods which fail to develop the skills of children. However, the former stresses the behaviour of individual families, the latter looks at patterns contained within certain social classes or sub-cultures. The focus away from the individual leads to the third explanation which has achieved prominence — a structural explanation. More popular amongst academics than politicians, it holds that social deprivation derives from certain social and economic mechanisms which make up the structure of society. Lack of space forbids an account of these mechanisms and the reader must be referred to Townsend's *The Concept of Poverty* and Coates & Silburn's *Poverty: The Forgotten Englishmen.*[64] The implication is that not individuals, not families, but the structures of society — the class system, the mechanisms for distributing power and income, the job opportunity structure, etc — need to be changed radically. Noticeably, structural arguments have gained ground in a period when the contrasts of society between rich and poor have gained unusual publicity. The withdrawal of free school milk for young children was associated with the closely timed decision to increase the subsidy to parents of children attending direct grant schools. Some social work journals have had no hesitation in pointing out, for instance, that tax reductions in the 1973 budget meant an extra £300 a year for those earning £50 or more per week and only £100 for the low wage earners.[65] A number of articles and at least one major book have demonstrated how income, wealth and other resources are disproportionately concentrated in the hands of a small minority.[66] The apparent injustices have provoked indignation and it is worth noting that the protagonists of the structural analysis are often committed not just to the abolition of deprivation but to an egalitarian society.

The major difficulty facing the structuralists is not just to formulate a programme for radical reform but to devise the means of implementing it. For if the analysis is carried through, it can be argued that the major political parties are themselves institutions which reinforce the existing situation and are therefore unlikely, for the present, to support structural changes. Consequently, it appears that many persons concerned with reform have turned away from national politics to community politics. The growth of community action in 1970-3 is the next point to which attention must be drawn.

Community action may be regarded as a general term to cover almost any collective activity which promotes broad social improvement. More narrowly, as Bryant explains, it denotes 'a particular approach to organising local groups and welfare publics'.[67] The latter view has gained prominence and its supporters would agree that it covers action frequently found in socially deprived areas, that it perceives society as a set of conflicting interests, that it involves the deprived themselves in collective action, and that its objectives include enabling participants to achieve greater control over their own lives and surroundings. Examples of community action are campaigns to rehouse families faced with eviction or forced to live close to motorways, mothers organising to obtain adventure playgrounds for their children, clients of the social services combining together to achieve more humane treatment, and tenants acting collectively to improve their housing standards. Not all activities are successful but clearly in many cases community action has enabled people to achieve changes which were previously beyond them. Possibly, in the long run, community action will contribute to the development of greater political consciousness amongst deprived persons which, in turn, may promote the radical reforms envisaged by the structuralists.

RESEARCH AND SOCIAL DEPRIVATION

Social research has thrown further light on the deprivations suffered by certain categories — motherless families, illegitimate children, large families, private foster children.[68] In addition, as Dr Wilson has pointed out earlier, research has identified the geographical areas and the kinds of children most in need of extra educational resources. But it has been less successful in determining how and if social services can overcome social deprivation as a whole. The Department of Health and Social Security is initiating studies to provide fuller understanding of the 'cycle of social deprivation' concept. This concept by no means finds favour amongst all social scientists and its selection for a research emphasis serves to underline the argument that the very choice of research projects (and the rejection of others) has political implications. A research concentration on one analysis and the social strategies which spring from it could lead to the exclusion of other analyses and strategies. The reasonable position would appear to be a number of research projects looking at alternative hypotheses.

Whatever the vices and virtues of government-sponsored research, it can be recorded that during 1970-3 a large independent research unit was established by a voluntary trust. The view was heard that the large amount of money involved would have been better spent on organisations which directly involved the poor but, in the long run, it is the hope that the Centre for Studies in Social Policy will provide directions which can be followed in order to overcome social deprivation.

Notes and references

1. Department of the Environment, Scottish Development Department, Welsh Office, *Housing and Construction Statistics,* no. 1, 1972, table 32, HMSO, 1972. For examples of studies of the administrative, social and economic issues in slum clearance see; D. Muchnick, *Urban renewal in Liverpool,* Occasional Papers in Social Administration, no. 33, Bell, 1970; N. Denis, *People and Planning,* Faber and Faber, 1970; H.W. Richardson, *Urban Economics,* Penguin, 1971 (especially chapter 5); National Economic Development Office, *New homes in the cities; the role of the private developer in urban renewal in England and Wales,* HMSO, 1971; L. Needleman, 'The comparative economics of improvement and new building', Urban Studies, vol. 6, no. 2, 1969; F. Medhurst and J.P. Lewis, *Urban decay: an analysis and a policy,* Macmillan, 1969.
2. DoE, SDD, WO, op.cit., supplementary table XXIII. Further information about the findings of the 1971 national house condition survey can be found amongst these supplementary tabulations.
3. Ibid, table 28. See also J. Morton, 'Improving slowly', *New Society,* 20 January 1972; Shelter, *Home improvement: people or profit?,* 1972; K.M. Spencer, 'Older urban areas and housing improvement policies', *Town Planning Review,* vol. 41, no.3, 1970.
4. DoE, SDD, WO, op.cit., table 28.

5. Ibid, table 30. See also J. Ferris, *Participation in urban planning; the Barnsbury case; a study of environmental improvement in London,* Occasional Papers in Social Administration, no.49, Bell, 1972; J.G. Davies, *The evangelistic bureaucrat,* Tavistock, 1972; Department of the Environment, *New Life in Old Towns,* HMSO, 1971; S. Pepper, *Housing Improvement: goals and strategies,* Lund Humphries, 1971.

6. See I.H. Welfeld, *European Housing Subsidy systems — an American perspective,* US Department of Housing and Urban Development, September, 1972; J. Greve, *Voluntary housing in Scandinavia,* Occasional Papers of the Centre for Urban and Regional Studies, University of Birmingham, no.21, 1971; also see the annual reports of the Housing Corporation and of the National Federation of Housing Societies.

7. *Report of the Committee on Local Authority and Allied Social Services,* Cmnd, 3703, HMSO, 1968; Central Housing Advisory Committee, *Council housing procedures and priorities,* HMSO, 1969; D.V. Donnison, 'A housing service', *New Society,* 11 November 1971; The Institute of Housing Managers, *The comprehensive housing service – organisation and functions,* 1972; J. Smith, 'Inquiry: housing aid centres', *Municipal Review,* vol. 43, November 1972, pp. 318-319.

8. See J.D. Stewart, *Management in local government – a viewpoint,* Charles Knight, 1971; P.A. Eddison, *Local Government, management and corporate planning,* Leonard Hill, 1973; P.A. Eddison, 'Comprehensive planning for local government,' in M. Stewart (ed), *The City,* Penguin, 1972.

9. The White Paper preceding the 1972 Housing Finance Act was entitled, *Fair deal for housing,* Cmnd, 4728, HMSO, 1971.

10. S. Cooper, 'Sites for gypsies, success or failure?', *Local Government Chronicle,* 10 November 1972.

11. Scottish Development Department, *Scotland's travelling people,* HMSO, 1971.

12. J. Greve, D. Page, S. Greve, *Homelessness in London,* Scottish Academic Press, 1971; B. Glastonbury, *Homeless near a thousand homes – a study of homeless families in South Wales and the West of England,* National Institute for Social Work Training Series, no.21, Allen and Unwin, 1971; K.M. Spencer, 'Homes, the homeless and the social services', in M.J. Brown (ed), *Social issues and the social services,* Charles Knight, 1973; R. Minns, 'Homeless families and some organisational determinants of deviancy,' *Policy and Politics,* vol. 1, no.1, 1972; D. Brandon, 'Homeless single persons', *British Journal of Psychiatric Social Work,* vol. 10, no.2, 1969; Shelter *The grief report,* 1972; BBC Television, *The Block,* a documentary film of temporary accommodation and its inhabitants, produced in 1972; D. Wilson, *I know it was the place's fault,* Oliphants, 1970.

13. D.V. Donnison 'No more reports', *New Society,* 27 May 1971.

14. South East Joint Planning Team, *Strategic plan for the South East,* studies volume 2, HMSO, 1971 (especially chapters 1 and 2); J. Morton, 'Housing', in J. Hillman (ed) *Planning for London,* Penguin, 1971.

15. The study group on local authority management structures, *The new local authorities: management and structure,* HMSO, 1972, (often referred to as the Bains Committee report).

16. For a discussion of the housing finance subsidies before the 1972 Act, see N.P. Hepworth, *The finance of local government* (Chapter 8), Allen and Unwin, 1970.

17. J.J. Atkinson, 'Housing Finance Bill – the assessment of fair rents', *Housing,* March 1972; W.M. Brook, 'The unit value scheme as applied to fair rents', *Housing,* March 1972.

18. For fuller details of the provisions of the Act and discussions of it, see, 'A guide, Housing Act, 1972', *New Society,* 28 December 1972; K.M. Spencer, 'The Housing Finance Act', *Social and Economic Administration,* vol. 7, no.1, 1973.

19. Prices and Incomes Board, *Increases in rents of local authority housing,* Cmnd, 3604, HMSO, 1968.
20. Cmnd. 4728. op.cit.
21. These powers were contained in the Birmingham Corporation Act, 1968, and allowances were given to unfurnished and furnished tenants, but not housing association tenants. See F. Cocks, 'Housing allowances for private tenants-Birmingham's experience', *Housing Review,* January/February 1972; A. Davies, 'Birmingham's rent rebate scheme for private tenants' *Housing,* July 1971.
22. For some of the arguments against the Act see A.A. Nevitt, 'A fair deal for housing', *Political Quarterly,* vol. 42, 1971; A.A. Nevitt, 'The new housing legislation', *Housing Review,* March/April 1972; A.A. Nevitt, *Fair deal for households,* Fabian Research Series, no.297, 1971; R.A. Parker, *The Housing Finance Bill and council tenants,* Child Poverty Action Group, 1972.
23. In this context see P. Townsend, 'Everyone his own home: inequality in housing and the creation of a national service', *Royal Institute of British Architect's Journal,* January 1973, which argues the case for social ownership of rented housing, the extension to tenants of the rights and privileges of owner occupiers, and a system of flat rate housing allowances. See also the Green Paper, *Proposals for a tax credit system,* Cmnd. 5116, HMSO, 1972.
24. Other references the reader may find of value are: P. Jephcott, *Homes in high flats,* Oliver and Boyd, 1971; J. Greve, 'Housing policies and prospects', in W.A. Robson and B. Crick (ed), *The future of the social services,* Penguin, 1970; E. Krausz, *Ethnic minorities in Britain,* Paladin, 1972; E.J.B. Rose, et al, *Colour and citizenship,* Oxford University Press, 1969.
25. Schools Council, *Project in Compensatory Education,* Field Report no.6, HMSO, 1968.
26. M. Chazan and S. Jackson, 'Behaviour problems in the infant school', *Journal of Child Psychology and Psychiatry,* 1971.
27. P. Widlake, 'Language and learning in the pre-school', *Remedial Education,* vol. 6, no.3, 1971.
28. H. Wilson, and G.W. Herbert, *Report on Socially Deprived Children.* In preparation.
29. J.W.B. Douglas, *The Home and the School,* Macgibbon and Kee, 1964; *All our Future,* Peter Davies, 1968.
30. *A Programme for Controlling Inflation: The First Stage.* Cmnd. 5125. HMSO, 1972.
31. *Social Trends, No.3,* HMSO, 1972.
32. J.R. Howe, *Two Parent Families,* HMSO, 1971.
33. P. Townsend, 'Politics and the statistics of poverty,' *Political Quarterly,* vol. 43, no.1, 1972.
34. Cited in *Journal of Social Policy,* vol. 1, part 3, 1972, p.260.
35. R. Davie, N. Butler and H. Goldstein, *From Birth to Seven,* Longmans, 1972.
36. *Reprieve,* Shelter, 1972.
37. B. Glastonbury, *Homeless Near a Thousand Homes,* Allen and Unwin, 1971.
38. J. Greve et al, *Homelessness in London,* Chatto, 1971.
39. See, D. Bull (ed), *Family Poverty,* Duckworth, second ed, 1972, pp. 176-183.
40. Sir F. Seebohm interviewed in *The Spectator,* 5 Febuary 1972.
41. The National Council for the Unmarried Mother and Her Child, *Annual Report,* 1972, p.5.
42. A. Sinfield, *Which Way for Social Work?,* Fabian Society, 1969.
43. BASW, 'Transmitted social deprivation', in *Social Work Today,* vol. 3, no.21, 1973,
44. *Left in the Cold,* Task Force, 1972.
45. R. Holman, 'The urban programme,' *Venture,* vol. 23, no.1, 1971.
46. A. Joseph and J. Parfitt, *Playgroups in an Area of Social Need,* National Foundation for Educational Research, 1972.

47. M. Meacher, 'A sandwich course', *The Guardian,* 21 December 1971: and Sir K. Joseph, 'Strategies of social justice,' *The Guardian,* 3 January 1972.
48. R. Mansley, *Areas of Need in Glasgow,* Glasgow Corporation, 1972, p.1.
49. Psychiatric Rehabilitation Associaton, *Poverty and Schizophrenia,* 1973.
50. National Association for Mental Health, *Mind,* 1971.
51. National Fund for Research into Crippling Diseases, *The Implementation of the Chronically Sick and Disabled Persons' Act,* 1973.
52. Cited in *Journal of Social Policy,* vol. 2, part 2, 1973, p.155.
53. See, M. Meacher, 'Scrooge areas', *New Society,* 2 December 1971.
54. T. White, 'Conflict of priorities', *Observer,* 10 January 1972.
55. See, Department of Education and Science, *Potential and Progress in a Second Culture,* HMSO, 1971, and H. Townsend, *Immigrant Pupils in England,* National Foundation for Educational Research, 1971.
56. R. Davie, N. Butler and H. Goldstein, op.cit., p.31.
57. See Professor Cullingworth's evidence to the *Select Committee on Race Ralations and Immigration,* HMSO, 1971.
58. P. Kemeny and G. Popplestone, 'Client discrimination in social welfare organisations', *Social Work,* vol. 27, no.2, 1970.
59. The opposing views are illustrated in R. Boyson (ed), *Down With the Poor,* Churchill Press, 1971; and P. Townsend and N. Bosanquet (eds), *Labour and Inequality,* Fabian Society, 1971.
60. Shelter Neighbourhood Action Project, *Another Chance for Cities,* 1973.
61. R. Page, *The Benefits Racket,* Stacey, 1971.
62. Sir Keith Joseph, speech to Pre-School Playgroups Association, 29 June 1972.
63. A. Halsey (ed), *Educational Priority,* vol. 1, HMSO, 1973.
64. P. Townsend (ed), *The Concept of Poverty,* Heinemann, 1971: K. Coates and R. Silburn, *Poverty: the Forgotten Englishmen,* Penguin, 1970.
65. *Social Work Today,* vol. 4, no.2, 19 April 1973, p.57.
66. For instance, A. Atkinson, *Unequal Shares,* Penguin, 1972.
67. For the general view, see R. Armstrong, 'Towards the study of community action', *Adult Education,* vol. 45; no.1, 1972. For the stricter definition, see R. Bryant, 'Community action', *British Journal of Social Work,* vol. 2, no.3, 1972 and R. Holman, *Power to the powerless, the role of community action,* British Council of Churches, 1972.
68. V. George and P. Wilding, *Motherless Families,* Routledge and Kegan Paul, 1972; E. Crellin, *Born Illegitimate,* National Foundation for Educational Research, 1971; H. Land, *Large Families in London.* Bell, 1970; R. Holman, *Trading in Children,* Routledge and Kegan Paul, 1973.